PHOTO: David M. Ice

Kuala Lumpur Monorail
Above traffic, moving people faster, cleaner and safer
PHOTO: Author

Monorails
Trains of the Future - Now Arriving

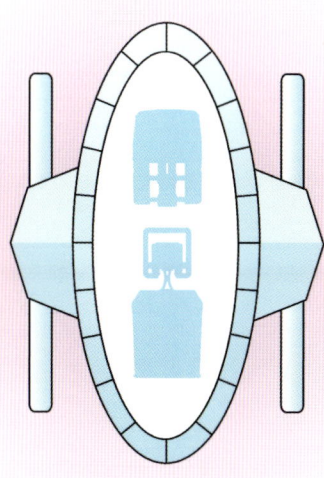

by Kim A. Pedersen

Foreword by Dale O. Samuelson

THE MONORAIL SOCIETY
Fremont, California

Dedication

To my wife, Carol
For sharing life's many adventures,
all while tolerating my unusual
passions and projects.

Acknowledgments

Donald & Lorrie Ballard: publication mentorship
Carlos Banchik: monorail engineering explained
Glenn Barney: Alweg vs. toy trains explained
Mike Chew: collecting explained
Harriet V. Commons: DTP skills advancement
Heather M. David: publication mentorship
Selwyn Eddy III: my 1st monorailist friend
Dick Falkenbury: grassroots champion
James Horecka: architecture explained
David M. Ice: Have camera-will travel
Thomas A. Jovick: Roberts collection preservation
Reinhard Krischer: Alweg history and legacy
Randy Lambertus: AMF/Safege research
Ellen F. Lyford: her grandfather's Schwebebahn collection
Paul M. Newitt: ideas, design and enthusiasm
Russell Noe': Alweg train preservation
Albert G. Nymeyer: engineer/monorailist
Carol E. Pedersen: "Carol is a Saint"
Kory and Skyler Pedersen: growing up in Dad's odd world
George D. Roberts Jr.: his father's story & collection
Dale O. Samuelson: word play, word work
Joshua C. Shields: Seattle knowledge/history
David B. Simons Jr.: WDW knowledge/history
Christine & Richard Sparks (Sparks Arts): graphics review
Luke Starkenburg: Have camera-will travel
Steven Stuart: life-altering 1987 sentence
Keith Walls: technology propagation plus
T.W. Weston: Texas knowledge/history
Teri-Lynn Wheeler: Mark V Blue

Copyright © 2015 by Kim A. Pedersen
Edited by Dale O. Samuelson
All rights reserved. No part of this book may be used or reproduced in any manner whatsoever without the written permission of the Publisher.

Library of Congress Control Number: 2014922177
ISBN: 978-0-9862494-8-8
First Edition

Published by The Monorail Society (www.monorails.org)

Printed in China by Four Colour Print Group, Louisville, Kentucky

Contents

Foreword...6
Introduction...7

1. **Basics**
   What is monorail and how is it perceived?...8

2. **Why not monorail?**
   Advantages and arguments...22

3. **History highlights**
   How the technology advanced...40

4. **Could have, should have**
   Missed opportunities, big ones that got away...80

5. **Where in the west**
   Today's monorails: Western Hemisphere...110

6. **Where in the east**
   Today's monorails: Eastern Hemisphere...138

7. **How to build monorail**
   In ten easy steps...194

8. **Monorailists**
   Promoters, believers and fans...208

9. **Trains of the future**
   What can we expect next?...226

Addendum... 244
Selected bibliography...245
Index...246

FOREWORD

One of my favorite business coaches, the quality guru Tom Peters, loves to quote the famous management guru Peter Drucker: "Whenever anything is being accomplished, it is being done, I have learned, by a monomaniac with a mission." Merriam-Webster defines monomania as a mental illness, but I prefer Wikipedia's description: "…a form of partial insanity conceived as single pathological preoccupation in an otherwise sound mind."

My favorite monomaniac calls himself a Monorailist. For the last two-and-a-half decades, this otherwise sound mind has been focused on presenting to the world the idea that the monorail is not just a theme park ride. In the 35 years I've known Mr. Pedersen, I've come to believe that it does indeed require someone with a single track mind, to persistently challenge the myths that plague monorail in the minds of those who promote mostly inappropriate systems (such as light rail) for our modern urban systems.

While monorails are often referred to as novelty rides, the simple truth is that monorails have been a wonderful way of giving billions of guests aerial tours of World's Fairs, zoos, and amusement parks for over 140 years! It is also true that a fine example of the urban transportation monorail has been in daily operation in Germany since 1901. Despite the efforts of hundreds of engineers, designers, architects and promoters, the seed of the modern monorail didn't germinate until 60 years later, when Walt Disney expanded his theme park ride to carry passengers to and from the Disneyland Hotel. After the Seattle Monorail opened for the 1962 World's Fair, Japan picked up the ball. Doubters of the feasibility of monorail need look no further than the history of Tokyo Monorail. In operation for 50 years, it serves eleven stations, and has carried over 1.75 billion passengers at a rate of more than a million passengers a week.

Since then, transit monorails have continued to be built around the world, at a rate equivalent to about one per year, continuing to prove and improve the technology. There is no one more qualified than Kim Pedersen to tell this story, as for half of those 50 years; The Monorail Society he founded has been instrumental in monorail development, through the exchange of information.

In writing this, I realized that the challenge was not what to write, but how to briefly wax poetic about monorail and the author's passion for it. I have great admiration for writers who can summarize a complex subject succinctly. So I was impressed when I read Dick Falkenbury's summation of the reasons to extend the Seattle Monorail: "It would be safe. It would be efficient. And it would be economical. It would move people, without accident, quickly. It would make money. It would avoid the taxpayer subsidies, which are the main support of all public transportation. It would not interfere with other transportation. It would be non-polluting and clean. The ride would be literally up-lifting."

In 2004 we finally opened such a system here in the USA. The Las Vegas Monorail was built with private funds, glides above a heavily trafficked corridor, required no lane removal, and brings in enough revenue from ridership to cover its operating expenses. Imagine that!

In the 45 years I've been driving, I've logged over a million miles behind the wheel, most often in traffic on the freeways of Southern California. For all those years I've had a recurring dream. As I sit there in traffic, I look up to see a sleek Disney-inspired monorail train speeding by, one after another; on a track system built in the medians of the vast network of existing L.A. area freeways. What could be more effective at getting people out of their cars, than seeing something going faster than them, repeatedly, day after day, completely indifferent to the traffic below? Even now, I have a vision that monorail is the future!

Dale O. Samuelson
Author of The American Amusement Park

PHOTO: Author

INTRODUCTION

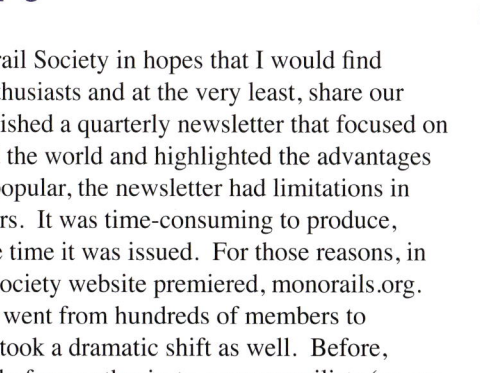

When someone says the word monorail in conversation, the first thing that comes up is usually Disney. In fact, my introduction to the word monorail came from Walt Disney. In 1959 he touted his then four-year old theme park's greatest expansion on a special live television show, *Disneyland '59*. With my young mind captured by his great story-telling ability, he showed spectacular views of something called the Disneyland-Alweg Monorail System. As a young boy already fascinated by trains, this strange Buck Rogers-inspired contraption running on a narrow beam was nothing short of magical. Most people had never seen anything like it. In the following years, Uncle Walt continually suggested to his television audience that someday these trains could be in many cities carrying passengers above the traffic in what he termed "a highway in the sky." I was convinced he was right and looked forward to that day. When the Seattle Alweg Monorail opened for the Century 21 World's Fair in 1962, it was further evidence that monorails were going to be everywhere.

Fast forward to 1987. Transit systems had been built in many places around the world, and my interest in rail transit never waned. In a casual conversation, an acquaintance pointed out the enormous waste of money being spent on the Los Angeles Metro Subway system, billions of dollars for what would only cover a short distance. He stated that with the billions of dollars they spent on the precious few miles of subway, they could have built monorail lines all over the entire Los Angeles area. This one short sentence was to alter my life dramatically. I asked myself, "What ever happened to monorail, the trains of the future?" I decided to find out.

I spent 1988 researching the subject and was pleasantly surprised to find out that in some places, monorails were indeed being built for transit. For whatever reason, few were being built in the Americas or Europe. I looked at the light rail systems that had become popular in the USA after San Diego Trolley debuted, but to me they didn't have the advantages of monorail. Putting trains in traffic seemed to be more of a step backward. I thought that perhaps an organization could be formed to bring more attention to transit monorails. On January 1, 1989, The Monorail Society came into being.

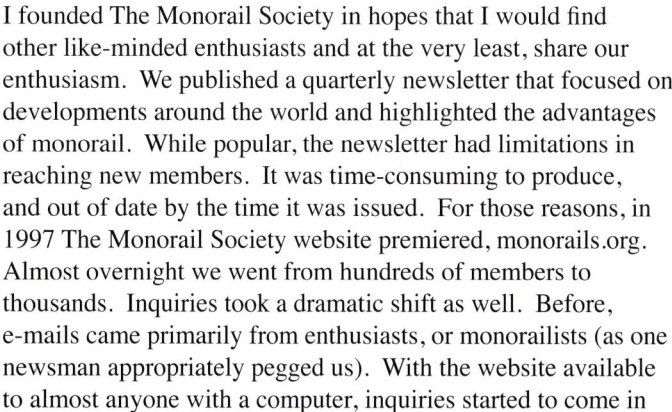

PHOTO: Carol Pedersen

I founded The Monorail Society in hopes that I would find other like-minded enthusiasts and at the very least, share our enthusiasm. We published a quarterly newsletter that focused on developments around the world and highlighted the advantages of monorail. While popular, the newsletter had limitations in reaching new members. It was time-consuming to produce, and out of date by the time it was issued. For those reasons, in 1997 The Monorail Society website premiered, monorails.org. Almost overnight we went from hundreds of members to thousands. Inquiries took a dramatic shift as well. Before, e-mails came primarily from enthusiasts, or monorailists (as one newsman appropriately pegged us). With the website available to almost anyone with a computer, inquiries started to come in from officials and promoters interested in monorail for their communities or developments. I am proud to say that in the past quarter-century The Monorail Society has played a part in the worldwide advancement of monorail, as systems have been developed with the aid of information gained from our website.

Why write a book? The last hardbound monorail-overview book came out in 1965, Derek G.T. Harvey's bright orange *Monorails* book. It was primarily geared toward school-aged readers and was a monorail 'bible' during my young years. Later it would help me find monorail systems, many of which I have now visited in person. Much has happened in the last 50 years, so a new book is long overdue.

This book is an overview and status update of monorails in the world today, which should demonstrate their validity as legitimate transit option. I am a strong believer in the adage *a picture is worth a thousand words*, and for that reason there is a liberal dose of pretty monorail images. No longer can adversaries deny the existence of successful transit monorails. As we have experienced with The Monorail Society website, the information gained from knowledge of different systems can result in more informed decisions by transit planners. At the same time I hope that this book becomes a monorail 'bible' for young people fascinated by trains. Perhaps it will inspire enthusiasm in them, just as that bright orange book did for me so many years ago.

Kim A. Pedersen
Fremont, California

MGM-Bally's Monorail
Before being expanded, the Las Vegas Monorail started as a stylish two-station shuttle.
PHOTO: Author

Lumber Monorail
FACING PAGE: An old postcard view of a lumber-carrying industrial monorail in Bogalusa, Louisiana

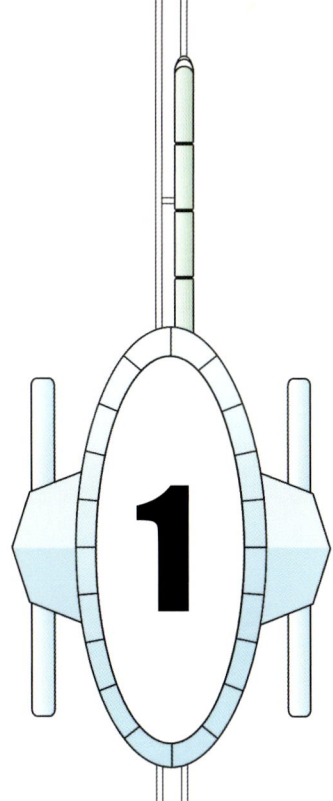

Basics

What is monorail and how is it perceived?

Before delving into the perceptions people have of them, it's a good idea to clarify exactly what a monorail is. The Monorail Society, the world's authority on the subject, defines monorail as follows...

MON*O*RAIL (mon-uh-reyl) n. 1. A single-rail serving as a track for passenger or freight vehicles. In most cases rail is elevated, but monorails can also run at grade, below grade or in subway tunnels. Vehicles are either suspended from or straddle a narrow track. Monorail vehicles are wider than the track that supports them.

MONORAILS

YES it is

Because of widely held misconceptions of what a monorail is or isn't, here are a few examples to illustrate the differences. The chart below compares the most common monorail technologies, and some corresponding monorail photographs. All clearly show that the guideway is narrower than the vehicle, a major advantage of monorail. The track is singular in structure (singular = one = mono).

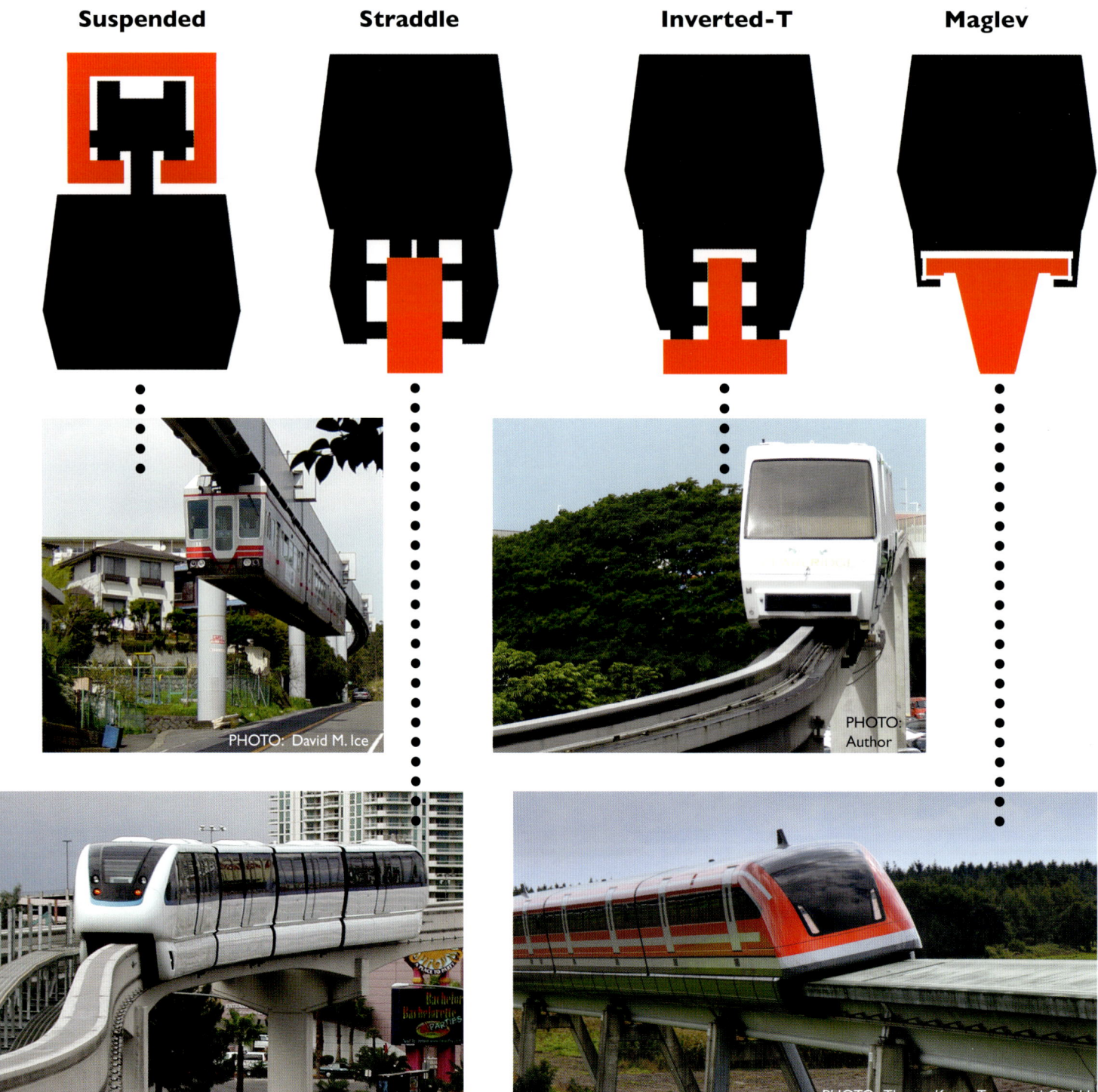

Suspended — PHOTO: David M. Ice

Straddle — PHOTO: Author

Inverted-T — PHOTO: Author

Maglev — PHOTO: ThyssenKrupp Transrapid GmbH

BASICS

NO it's not

The mislabeling of non-monorails comes from the perception that any rail system that is sleek and/or elevated is a monorail. Not so! Most mislabeled non-monorails have massive guideways that are wider than the trains and are double-tracked, which puts them outside the definition parameters.

No, it's elevated conventional rail

From a distance some subway trains might fool you, but up close you'll seen much more concrete than monorail, plus two steel rails.

PHOTO: Author

No, it's elevated light rail

Detroit's People Mover is often confused with monorail. PHOTO: Gepapix/Dreamstime

No, it's u-track maglev

Unlike maglev trains that wrap around a guideway, this one has a much larger trough-like track.

PHOTO: JR Central

No, it's automated guideway transit (AGT)

Many airport peoplemovers are mistaken for monorail, but essentially they're guided busses on huge tracks.

PHOTO: Author

No, it's cable car

Sleek train, but not the track

PHOTO: James Horecka

11

MONORAILS

Industrial Monorails

Monorails are everywhere, which might come as a surprise to many. While the main focus of this book is on transit monorails, it should be noted that thousands of monorails go unnoticed. They carry things, not people. The word 'monorail' isn't usually connected with them, but that is exactly what they are. Industry has used the monorail since the beginning of the Industrial Revolution. They carry your laundry to the front desk of the dry cleaner, they hold almost every imaginable part or product along assembly lines in factories and tiny monorails even hold the sliding curtain that surrounds hospital beds.

Why are there so many of them? It's the simplicity of monorail design, the ease of installation and the amazing carrying capabilities they offer. The majority of industrial monorails are suspended, where the load-carrying vehicle hangs below a simple I-beam track, yet a good number of industrial monorails are straddle-type as well. Straddle monorails have the freight carriers straddling the top of a single rail. The largest are shipping container monorails recently developed in Indonesia.

ABOVE: I-beam monorails move just about anything, including torpedoes on the carrier USS Hornet.
PHOTO: Author

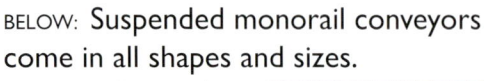

BELOW: Suspended monorail conveyors come in all shapes and sizes.

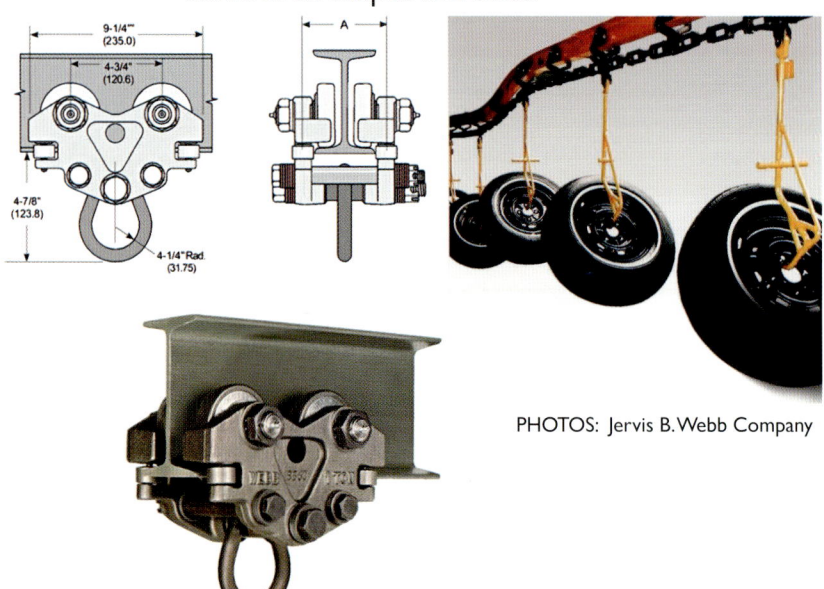

PHOTOS: Jervis B. Webb Company

ABOVE: British-firm Road Machines Ltd. carried all sorts of items with their portable, industrial monorails. This restored vehicle operates at Amberley Museum in England.
PHOTO: Tim Edmonds

BASICS

ABOVE: Historic photo of Indonesian workers pushing lumber along a bargain-basement track

BELOW: 21st Century prototype Automated Container Transporter developed in Indonesia

PHOTO: PT Adhi Karya Persero Tbk

RIGHT: Automobile parts being automatically monorailed along an assembly line.

BELOW: Hospital privacy curtain monorail

PHOTO: Author

PHOTO: MD-MAX, s.r.o.

ABOVE: Monorails carry their weight for industry worldwide.

PHOTO: Klass Teknofabs

13

BASICS

Novelty Monorails

While industrial monorails are everywhere, people-carrying monorails also dot the planet. The vast majority of them carry people in recreation-related venues. As far back as the 1800s, monorails were installed at fun parks. This history has helped associate monorails with a pop culture status of futurism. While conventional, two-rail passenger systems quickly caught on and were standardized, for the most part transport monorails continued to be delegated to expositions and fairs.

Much progress was made in the improvement of monorail technology in the 1950s. The development of Alweg and Safege accelerated interest in transit monorail implementation. Since they were still a novelty to the general public, entertainment venues like fairs, zoos, amusement parks and theme parks scrambled more than ever to give their patrons the unique experience of riding a monorail.

A new breed of novelty monorail was developed, often referred to as minirail. 'Mini' explains it all. They are small novelty rides that are affordable to smaller entertainment destinations, yet they still provide the fun experience of simulating low-level flight.

The result of so many monorails in fun parks, fairs and zoos has been that the general public has typecast monorails. The nonsensical claim by detractors, "Monorails: trains of the future, always have been, always will be," hasn't helped either. There are more and more successful transit monorails opening, despite any catchy phrases opponents espouse.

ABOVE: **This 1955 monorail roller coaster at a Hamburg fair was inspired by the German Alweg test track.**

LEFT: **Novelty monorail postcards.**

15

MONORAILS

ABOVE: Elvis Presley gets a manicure on Seattle's Red Train during the 1962 filming of *It Happened At The World's Fair*.
PHOTO: MOHAI/Seattle Post-Intelligencer Collection

Monorails in Pop Culture: Film and TV

Proponents have formidable challenges getting transit monorails built, but there is no such problem in getting them included in films, books or on television. Even though monorails have existed for well over a century, science fiction and other film/TV productions continue to feature monorails as an illustration of the world of the future.

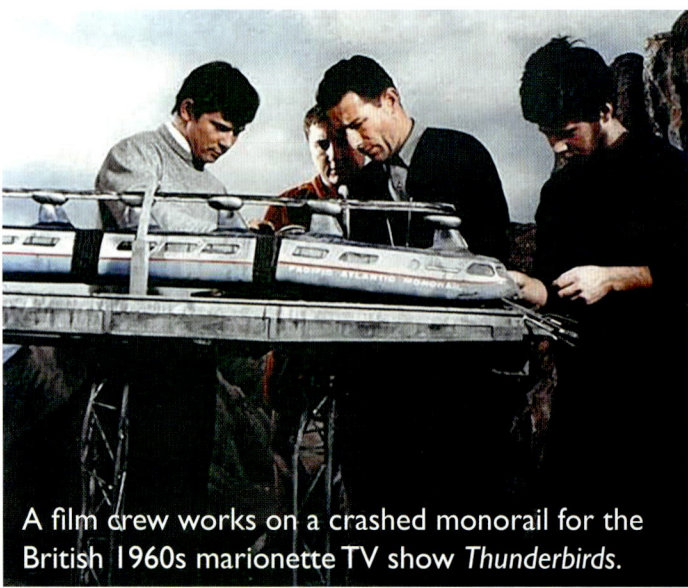

A film crew works on a crashed monorail for the British 1960s marionette TV show *Thunderbirds*.

LEFT: *You Only Live Twice* featured a low altitude monorail in evil Ernst Stavro Blofeld's (Donald Pleasence) volcano interior facility.

BELOW: James Bond (Sean Connery) holds onto monorail track during the final battle scene. The monorail was built by industrial monorail builder Road Machines Ltd.

PHOTOS: United Artists

BASICS

Julie Christie and Oskar Werner walk under the Safege test track in the 1966 Francois Truffaut film *Fahrenheit 451*.

PHOTO: 1966 Vineyard Films, Ltd.

LEFT: *Grassroots*, the highly-fictionalized 2012 film on politics in Seattle, touts the advantages of monorail from beginning to end

PHOTO: MRB Productions

ABOVE: The infamous Simpsons *Marge vs. the Monorail* episode, written by Conan O'Brien. Funny? Yes, but unfortunately some people actually judge monorail based on cartoons.

PHOTO: 20th Century Fox

Avatar included suspended monorails in the special collector's extended-cut DVD.

PHOTO: 20th Century Fox

17

MONORAILS

Monorails in Pop Culture: Advertising

The public likes monorails and advertising agencies have figured that out. Their futuristic look captures attention, and capturing attention is important to advertising. The odd thing is that many print ads have been used to sell things totally unrelated to monorail. Evidently monorails help sell everything from whiskey to adding machines.

NEW DEPARTURES OF TOMORROW
Trip-a-matic 1960?
AERO TRAIN
MONO RAIL
TOMORROW: Get your travel information, accommodations, and tickets in an instant—electronically!
Imagine the ease . . . the simplicity! Trip-a-matic, activated by push buttons and your charge plate, checks accommodations, makes reservations, prints tickets, and bills you later!
Jules Verne himself never imagined it this quick! Nor this reliable! For when Trip-a-matic becomes a reality, its designers will look to New Departure for ball bearings of unerring accuracy . . . even today, the best way to keep moving parts operating smoothly in perfect alignment.
If you have a "dream" on the drawing board, call on New Departure's engineering service for the ball bearings that will help make it come true.
NEW DEPARTURE • DIVISION OF GENERAL MOTORS • BRISTOL, CONNECTICUT
GM GENERAL MOTORS
NEW DEPARTURE
BALL BEARINGS
TODAY: New Departure "sealed and lubricated-for-life" ball bearings help semi-automatic ticket vendors, used by railroads and airlines, to sustain day-in, day-out service.

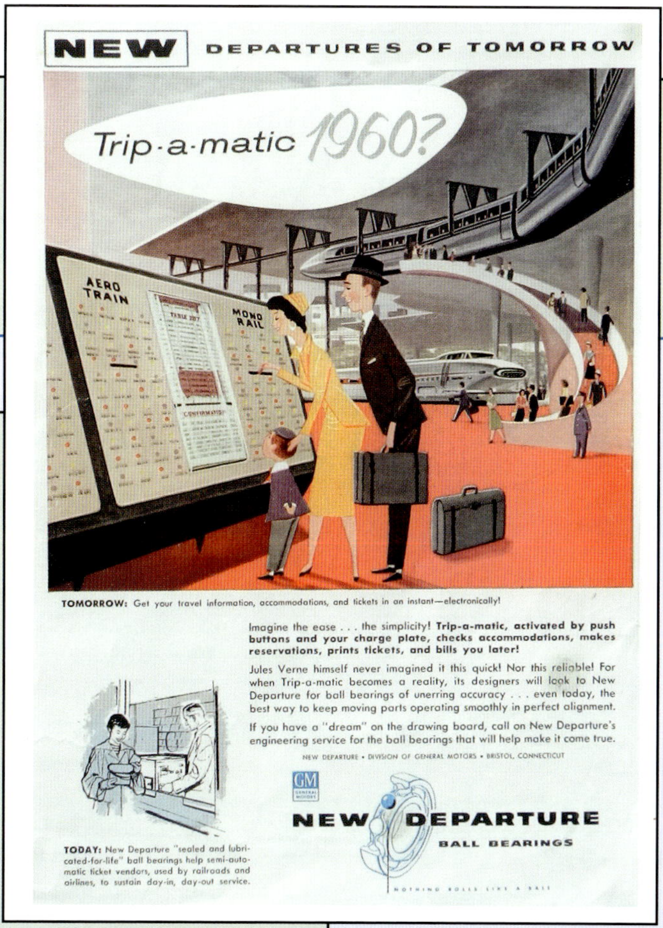

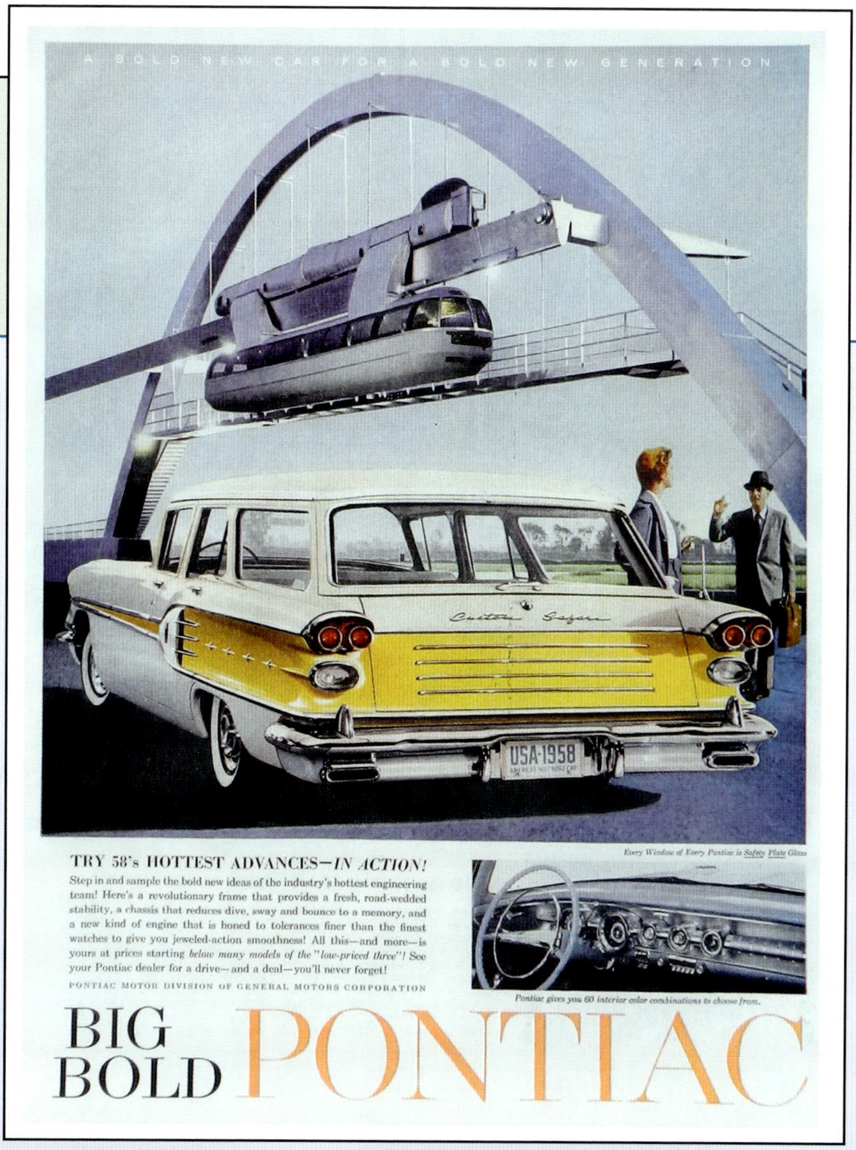
A BOLD NEW CAR FOR A BOLD NEW GENERATION
USA-1958
Every Window of Every Pontiac is Safety Plate Glass
TRY 58's HOTTEST ADVANCES—IN ACTION!
Step in and sample the bold new ideas of the industry's hottest engineering team! Here's a revolutionary frame that provides a fresh, road-wedded stability, a chassis that reduces dive, sway and bounce to a memory, and a new kind of engine that is honed to tolerances finer than the finest watches to give you jeweled-action smoothness! All this—and more—is yours at prices starting below many models of the "low-priced three"! See your Pontiac dealer for a drive—and a deal—you'll never forget!
PONTIAC MOTOR DIVISION OF GENERAL MOTORS CORPORATION
Pontiac gives you 60 interior color combinations to choose from.
BIG BOLD PONTIAC

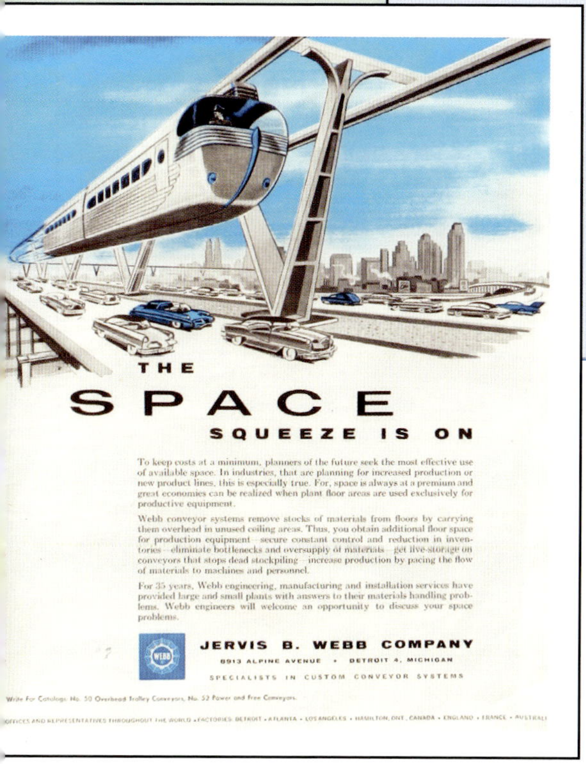
THE SPACE SQUEEZE IS ON
To keep costs at a minimum, planners of the future seek the most effective use of available space. In industries, that are planning for increased production or new product lines, this is especially true. For, space is always at a premium and great economies can be realized when plant floor areas are used exclusively for productive equipment.
Webb conveyor systems remove stocks of materials from floors by carrying them overhead in unused ceiling areas. Thus, you obtain additional floor space for production equipment—secure constant control and reduction in inventories—eliminate bottlenecks and oversupply of materials—get live-storage on conveyors that stops dead stockpiling—increase production by pacing the flow of materials to machines and personnel.
For 35 years, Webb engineering, manufacturing and installation services have provided large and small plants with answers to their materials handling problems. Webb engineers will welcome an opportunity to discuss your space problems.
JERVIS B. WEBB COMPANY
8913 ALPINE AVENUE • DETROIT 4, MICHIGAN
SPECIALISTS IN CUSTOM CONVEYOR SYSTEMS

As transportation goes more and more electric...you can see the future happening.
The people at your Investor-Owned Electric Light and Power Companies*

BROOKLYN-BRONX-N9
MIDTOWN NX 5
NOT AS "Jules Verne" AS IT LOOKS!
Building a high-speed monorail transit system like this is not a postwar project here at Goodyear Aircraft. But we show you this picture to illustrate a point. Fantastic as it looks, its construction is well within the range of our wide experience.
For Goodyear Aircraft Corporation is no stranger to advanced ideas. We are the nation's only builder of giant rigid airships. We engineered the cars of the famed Sky Ride of the Chicago World's Fair; and the most completely aerodynamically streamlined train incorporating aeronautical features. In war we built thousands of swift Corsair fighters and major components for many other airplanes.
Such pioneering has given us expert knowledge in the use of light metals, plastics, fabrics — a special skill we call aircraftsmanship. It can serve you, profitably, in the design, engineering and construction of your postwar product, whether it be a monorail railroad or a monopiece cabinet, a milking machine or a milk bottle cap.
If the design of your new product makes extreme lightness or strength desirable, if it calls for manufacture from metals, plastics, fabrics — or any combination — Goodyear aircraftsmanship may be your answer. Just submit your problem to Goodyear Aircraft Corporation, Akron 15, Ohio.
This is GOODYEAR AIRCRAFTsmanship:
— one of America's dynamic engineering organizations
— a corps of able engineers; master tooling experts; skilled management
— more than a million square feet of floor space; most modern equipment for working metals, plastics, fabrics
— high production capacity geared to meet your sales requirements.
GOODYEAR AIRCRAFT

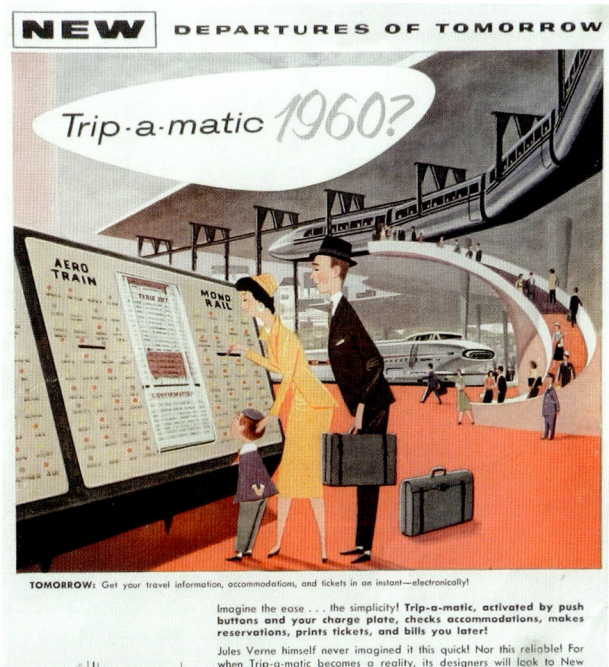

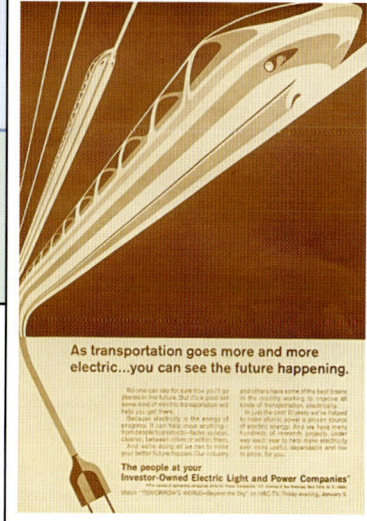

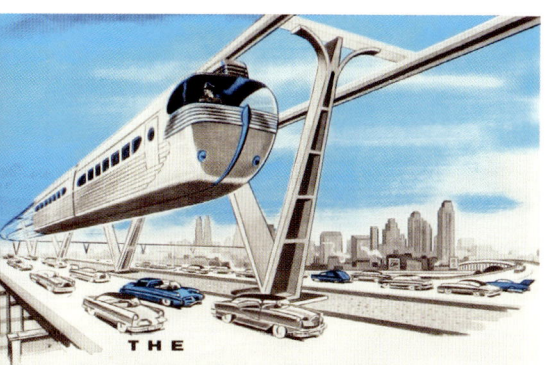

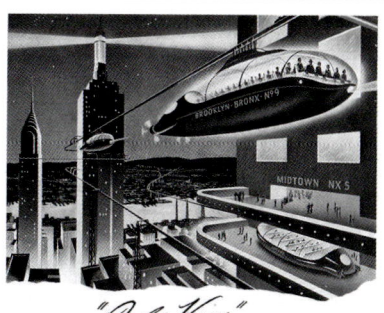

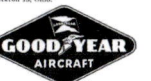

Despite having a perception as a fun ride, Disneyland Monorail continues to demonstrate its over-traffic advantages.

PHOTO: Author

Monorails are everywhere. They are used in industry in thousands of ways, yet go unnoticed. The ones that usually gain attention are the novelty monorails at zoos, fun parks and fairs. Monorail's true potential for transit applications is too often ignored, mostly because of their fun park typecasting. This chapter ends with images of a famous theme park and World's Fair monorail. While they could both be lumped into the 'just for fun' perception many have, ironically these monorails continue to inspire and set the example that *monorails are not just a ride*. They are proving so more than fifty years after their openings.

Both the Disneyland Alweg Monorail System and the Seattle Century 21 World's Fair Monorail were built to demonstrate the amazing capabilities of monorail. They have succeeded, but not everyone recognizes this. Consider that Seattle's monorail was reverse-engineered and resulted in the Kuala Lumpur Monorail in Malaysia, and Mumbai Monorail in India. There are many more to come. Monorail technology is now enjoying a growth spurt. In fact, they are being built in increasing numbers too large to be ignored. This book intends to shed light on existing and new systems. But first, what really are the advantages of monorail?

BASICS

One of the most iconic monorail photographs ever taken, this view of Alweg's monorail at Seattle's Century 21 World's Fair donned the cover of Life Magazine in 1962.
PHOTO: Ralph Crane

Chongqing Monorail
Monorail in greenery, and monorails *are* green
PHOTO: ImagineChina

Shonan Monorail
FACING PAGE: Red lights and traffic don't hinder monorail.
PHOTO: Author

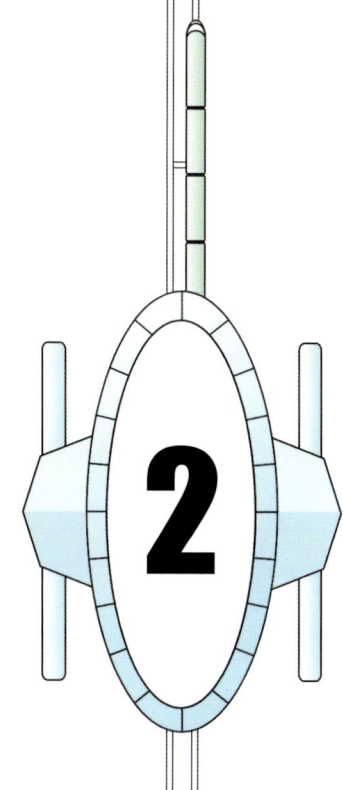

Why not monorail?

Arguments and advantages

As traffic woes increase around the world, the debate over the best way to mitigate congestion continues. There are numerous options, and *no single mode is good for every situation*. However, monorail is often completely left out of the mix. This chapter brings to light some interesting facts to ponder.

MONORAILS

The problem and one solution

Traffic is an every day fact of living in today's world. It's the price we pay for our love of the automobile, as well as our growing needs for mobility. To take on this challenge a variety of solutions to transport needs are being implemented. However, for reasons mentioned in Chapter One, one solution is far too often completely overlooked; monorail.

Monorails are proven. Each and every day hundreds of thousands of passengers are carried on monorails. Many of the world's transit monorails exist in Japan, eight of which are full-scale urban systems. Others exist in all corners of the world. Numerous additional monorails are either in advanced planning or under construction (see Addendum, page 244).

Monorails can be built quickly, using the space above public roads without disturbing surface vehicular traffic or that of pedestrians. Most monorails make use of rubber tires, producing little noise or vibration.

Monorails are not only a great way to move people, they are also extremely environment-friendly. As an example, in 2013 the Las Vegas Monorail aided in the annual removal of an estimated 1.9-million vehicle miles from Southern Nevada's major roadways, reducing emissions by more than 24 tons of carbon monoxide (CO), volatile organic compounds (VOC) and nitrogen oxides (NOx) over the course of the year. All this from a relatively short 6.3-kilometer system. Consider the similar results by the growing number of monorails and you can imagine the positive impact on their communities.

PHOTO: Eagleflying / Dreamstime

With a surface footprint less than two meters wide, a typical monorail system is capable of handling rush hour traffic equivalent to many lanes of freeway.

ART: Alweg/Author

WHY NOT MONORAIL?

Fast

Mass transit officials are charged with getting Joe Citizen out of his automobile and into their busses and trains. One of the great enticements is the ability to get Joe to his destination as fast or faster than he can by car. Are they successful? If the mass transit is located in the same space as street traffic, the answer is no. In that case, riding bus or light rail can take as much as double the time of his automobile. That's not exactly an enticement. On the other hand, if the transit is grade-separate from traffic, chances are much better Joe can get downtown, or wherever he's going more quickly. There are grade-separate trains other than monorail that can be fast, such as subway, but the time to build them is far longer and they are much more expensive to construct and operate. Subway doesn't provide riders with views along the route either. Meanwhile, monorail gives demonstrable views of the traffic they are speeding past. The result is that riders immediately put two and two together, "We are travelling faster than we would in our car." Most rubber-tired monorails travel up to 89-kilometers per hour, which is plenty fast for systems with stations about one to two kilometers apart. Joe would use it.

ABOVE: Monorails run red lights all the time, and they do it legally.

PHOTOS: Author

LEFT: Kuala Lumpur's KL Monorail speeds along over busy streets below.

Reliable

What good is a transit system if passengers can't rely on it? If there has been an accident with pedestrians or an automobile somewhere on the line, an entire system is affected with delayed service and lower reliability percentage numbers. Do commuters enjoy having to repeatedly explain to their employers why they are late to work? They certainly don't like waiting in stations or on stalled trains for delayed service. One of the great advantages of monorail systems is their reliability. Monorails regularly operate at reliability percentages higher than 99%. Other forms of transit have a tough time reaching numbers like that. Monorail rubber tires get little wear running on smooth guideways. Typically, each load tire gets over 160,000 kilometers of travel before being replaced. Florida's Walt Disney World Monorail System has a total of twelve trains. During peak seasons at least ten of them are on the beamway, serving passengers 18 hours a day. It's not unusual for all twelve trains to be operating at the same time. The system carries on average over 150,000 passengers a day. No other form of transit is as reliable. With steel rail, there are almost always trains and track segments undergoing maintenance because of the wear and tear by friction.

Cost Effective & Sustainable

When transit systems are proposed and debated, one immensely important factor is usually not included. If long-term cost effectiveness was considered seriously, it is likely far more monorails would be in our midst. Case in point: The Tokyo-Haneda Monorail has been operating since 1964. This 17.8-kilometer dual-beam system is privately owned and turns a profit. The Seattle Center Monorail is owned by the City of Seattle and operated under a concession agreement by

LEFT: **Disney's Contemporary Resort and the Transportation Ticketing Center at Walt Disney World Resort**
PHOTO: Anthony Aneese Totah Jr/Dreamstime

WHY NOT MONORAIL?

Seattle Monorail Services (SMS) with independent leadership and staff. The monorail is not given any operating funds from taxpayers. All operations costs and profits which the City and SMS receive are generated through ticket sales. In return for the concession to operate the line, the SMS splits profits with the city 50-50 every year. What private business would take on a contract like this unless a profit was guaranteed? Profit is indeed an oddity in the transit world, as most transit technologies require enormous subsidies from taxpayers. Studies have found that construction costs of monorail are comparable to light rail. However, monorail requires *less* concrete, steel, rail, ties, cables and all other types of hardware. Bombardier, a major multi-technology rail supplier, suggests in their monorail literature, 'where more than 25% of the route must be elevated, [monorail] will cost less to build and maintain than any other elevated transit technology with similar capacity.' A huge cost benefit will be realized during operation. If you're planning a transit system, insist upon a long-term Life Cycle Cost Analysis comparison of monorail vs. the other transit systems, then judge which one is the most sustainable.

ABOVE: Rubber tires on concrete beams require minimal care. Here a technician works on a Tokyo Monorail bogie.

PHOTOS: Author

Two controllers oversee the entire Las Vegas Monorail system. Drivers aren't needed when trains don't mix with traffic.

MONORAILS

Environment Friendly - Construction

Most rail construction includes long-term and space-constraining disruption of the surrounding area. Monorail construction progresses down the alignment far quicker than other rail systems, minimizing the disruption time. The land space required for monorail supports isn't much; so fewer traffic lanes are closed while posts are installed. Additionally, beams are built offsite, trucked in and lifted into place very quickly. This topic warrants more attention; hence Chapter Seven is entitled 'How to Build a Monorail.'

LEFT: Monorail construction is the least disruptive, and takes the least amount of time.

Environment Friendly - Less Intrusive

To this day the existence of the Chicago L (elevated) contributes to the notion that all elevated rail produce darkened streets and noise. Monorail has been unfairly lumped into this image. The monorailist's battle to convince the public otherwise continues. While the L is conventional steel rail built on massive structures that almost completely cover the streets, monorail features far less-imposing narrow posts with track less than a meter wide. In fact, monorail usually creates less shadow than any other structure or building nearby.

LEFT: The Chicago L is not monorail, yet its negative image for elevated rail is unfairly shared.

RIGHT: Does monorail create the most imposing, street-darkening shadows in downtown?

WHY NOT MONORAIL?

Environment Friendly - Quiet

Disney's Contemporary Resort in Florida includes room rates of over $500 per night. Why would any guest pay for such a room if an operating train system were located on the floor below them? In the case of monorail, they are so quiet that trains continuously enter the concourse without disturbing any guests. Running on rubber tires, they glide almost silently on their concrete beams. Since they are this quiet *inside* a building, they are just as quiet outdoors. Where monorails are located above city streets, the sound of the trains is drowned out by surface traffic below. They don't have wheels that squeal, and their electric motors are nearly silent.

BELOW: In an unusual demonstration of quietness, Inuyama Monorail didn't disturb the dearly-departed during its 46-year run.

PHOTO: Author

ABOVE: A quiet Mark VI train enters the luxury Disney's Contemporary Resort in Florida.
PHOTO: Keith Walls

MONORAILS

Environment Friendly - 'Green'

Elevated rail can be attractive. Really, it can! Good-looking trains are a staple of the monorail family, and that will continue. However, rail alignments are not immune to creative aesthetic improvements. In the first place, minimal space is needed for monorail. There is much airspace below track that can be filled with fountains, lighting and most importantly, the greenery of plants. The desire for green belts in urban environments has grown in recent decades. Landscaping under monorails likely originated in fairs and theme parks, but the idea has spread to most non-resort systems. New urban monorails feature extensive use of landscaping beneath the track, and in some cases vines grow freely up the pylons.

ABOVE: Daegu Monorail, South Korea; developed in parallel with numerous linear parks along the route

LEFT: Tokyo Monorail by night; extensive landscaping below monorails is possible because of minimal space taken by track supports.

WHY NOT MONORAIL?

Environment Friendly - Aesthetic

While monorailists may adore the look of clean, minimal structures of monorail, the general public can have 'attitude' when it comes to any over-street trains, no matter how quiet they may be. Architects deal with the challenge in clever ways. First off, a monorail station can look like just about any building you want it to. If the surroundings call for a Victorian turn-of-the-century structure, no problem. If the station serves a tropical resort, a Polynesian flavor can be added. If the surroundings are contemporary, there are literally thousands of building designs that will fit the bill. But what about the track stretching between stations? Monorail track structures are as simple and classic as Stonehenge and the Roman arches. Virtually any surface, color or lighting can be applied; only limits of the imagination can hinder the possibilities.

LEFT: **Decorated pylons can not only support monorail track, but they can double as light posts.**

PHOTOS: Author

ABOVE: **Marbleized bases and metal-framed, mirrored pylons can enhance pylon aesthetics in urban areas.**

LEFT: **Several monorails, including this one in Australia's Broadbeach, have attractive neon-like lights under the beams. Rather than hide track, the lights enhance them.**

MONORAILS

RIGHT: In 1999 Wuppertal's Schwebebahn suffered five passenger fatalities. Construction workers left a temporary clamp on the track and no safety check runs were made before the first passenger train of the morning.

PHOTO: Wikipedia

Safety - Sparse Accident History

Is monorail history perfect? No, there have been unfortunate accidents, but they remain few and far between. The entire accident history of monorails is less in number than one year of many individual conventional rail transit lines. Monorail accidents are so rare that when they happen they receive worldwide press attention. There have been only three accidents resulting in passenger fatalities in over one hundred years of monorail history.

BELOW: Hemisfair 68's minirail suffered a driver caused collision, resulting in the Western Hemisphere's only monorail passenger fatality in the entire 20th century.

PHOTO: Robert E. Weston Jr.

Safety - Evacuation

Evacuation of trains in emergency situations is often cited as a negative for monorail. While monorail evacuations are extremely rare, builders and operators have established a number of ways to rescue passengers in the unlikely event of power failure or fire. Train-to-train evacuation ramps are available on many monorails. Ladder trucks provided by fire departments are a common method; evacuation slides on board trains are another. Nowadays, many new monorails feature emergency walkways.

ABOVE: For monorails without emergency walkways, ladder trucks are used when train-to-train ramp evacuations aren't possible.

PHOTOS: Chiba Urban Monorail Col., Ltd.

RIGHT: On board train chutes are available in emergencies on Mitsubishi suspended monorails.

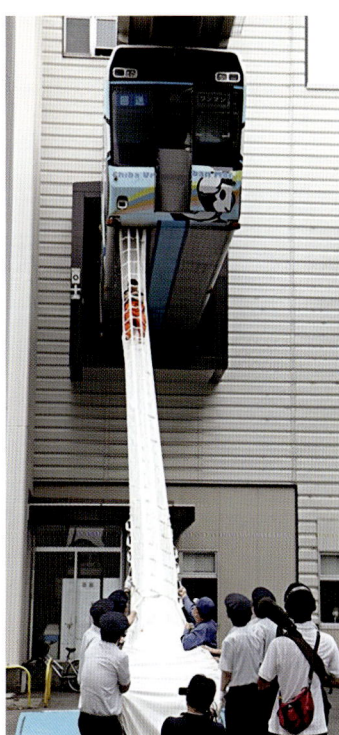

Like most new systems, Las Vegas Monorail features emergency walkways between the tracks.

PHOTO: Author

MONORAILS

ABOVE: Automobile drivers or pedestrians are almost always blamed, but blame doesn't stop frequent light rail accidents from happening.

Why not Light Rail?

Light Rail Transit (LRT) has enjoyed several decades of growth, most notably in the United States. LRT is a fancy new name for streetcars or trams. The word 'light' refers to passenger capacity and has nothing to do with weight. In fact, light rail trains are very heavy. They are built heavy to withstand collisions, and for good reason. Light rail operates primarily at ground level, and more often than not the track is embedded in public streets. LRT trains share space with automobile and pedestrian traffic. While LRT proponents tout the easy access to trains via ground level stations, its proximity to traffic leads to far too many accidents. For example, Houston's Metrorail LRT suffered 70 accidents in its first year. Accidents reduce reliability and worse yet, they hurt and kill people. Light rail has other problems as well, including prolonged and disruptive construction time. Automation isn't possible, since drivers are required to operate trains in hazardous surroundings. Ground space takes away traffic lanes, adding to congestion. Speed is not an advantage since trains must also wait for signal lights and traffic. Like bus and subway, LRT operational costs make profit unheard of.

ABOVE: Light rail drivers striking, not a problem with an automated monorail

PHOTOS: Author

RIGHT: The aesthetics of light rail warning signs, catenary lines and posts

34

WHY NOT MONORAIL?

Ground space: which takes up more, monorail or light rail?

Why not Subway?

Ray Bradbury said it best, "Subways take forever to build and, because the tunnels have to be excavated, are incredibly expensive. The cost of one subway line would build ten monorail systems. Along the way, subway construction destroys businesses by the scores. The history of the subway from East L.A. to the Valley is a history of ruined businesses and upended lives." Then why are so many built? Follow the money. Much more can be made from conventional rail.

Why not Bus Rapid Transit?

Bus Rapid Transit (BRT) suffers the same issues as light rail. BRT is simply a bus with exclusive ground and road space, yet it's been given a carefully contrived, appealing name. That exclusive road space is rarely 100% of the alignment, and BRT still mixes with auto and pedestrians in negative ways. When Los Angeles officials decided against monorail for the San Fernando Valley, the area got an accident-prone, ground-space-hogging bus path instead. And like light rail, each BRT vehicle requires a driver.

ABOVE: Grim, dark and expensive tunnels of subway

ABOVE: BRT gobbles up a lot of ground space.

MONORAILS

What about the weather?

Inclement weather is a factor that challenges all forms of transit. How does monorail hold up to these challenges? Modern 20th century monorail technologies now have more than a half a century of experience to prove their abilities. Straddle monorails operate well in cold weather because of the tractive qualities of their rubber-tired trains on concrete. The narrowness of the guideway structure is also a plus. The beam is free of any fixtures that can trap snow or ice and most snow is blown off the guideway surface. Frequency of train service usually prevents build-up, however any snow on the beam is easily removed with rotating brushes or scrapers mounted on the front car. Japanese monorail systems demonstrate this by continuing to operate without interruption during snow and ice storms. In areas that experience severe ice accumulation, resistance heating elements can be embedded in the top surface of the beamway, especially where there are grades. Safege suspended monorails have a similar successful inclement weather history, with the added benefit that all running surfaces are enclosed inside the box-beam track. The complete enclosure of the bogies inside the track protects them from the weather, so the system is unaffected by rain, frost or snow. In fact, it's not unusual for monorails to continue operating while weather creates gridlock on the streets below.

ABOVE Chiba Urban Monorail operates in adverse conditions from typhoons to blizzards. The running surfaces are on the interior of the box-beam track, a strong selling point for inclement weather capabilities of Safege technology.

PHOTO: Sakakura Toru/Chiba Urban Monorail Co., Ltd.

RIGHT: Kuala Lumpur's KL Monorail each year endures massive downpours of the Monsoon season without hindrance of service.

PHOTO: David M. Ice

WHY NOT MONORAIL?

While not an annual event, Seattle Center Monorail has weathered snowstorms on many occasions. Load-bearing tires flatten any fresh snow on the beam and repeated runs prevent snow or ice buildup. The same can't be said for surface-running busses and light rail, which under these conditions often come to a standstill.

PHOTO: Megan Ching/Seattle Monorail Services

MONORAILS

Fun and Popular

Monorails are popular with people. Monorail travel gives riders the sensation of low-level flight. Like an airplane, trains bank slightly from side to side in turns and provide great views due to a virtually invisible track. A common rider phrase heard by monorail operators at Disney parks in the USA is, "Why don't we have one of these back in our city of ____?" In fact, voters have demonstrated their preference for monorail on more than one occasion. In Los Angeles, they voted five to one in favor of monorail in a 1990 referendum on transit for San Fernando Valley. LA transit officials and politicians ignored them and continued to build light rail, bus rapid transit and subways. In November of 1997, approximately 93,000 Seattle voters said yes to a grassroots-produced initiative for a 64-kilometer citywide monorail system. A subsequent Seattle ballot initiative to tax automobile owners for a starter line in 2002 passed as well. Although voters supported the monorail on no-less-than four separate ballots, controversy over financing and lack of mayoral support resulted in the cancellation of the project in 2005 (see Chapter 4). Undeterred, Seattle monorail proponents continue efforts to revive the project. Monorails continue to remain popular with people and slowly but surely, more are being planned and built.

Monorails are fun and popular. Does this mean their advantages should be taken less seriously?

Some things never change; children excitedly wait to ride the 1956 Goodell monorail in Houston.

Why not More?

You might be asking, "If monorails are so wonderful, why aren't there more of them?" It's a very good question! A multitude of reasons can explain why you don't see as many monorails as other transit systems. Some have said, "There aren't any transit monorails and we shouldn't build something that hasn't been proven." It's flawed reasoning, but thanks to lack of knowledge, it continues. Monorails are still perceived as new, experimental and untried. Not enough people are aware of the many monorails in operation today. The more fallacious reasoning for less monorails is, quoting numerous professionals from within the industry, "There's just not enough money in monorails." The conventional rail industry has established a stronghold and monorail is often discouraged by consultants. Seeking more lucrative steel rail contracts, they recite repeated untruths about monorail in city after city when rail is initially studied. Using these deceitful tactics, they succeed in eliminating monorail in early stages of planning. Despite the understandable desire to maximize profit, manufacturers will line up to build whatever you want. If your city wants a more expensive-to-build, more costly-to-operate technology than monorail, manufacturers are happy to oblige. Despite the claims of monorail critics, as you will see in this book, there are many successful transit monorails around the world and more are coming.

Chongqing Monorail speeds past traffic.

PHOTO: Bo Li/Dreamstime

Enos Electric Railway
The one-kilometer track by Enos Electric Railway Company in South Park, Minnesota
PHOTO: Minnesota Historical Society

Torino Alweg Monorail
FACING PAGE: Alweg's first full-sized monorail for paying passengers at Italia 61 Expo.
PHOTO: Author's Collection

3 History highlights

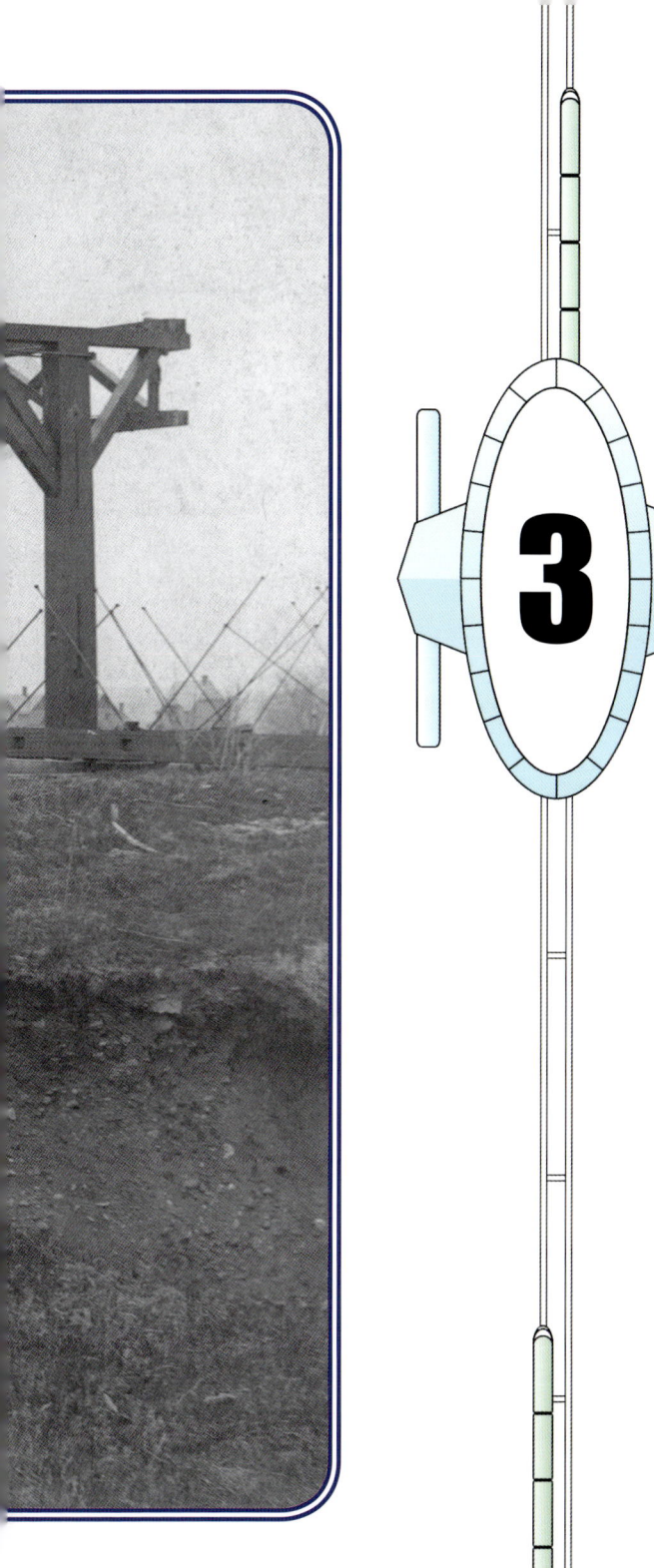

How the technology advanced

Monorail history could fill volumes of books. This chapter offers only highlights of that rich history. Included are notable monorails from the beginning that either advanced the technology, or at the very least brought attention to the idea of monorails for transit. Surprisingly, the 'train of the future' has been around for a long time.

MONORAILS

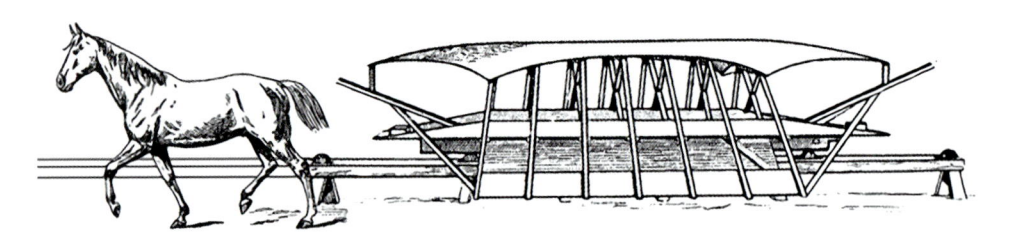

1820: Elmanov

Although it's possible that others preceded him, Russian inventor Ivan Kirillovich Elmanov has been credited with building the world's first monorail. His 'road on pillars' was built in the village of Mychkovo, near Moscow. Carts straddled a low, elevated track made of wood. Wheels were placed on the track and not on the car. Horses would walk alongside the track and pull the carts. Salt mines in Crimea are said to have used Elmanov's monorail design.

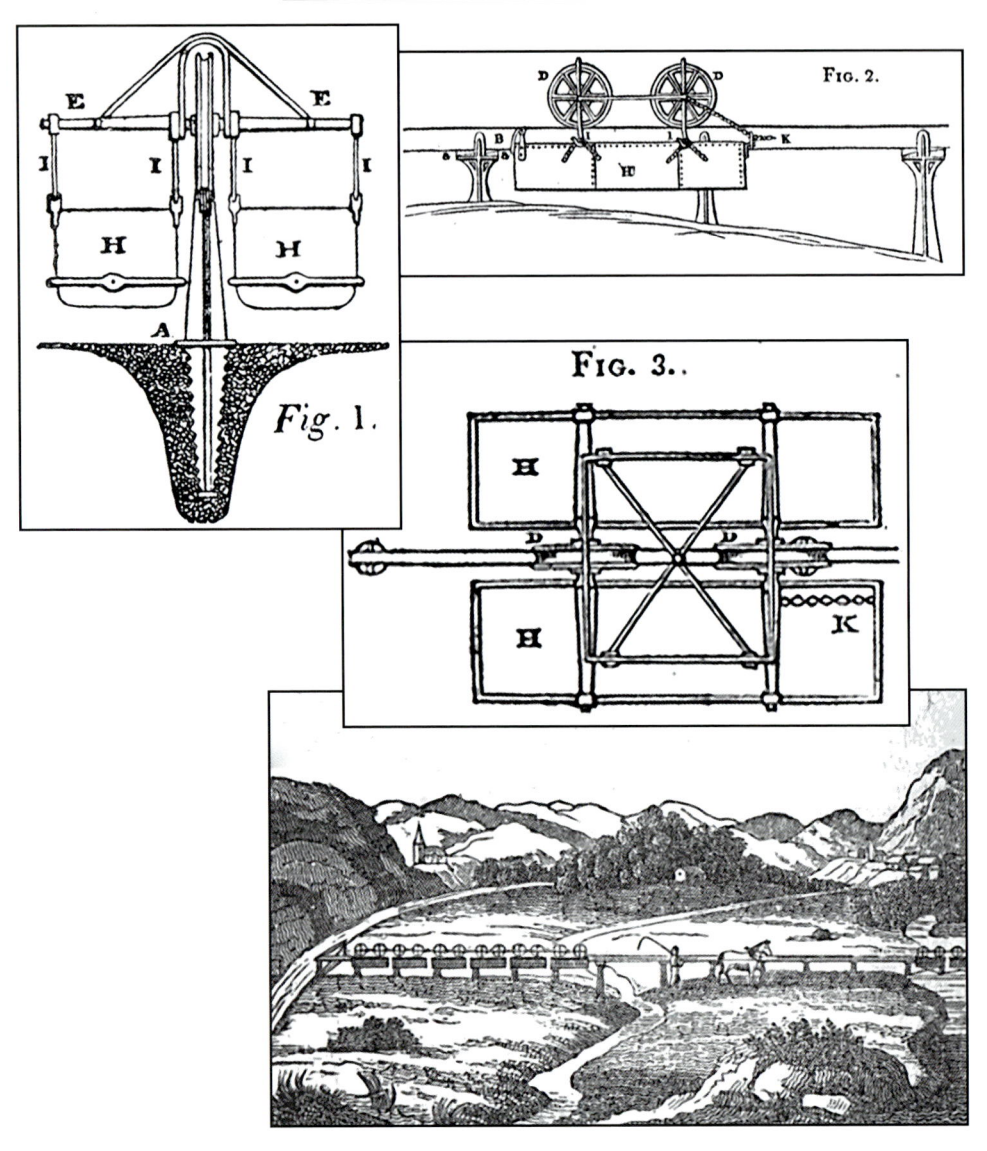

1824: Palmer

The distinction of obtaining the first monorail patent is given to Englishman Henry Robinson Palmer. As an engineer for the London Dock Company, Palmer applied his 1821 patented monorail concept to the loading and unloading of vessels. Palmer published a book entitled 'Description of a Railway on a New Principle' in 1823, which was popular enough to go into a second edition in 1824. The advantage of the Palmer monorail was that while the rail was essentially level, the ground did not require extensive grading. Wooden posts varied in height depending on need. 1824 is also when the first Palmer monorail line carried goods between the Thames River and the warehouses of Royal Victualling Yard. The second line opened the next year to carry bricks across the Cheshunt marshes from the brickworks to the River Lee where they were loaded onto barges.

Although the line carried bricks, it has been given the distinction of the first passenger-carrying monorail in the world. During the grand opening of the Cheshunt Monorail, a special carriage built in the barouche style carried officials of the company for that one day. Seven cars, each with two cast-iron double-flanged wheels, were pulled by horses walking alongside the track. In 1826 Palmer exhibited a model of his monorail in Elberfeld, Germany. A company was formed for a Palmer monorail to carry coal between Elberfeld and Barmen, yet no such monorail was built. However, 75 years later, Elberfeld and Barmen would be connected by a world-famous suspended monorail.

HISTORY HIGHLIGHTS

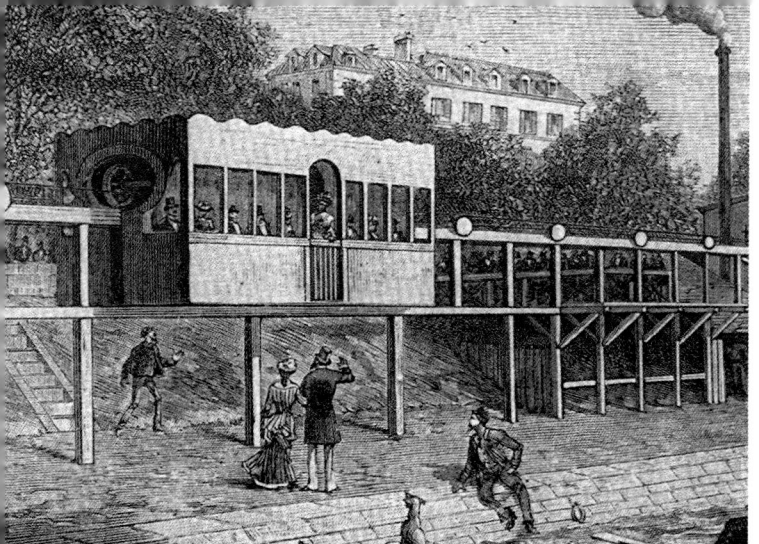

1872: Lyon Exposition

Designed by Monsieur Duchamp, an elevated monorail was put into service at the Exposition Universelle et Internationale in Lyon, France. The car was mounted on the sides of a one-kilometer guideway, and elevated approximately four meters above the ground. A cable moved the car along the track. 3,500 passengers per day rode the monorail during the exhibition. After Lyon, monorails at fairs would become commonplace.

1876: Philadelphia Centennial

The United States of America saw its first monorail on the occasion of its 100th anniversary in 1876. General LeRoy Stone demonstrated a steam-driven monorail at the United States Centennial Exposition in Philadelphia. Almost ten million visitors went to the fair between May and November of that year. The grounds were on 285 acres of land. Stone's ornately designed double-decker vehicle had two vertical double-flanged wheels that rolled on the single load-bearing rail. The rear wheel was driven by a rotary steam engine. Side wheels stabilized the train against the A-frame of the wooden track. The short demonstration line was located over a gorge in Fairmount Park on the exhibition grounds.

ABOVE: Stone's monorail as imagined for city use

MONORAILS

1878: Bradford & Foster Brook

A modified version of General Stone's Centennial monorail was put into use on a 6.4-kilometer line between Bradford and Gilmore, Pennsylvania. It was built to transport oil drilling equipment and personnel to Derrick City. One of the rare monorail disasters in history occurred on January 27, 1879. Coupled to a flat car full of officials, the train ran at high speed to demonstrate its capability. The boiler exploded and the train crashed into a creek, killing the driver, fireman and three passengers. Other passengers were severely injured. The line was sold and abandoned shortly thereafter.

1869-1924: Haddon and Lartigue

While the monorails in Pennsylvania garnered much of the attention in North America, similar A-shaped trestle monorails were already being utilized elsewhere in the world. British civil engineer J.L. Haddon modified mule-pulled monorails to include steam-powered engines in Syria. Yet no one was more successful in spreading the technology than French engineer Charles Francois Marie-Therese Lartigue. Lartigue improved upon Palmer's design and demonstrated his ideas in 1884 in Paris. In the following years he also showed the technology in Westminster, Tours, St. Petersburg, Long Island and Brussels. Several lines were built as a result of his efforts, including in Guatemala, Peru, and Russia.

Feurs-Pannisière line in central France

HISTORY HIGHLIGHTS

ABOVE: **The re-created Lartigue Monorailway in Ireland.**

Probably the most famous of railways built upon Lartigue technology was the Listowel & Ballybunion Railway in Ireland. Starting in 1888, trains covered a distance of 14.5-kilometers between Listowel and Ballybunion at speeds up to 42 km/h. It operated for 36 years. A 16.8-kilometer Lartigue line opened in central France in 1894 linking Feurs and Pannisière. The last of the Lartigue lines was known as the Magnesium Monorail. The 48-kilometer line began operating in 1924 near Trona, California. The gas-powered monorail carried magnesium salts from the mine of the Sierra Salt Corporation through rugged terrain to the Searles Valley, before desert conditions took their toll on the wood track structure. It ceased operations in 1926 and was abandoned. In recent years, a Lartigue train and a 1000-meter section of track were painstakingly re-created in Listowel.

Magnesium Monorail

MONORAILS

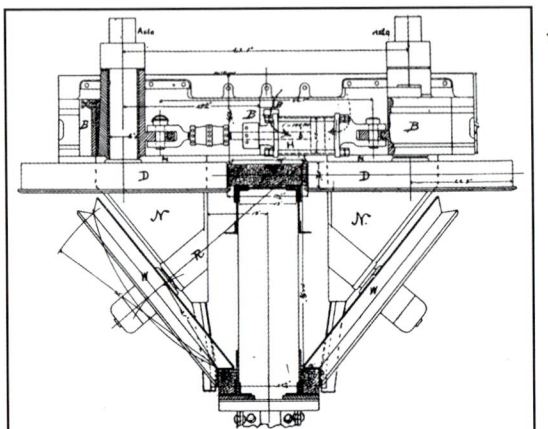

1886: Meigs

Captain Joe V. Meigs seemed to understand the possibilities of monorail like no other inventor preceding him. The importance of separating rail from street traffic was the basis for the Meigs Elevated Railway. Another advantage of his design was the narrowness of the guideway; it wouldn't darken the streets with massive structures as the conventional elevated railways being built at the time. Meigs managed to go where many proposed designs fail to go even today, to a full-sized test track. About 1.6-kilometer of track was built to test and demonstrate his radically new design in East Cambridge, Massachusetts. Meigs Monorail was way ahead of its time with aerodynamic coaches, angled load bearing double-flanged wheels and hydraulic brakes on the vertical wheels that squeezed the track. Meigs tested his train to 48 km/h, but claimed in regular use it would be capable of up to 160 km/h. This is remarkable considering it was the 1880s. The technology might have been too far ahead of its time, no Meigs monorail was ever used in revenue service.

46

HISTORY HIGHLIGHTS

1887: Enos

The first suspended monorail was tested on the grounds of the Enos Electric Company in Greenville, New Jersey. The Greenville demonstration track attracted considerable publicity in the press, but only one short line was built based on the technology. The design may have influenced Eugen Langen in Germany, as the Enos Monorail bears a likeness to the later-built Wuppertal Schwebebahn. After proving the concept at the Greenville test track, a 1.2-kilometer line was built in 1888 in South Park, a suburb of St. Paul, Minnesota. Enos called for steel construction and track elevated 4.2 meters above the ground, yet the short line was built of wood and ran barely above the surface. Plans to extend the line across the Mississippi River into St. Paul evaporated after running into strong local opposition.

1900: Romanov

In March 1895, Russian engineer Ippolit Romanov built a prototype electric monorail in Odessa. He demonstrated a functional model of his monorail at an 1897 meeting of the Russian Technological Society. Romanov received approval from Empress Maria Fedorovna to built an experimental electric line in Gatchina. The steel track was a short .2-kilometers long. The one car vehicle was first tested on June 25, 1900. The fully loaded vehicle was only capable of a modest 15 km/h, yet riders said the monorail gave a very smooth ride, free of 'jerks and jolts.' Romanov suggested his monorail could be used for movement of light and/or heavy freight of mail, grain crops, stone, ore, earth and cement, and for transportation of people. He also suggested that the military could use quickly-installed military monorail lines using tripods made from trees.

MONORAILS

1901: Wuppertal

Civil Engineer Eugen Langen of Cologne, Germany left his mark on the history of monorails like few others have. His Schwebebahn (swinging railway) has operated successfully along the Wupper River for over 100 years. Langen's invention has survived two world wars and continues to operate today. Langen conceived of his suspended rail line for passengers after success with his invention of small freight monorails attached to the ceiling of his sugar refinery in Cologne. Industrial monorails based on his invention are easily the most common monorail conveyances found in the world. Wuppertal's trains are suspended from bogies with double-flanged wheels. A passenger-carrying demonstration line was first built at Cologne-Deutz. Unfortunately Langen died in 1895 and never saw his monorail completed. One of the first dignitaries to test ride the Schwebebahn was Kaiser Wilhelm II, six months before the public had a chance to ride. The first 4.4-kilometers opened with great fanfare on March 1, 1901, with additions shortly thereafter. Trains have been replaced over the years, but the meticulously-maintained 'Kaiserwagen' provides special runs for tourists and rail fans along the 13.3-kilometer line.

PHOTO: James Pierce Fox Collection

Langen test track featuring single pylon supports

Schwebebahn's double-flanged wheels banking over the curving river

HISTORY HIGHLIGHTS

PHOTO: James Pierce Fox Collection

Finely-dressed passengers at Döppersberg Station

MONORAILS

Four examples out of hundreds of postcards that well document over a century of Schwebebahn history

HISTORY HIGHLIGHTS

PHOTO: United States Library of Congress

ABOVE: The Wuppertal Schwebebahn in 1913
A train of the future in an era of horsecarts

LITHOGRAPHY: Friedrich Brockhaus Co. Ltd.

51

MONORAILS

1909: Brennan

Louis Brennan patented his invention for a gyroscopically-balanced car in 1903. His first prototype could carry one child on a tensioned cable. A full-scale demonstration was presented to the press on November 10, 1909 at Gillingham, England. Brennan's 22-ton vehicle was promoted primarily for the military, due to the quickness that track could be laid. Even with 40 passengers on one side of the vehicle, the two onboard gyroscopes were strong enough to keep the car level. If the gyroscope power failed, gyro momentum was said to be sufficient for the train to stop and rest on side-mounted stands.

1909: Scherl

At the same time that Brennan developed his gyro-monorail, German pioneer August Scherl worked on his own design. Not by coincidence, both inventors first demonstrated their prototypes on the same day, November 10, 1909. Despite a series of successful demonstrations to scientists, engineers and military officers, the fear of gyroscope failure prevented both Scherl's and Brennan's designs from ever being used for transportation. Other attempts to develop gyroscope monorail systems would later be made without success; Peter Schilovsky in Russia in the 1920s and brothers Louis and Ernest Swinney with friend Harry Ferreira in the United States in the 1960s.

HISTORY HIGHLIGHTS

1911: Boyes

Inventor and entrepreneur William H. Boyes built a straddle-beam monorail test track on the Tacoma tide flats in Washington State. The International Monorail Company used wooden beams and promised a cost of only $3,000 per 1.6 kilometers. Financial backing fell through, but the Boyes design predicted the look of monorails to come decades later.

PHOTO: United States Library of Congress

1914: Genoa

Built for the 1914 Esposizione Internazionale di Igiene, Marina e Colonie, the monorail also resembled designs to come many years later. Taking the technology a step further than Boyes, Genoa's monorail featured concrete track. The line linked the exhibition site with a central square of the city. The electric train was built by the Italian manufacturer Carminati & Toselli and consisted of four passenger coaches. The monorail operated for a couple of years and was then dismantled.

MONORAILS

1952: Alweg

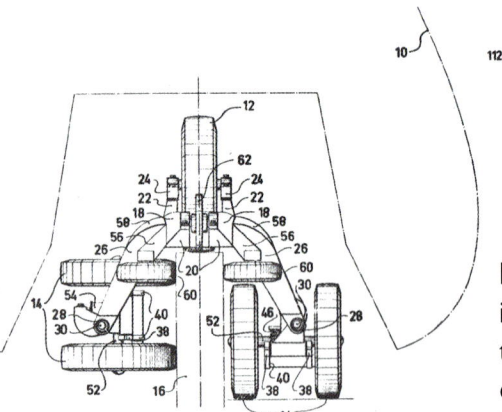

Early Alweg patents included multi-modal trains that could run on both concrete beams and conventional rails. Patents also existed for Alweg monorail trains that could convert to surface road vehicles.

Illustrations in one of the first Alweg brochures suggested a double-decker inter-city transport, as well as an industrial freight train

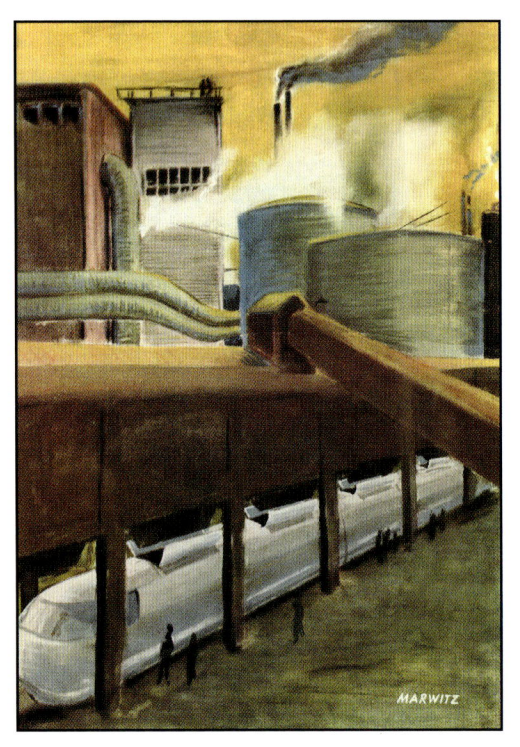

Swedish industrialist and financier Axel Lennart Wenner-Gren was the first to build a monorail test track after World War II. The system was called Alweg, an acronym of his name. Wenner-Gren's first monorail was aimed more toward a high-speed city-to-city rail, capable of carrying either passengers or freight. Designs revolved around very large trains, double-decked for passenger use.

A post-war upsurge in the use of automobiles and increase in traffic jams led to Wenner-Gren's efforts to study new ways of moving people and product. The Alweg system was the result of studies he began in 1950. To avoid potential collisions, the design called for grade separation from all surface traffic. Another goal of Alweg GmbH was to speed up construction methods. Modular construction methods were patented and they have been incorporated in every Alweg-type monorail, from the first prototype up to and including new monorails being built today.

The test track was built in less than a year in Fühlingen, Germany. Using new aircraft building techniques that kept weight levels low, Alweg engineers designed a sleek, aerodynamic train. The two-fifths scale train attained speeds up to nearly 160 km/h on a test track. Promotional materials from Alweg claimed full-sized trains would be capable of speeds up to 322 km/h. The steepest conventional rail grades of the day were less than 6 percent, yet Alweg was designed to handle grades up to 15 percent. The proposed 300+ km/h Alweg system would also use 27% less energy than that of conventional trains operating at 80 km/h.

When it debuted to the press on October 8, 1952, the Alweg system garnered so much press attention

HISTORY HIGHLIGHTS

around the world that it heralded new era of excitement for monorail. Others would follow Alweg in an effort to cash in on the new hopes for monorail. While impressive in breaking new ground, an Alweg high-speed, intercity system was never built. Wenner-Gren continued to fund experimentation and development. The Alweg system would soon evolve into something less speedy, yet far more successful (page 58).

Alweg's first test track, located in Fühlingen, Germany, featured a 2/5 scale train running on a two-kilometer oval loop. Turns were banked at a severe 45-degree angle for speed. This tilt was fine while being negotiated at high-speed, but was perhaps a bit uncomfortable for passengers should the train ever need to stop in a turn.

MONORAILS

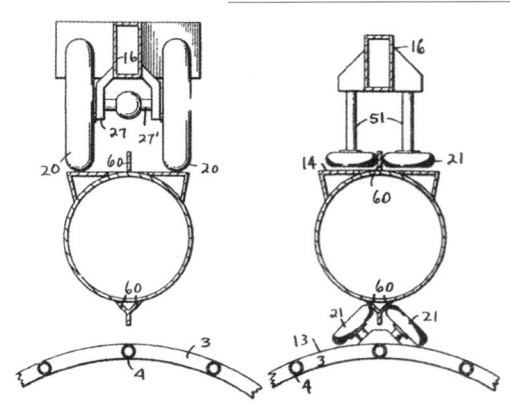

1956: Goodell

Murel Goodell's Monorail Incorporated built a short test track of their suspended Skyway system at Arrowhead Park in Houston, Texas. The demonstrator was powered by two Packard 352 automobile engines. The driver was seated high above the passenger carriage on one of the two bogie compartments. The Trailblazer passenger compartment featured the latest technologies of the time, including a fiberglass skin and seats. Goodell's monorail was also the first suspended monorail to use rubber tires. Track was made up of a steel tube with added running surfaces. The test track cost $125,000. Promoters said that revenue systems could

Roy Rogers at the grand opening

Hostesses on the inaugural Trailblazer run were Kay Bright, a former Pan American Airlines stewardess, and Dorothy Buell, owner of the Studio of Charm.

The 1956 Skyway test track on opening day
PHOTO: Peter Whitney

HISTORY HIGHLIGHTS

Texas State Fair

Hobby Field

be built for $500,000 for every 1.6-kilometers. With great fanfare, the grand opening of the 295-meter test run took place on February 18, 1956. The event and subsequent demonstration runs brought America into the monorail publicity battle, which began after the opening shot of Germany's Alweg in 1952. After eight months of testing, the track was dismantled and rebuilt at the Texas State fairgrounds in Dallas with some curves added. It operated at the fairgrounds until 1964. Only one Skyway transit installation was built, a short line at Houston's Hobby Field Airport. The Hobby Field Sky Taxi monorail served a remote parking lot and was dismantled in 1967 as a result of low ridership.

1958: Ueno

The first Japanese prototype transit monorail was produced by the Transportation Bureau of Tokyo Metropolitan Government. Tokyo's Ueno Zoo Monorail construction began in 1957 and it debuted in 1958. To save costs and keep the system simple, the 331-meter demonstrator line used parts including rubber tires and off-the-shelf steel parts for track. Japan would later adopt the Alweg and Safege monorail systems to build more transit monorails than any other country in the world.

An early test run at Ueno Zoo resulted in all eyes pointed upwards

MONORAILS

1957: Alweg

Using knowledge gained from the original test track of 1952, in 1957 Alweg GmbH unveiled what has become the most successful monorail technology in the world. The Fühlingen test line was Alweg's first full-scale monorail. The train rode on dual pneumatic rubber tires with smaller tires pressing against the sides of the beam for stability and guidance. Quieter than conventional rail, the rubber pneumatic tires performed better, allowing more than three times than traction of steel wheels on steel rail. The simplicity of the track design allowed much quicker and more economic construction, a key goal of Alweg GmbH. The test track caught the attention of Walt Disney, who visited it while on vacation with his wife Lillian in 1958. That visit resulted in the 1959 opening of the Disneyland-Alweg Monorail System, using trains built at his studio. Many more lines would follow.

PHOTO: E.A.S. Cotton

On July 23, 1957, the world got its first glimpse of Alweg's full-scale urban monorail demonstrator

HISTORY HIGHLIGHTS

LEFT: The test track station was a simple one-sided platform.

RIGHT: Flexible switches were first demonstrated at the Alweg test facility.

PHOTO: Reinhard Krischer Collection

Alweg's test track at Fühlingen, Germany. Supports of the original 1952 oval test track are visible. The facility was demolished in 1967.

59

MONORAILS

1957: The Wenner-Gren/Appelt monorail

In November of 1957, a little-known secret prototype monorail was tested near Houston, Texas. That same month, Alweg pioneer Axel Wenner-Gren announced the purchase of a controlling interest in Goodell's Monorail, Inc., which had already developed suspended monorails. Weldon Appelt was the designing engineer for Monorail Inc., and Wenner-Gren had already used his talents to improve his Alweg monorail. Appelt's input helped change it from an intercity monorail to an intracity system. Appelt had also secretly reported to Wenner-Gren that he had a better design for supported monorails, the inverted-t. Inverted-t monorails have the load-bearing wheels running on lips at the bottom of the beam and not on top, freeing up important space for the passenger cabin while also simplifying switches. Another advantage was the strength of the t-track. Spans up to 60-meters long were possible, reducing the number of pylons.

A secret meeting outside of Houston where Axel Wenner-Gren (center in suit) first inspected the results of his investment. Representing Monorail Inc. was, from left, LeRoy Laycock (1), Felix Davis, VP (2), Weldon Appelt (3), Murel Goodell (5), illustrator L.C. Mitchell (9) and other project technicians.

PHOTO: LeRoy Laycock collection

HISTORY HIGHLIGHTS

Appelt had a legal skirmish with Alweg after Wenner-Gren's death, but subsequently won rights to his own technology. Appelt and his business associate, T.W. Weston, continued to promote his design for decades. Both Atlantic City and Houston came close to producing the monorail, then marketed under the name of Advanced Rapid Transit Systems, Inc. The inverted-t design would be reintroduced in later decades by Eurotren of Spain and by promoters of a high-speed Colorado Monorail from Denver to Rocky Mountain ski resorts.

RIGHT: After Wenner-Gren funds dried up, so too did the prototype in the Texas sun

LEFT: From this angle, the Appelt test vehicle appears to have been made up of a patchwork of available parts

BELOW: Project engineer LeRoy Laycock at the helm of the Appelt Monorail

PHOTO: LeRoy Laycock collection

MONORAILS

1960: Safege

In the 1940s, French engineer Lucien Félix Chadenson became interested in suspended rail. Impressed by the Paris Metro Route 11, which used rubber tires instead of steel, he decided to include that in his design. The result was a suspended monorail in which the bogies are protected from weather conditions. A 1370-meter test track operated from 1960 to 1967 in Châteauneuf-sur-Loire, south of Paris. S.A.F.E.G.E. is an acronym of Societe Anonyme Francaise D'Etudes, De Gestion Et D'Entreoprises. The Safege group included numerous prestigious French firms, including Renault and Michelin. Safege technology has to date not been used in France, but the Japanese built three Safege lines. The Shonan and Chiba City Monorails continue to operate today. In the 1970s, Siemens AG of Germany developed a smaller scale system very similar to the Safege Monorail, currently in use at Dortmund University and Düsseldorf Airport. Several companies have proposed variations of the Safege system, including steel-wheel versions for higher speeds featuring smaller guideways.

ABOVE: **The Châteauneuf Safege test track featured both steel and pre-stressed concrete guideway..**

RIGHT: **Standard subway controls of the test vehicle**
PHOTO: Albert G. Nymeyer

The Safege test track was featured prominently in the 1966 Francois Truffaut film *Fahrenheit 451*

HISTORY HIGHLIGHTS

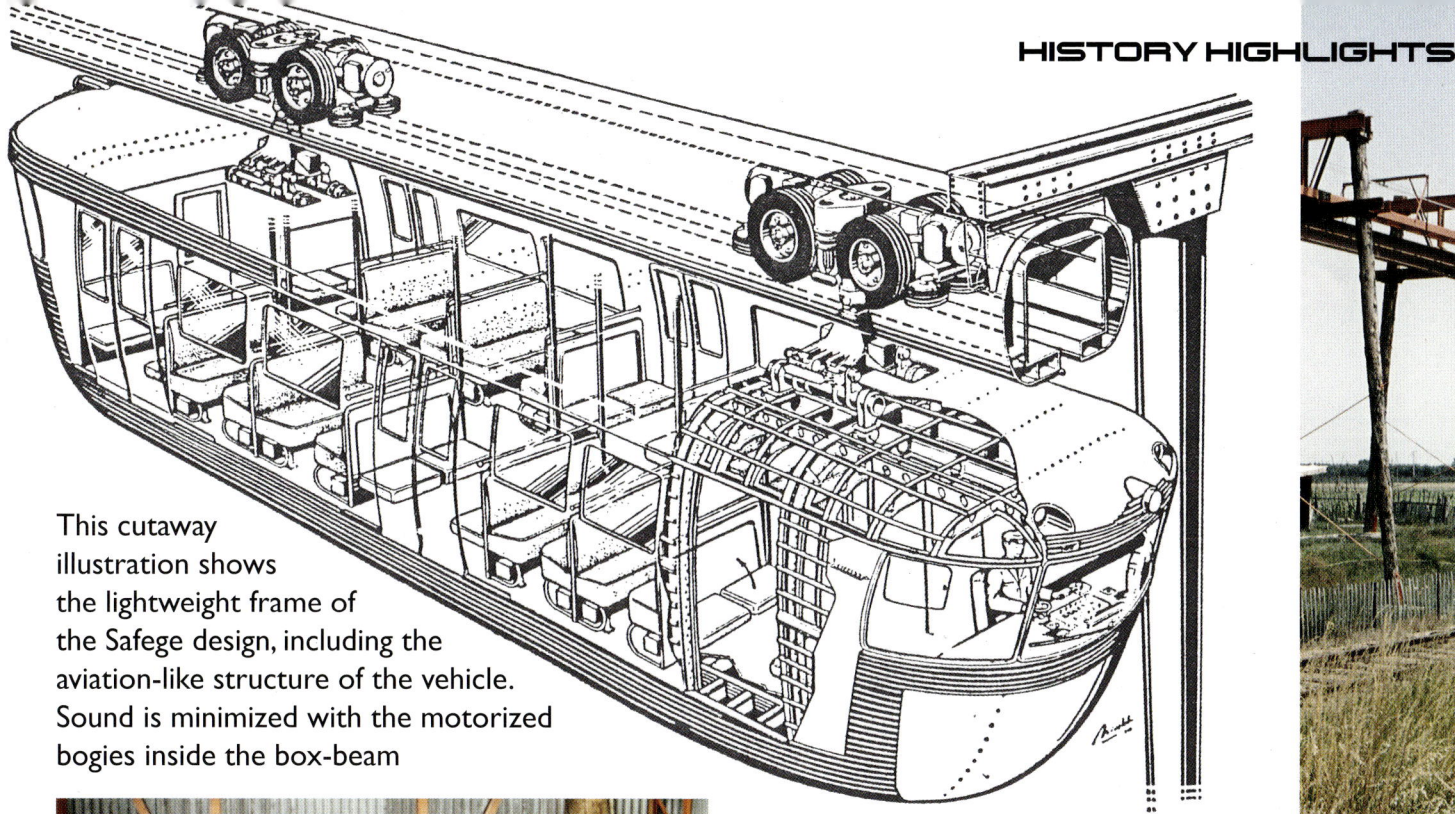

This cutaway illustration shows the lightweight frame of the Safege design, including the aviation-like structure of the vehicle. Sound is minimized with the motorized bogies inside the box-beam

Safege bogie utilized Michelin tires, which had proven to be capable of a useful life of over 400,000 kilometers on Paris subways.

BELOW LEFT: Safege switch prototype, not enclosed for easier research. The Japanese developed a simpler switch design for their Safege lines.

PHOTOS: Albert G. Nymeyer

A portion of the test track was supported by wooden poles, proving that temporary re-alignments could be constructed in a matter of days.

ABOVE: The Safege test facility included this scale bridge model, which combined the monorail technology with engineer Chadenson's considerable suspension bridge experience.

63

MONORAILS

1961: Nihon-Lockheed

Lockheed Aircraft Corporation teamed up with Kawasaki Aircraft and six other Japanese firms to form the Nihon-Lockheed Monorail Company in 1961. In 1963 a test track was built in cooperation with the Nihon Company in Gifu, Japan. Nihon-Lockheed's technology was selected for both the Century 21 Exposition in Seattle and the Tokyo Monorail, but Alweg ended up building both milestone monorails. The Lockheed design is similar to Alweg with use of a concrete beam, yet the track and wheels are steel. Despite numerous proposals for major Nihon-Lockheed systems, only two single-rail shuttles were built in Himeji and Mukogaoka, Japan. Both were rail station to amusement park shuttles. Himeji's monorail was a financially unsuccessful and closed in 1974, while Mukogaoka's monorail operated for 35 years.

LEFT: The original test train vehicle ended up operating as the Mukogaoka Monorail from 1966 until the destination amusement park closed in 2001.

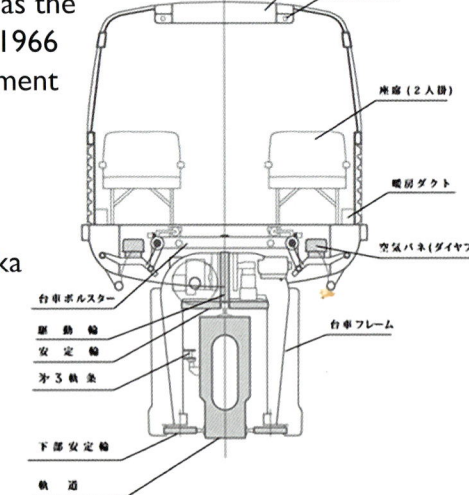

LEFT: A close-up of the Nihon-Lockheed concrete and steel track at Mukogaoka Monorail, after years of exposure to the elements.

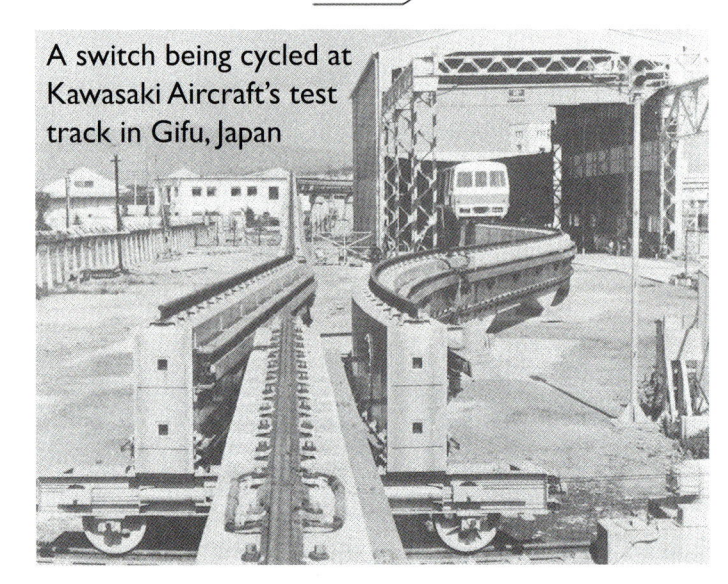

PHOTO: Author

A switch being cycled at Kawasaki Aircraft's test track in Gifu, Japan

HISTORY HIGHLIGHTS

The Himeji Monorail, as seen in 1966. The 1.6-kilometer line ran from Himeji Rail Station to Tegarayama Central Park with one intermediate stop. Some of the abandoned track still stands today and two cars have been preserved for a museum display.

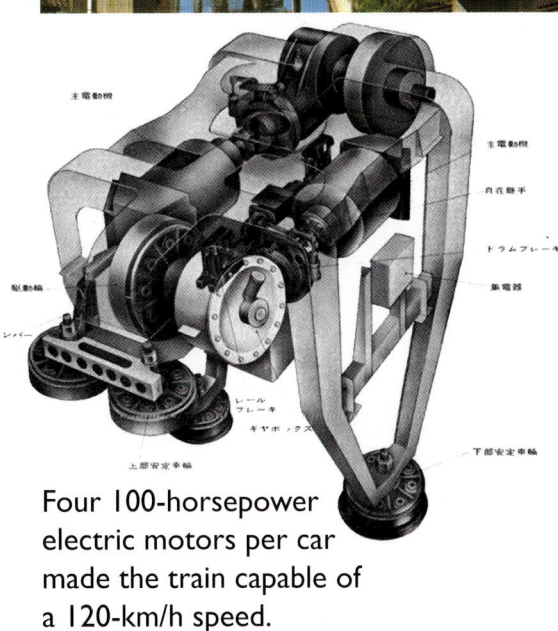

BELOW: Mukogaoka Monorail had aggressively-banked track on its curves, yet the ride was rocky when the train changed angles.

Four 100-horsepower electric motors per car made the train capable of a 120-km/h speed.

PHOTO: Author

MONORAILS

1961: Alweg

The irony is that despite the many Alweg-type monorails that now exist, Alweg GmbH only built two public monorail lines. One was in Torino, Italy for the six-month Italia '61 Exposition. 1.3 million passengers traveled on the monorail line during the fair. The line was 1.2 kilometers in length. The three-car train could carry 80 passengers seated and 120 standing. The monorail is visible in over 70 postcards of the fair. Plans to operate the monorail on a permanent basis and extend it three kilometers to Moncalieri never came to be. A month after the fair closed, the founder and driving force of Alweg, Axel L. Wenner-Gren, died on November 24, 1961. After the exposition, the train sat quietly for nineteen years inside its maintenance garage. In November of 1980 vandals set fire and destroyed the historic train. The station structures and over-lake track remain standing.

PHOTO: Albert G. Nymeyer

Smartly uniformed monorail hostesses and driver as shown on an Italia '61 postcard.

PHOTO: Albert G. Nymeyer

Alweg used a few design tricks learned from Disney, with a more bubble-like nose and a driver cockpit that protruded above the cabin

PHOTO: Albert G. Nymeyer

HISTORY HIGHLIGHTS

ABOVE: Seattle's Red Train during the 1962 Century 21 Exposition

1962: Alweg

The second and final Alweg GmbH-built monorail trains went to the iconic Century 21 Exposition in Seattle. During the six-month fair, the monorail shuttled over eight million people between downtown and the fairgrounds. Alweg spent $3.5-million to build the 1.5-kilometer line to garner attention for their technology. Revenue from ticket sales during the fair paid for the entire system cost. The Alweg company had proposed many systems throughout the world, yet built no more itself. However, Alweg technology continues to flourish today, with numerous companies offering a variety of derivative systems.

Elvis Presley flirts while riding the Red Train in MGM's campy film *It Happened at the World's Fair*

PHOTO: Metro-Goldwyn-Mayer Pictures, Inc.

Young passengers enjoy riding up front with the driver

67

MONORAILS

1964: I-Beam Monorails / New York World's Fair

I-beam monorails are easy to build, due to the commonality of I-beam steel parts. As shown in Chapter One, most I-beam systems are used for non-passenger industrial applications. American Machine and Foundry (AMF) built an I-beam excursion monorail for the 1964-1965 New York World's Fair. Oddly, AMF was promoting their then-licensed Safege technology. AMF never sold any monorail systems, but they were responsible for first monorail rides for many Americans.

Pre-fair art highlighted the futuristic-looking monorail to be built in Queens.

The AMF Monorail approaching its one and only world's fair station.

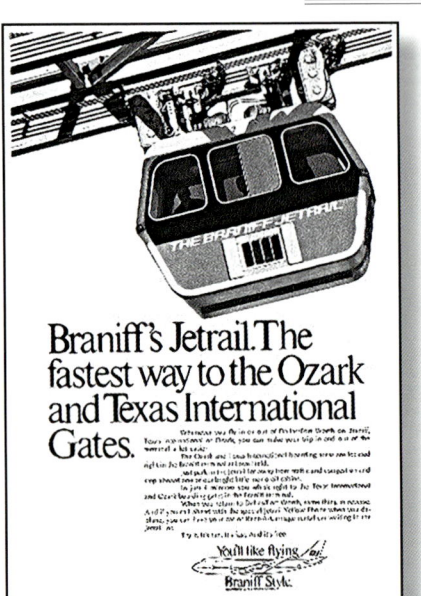

1970: I-Beam Monorails / Braniff Jetrail

Jetrail was a 3-station, 2.8-km monorail built for Braniff International Airlines at Dallas Love Field. The system was invented by George Adams and built by Stanray Corporation and American Crane Corporation. It was the world's first totally automated monorail system. It closed in 1974 when the Dallas/Fort Worth International Airport opened and Braniff moved. The U.S. Department of Transportation studied the system and in 1977 reported, "Over six million passengers were carried 2.1 million kilometers by the system over a four-year period without a fatality or major mishap, and with an overall availability of 99.7%."

HISTORY HIGHLIGHTS

1970: I-Beam Monorails / Aerobus

With a unique hybrid design, a full-scale Aerobus 1.6-kilometer line was first tested in Switzerland in 1970. The invention of Gerhard Mueller, Aerobus is part monorail and part cable-suspended rail. Aerobus utilizes slender steel pylons to elevate suspension cables, similar to those used in the Golden Gate Bridge. Pylons can be separated as much as 600 meters. When a turn in the track is required, monorail track similar to other I-beam monorails is used. To date the largest Aerorail installation was for a 1975 horticultural exposition in Mannheim, Germany. The 3.2-kilometer, dual-tracked line carried 2.5-million passengers during the six-month event. Due to the design of the guideway, costs are low and installation is fast.

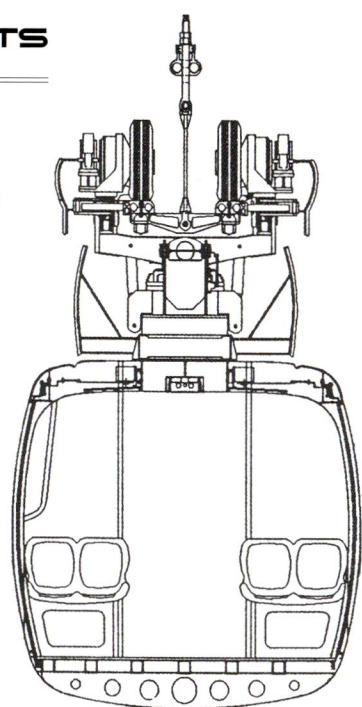

Aerobus at the 1975 Bundesgartenschau Mannheim

PHOTOS: Jean-Henri Manara

I-beam track at Mannheim

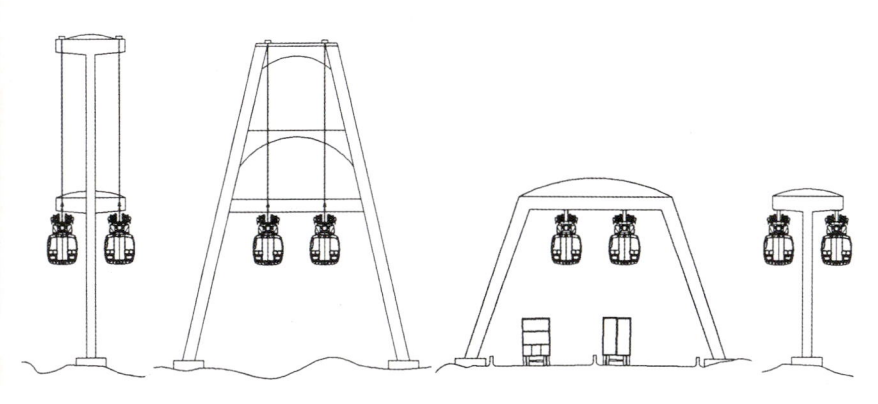

Different Aerobus designs, both cable-supported and conventional monorail supported

DIAGRAMS: Aerobus International Inc.

Long pylon-free span above urban street

69

MONORAILS

1978: I-Beam Monorails / Titan PRT Systems

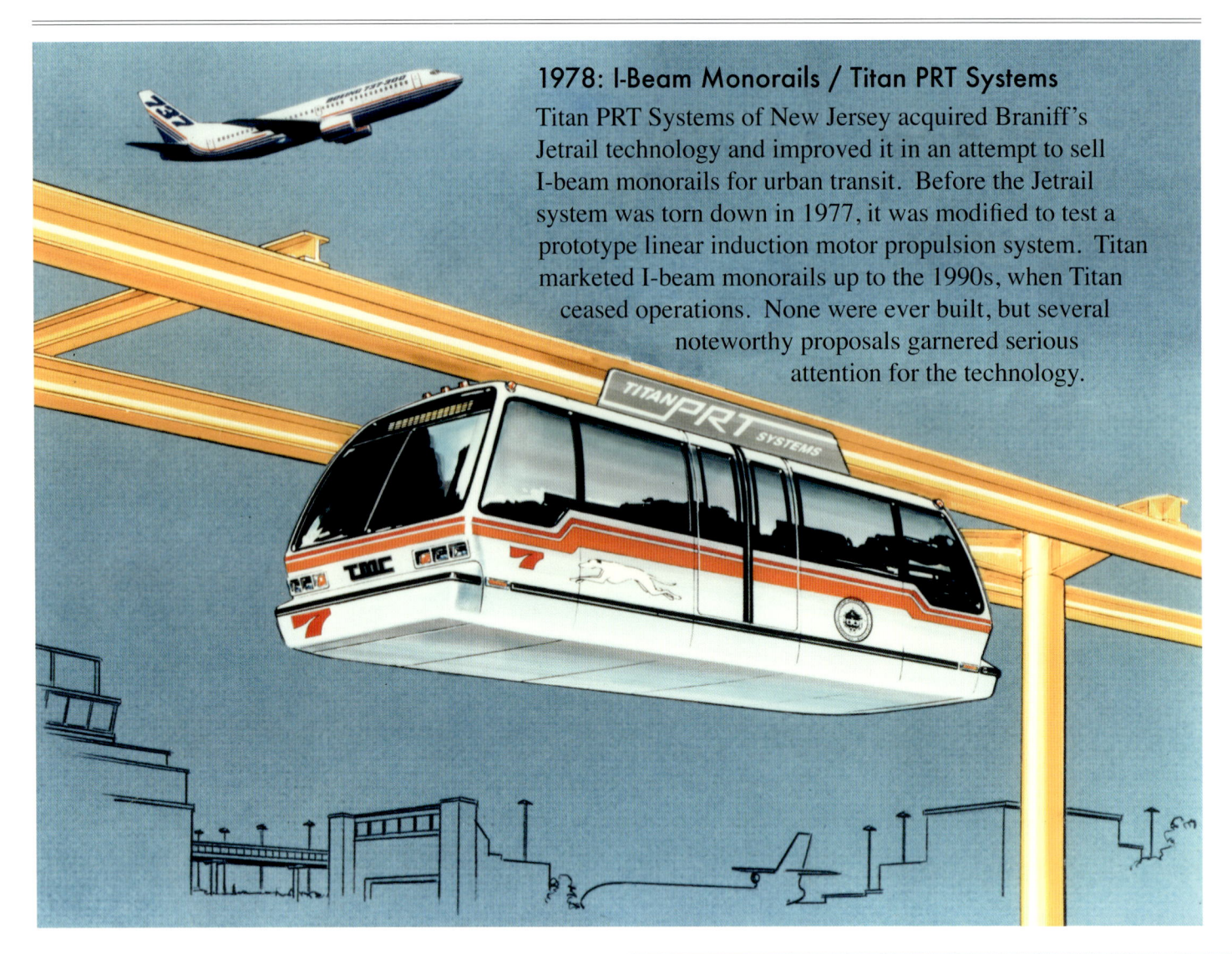

Titan PRT Systems of New Jersey acquired Braniff's Jetrail technology and improved it in an attempt to sell I-beam monorails for urban transit. Before the Jetrail system was torn down in 1977, it was modified to test a prototype linear induction motor propulsion system. Titan marketed I-beam monorails up to the 1990s, when Titan ceased operations. None were ever built, but several noteworthy proposals garnered serious attention for the technology.

A scale mockup of a Titan bogie on a short piece of I-beam. Vehicles would be propelled by maintenance-free linear induction motors.

Titan technology was based on the slender track of Braniff's Jetrail at Love Field in Dallas.

HISTORY HIGHLIGHTS

1993: I-Beam Monorails / Luxor-Excalibur

Arrow Development/Dynamics provided successful suspended monorails for two Busch Garden parks in the 1960s. In the 1990s they began offering larger scale I-beam monorails. In 1990 they replaced Los Angeles County Fair's monorail cars and in 1993 they completed a short two-hotel shuttle line in Las Vegas, Nevada. Both the LA Fair and Luxor/Excalibur Arrow systems were plagued with track problems and were closed and demolished.

An Arrow train crosses over East Reno Avenue in Las Vegas

PHOTOS: Author

Luxor's short-lived suspended monorail station

Above traffic, the sleek Arrow train mimics the shape of the Luxor Hotel

Track stress troubles began shortly after opening in 1993

71

MONORAILS

I-Beam Monorails / 100 years of Novelty Rides

I-beam steel has been a favorite of amusement establishments to carry guests for a century. The suspended vehicles below the track have been shaped as flying carpets, pirate ships, bumble bees and miniature representations of future trains. The ease of shaping track and the availability of steel I-beams make it a natural for creative entrepreneurs.

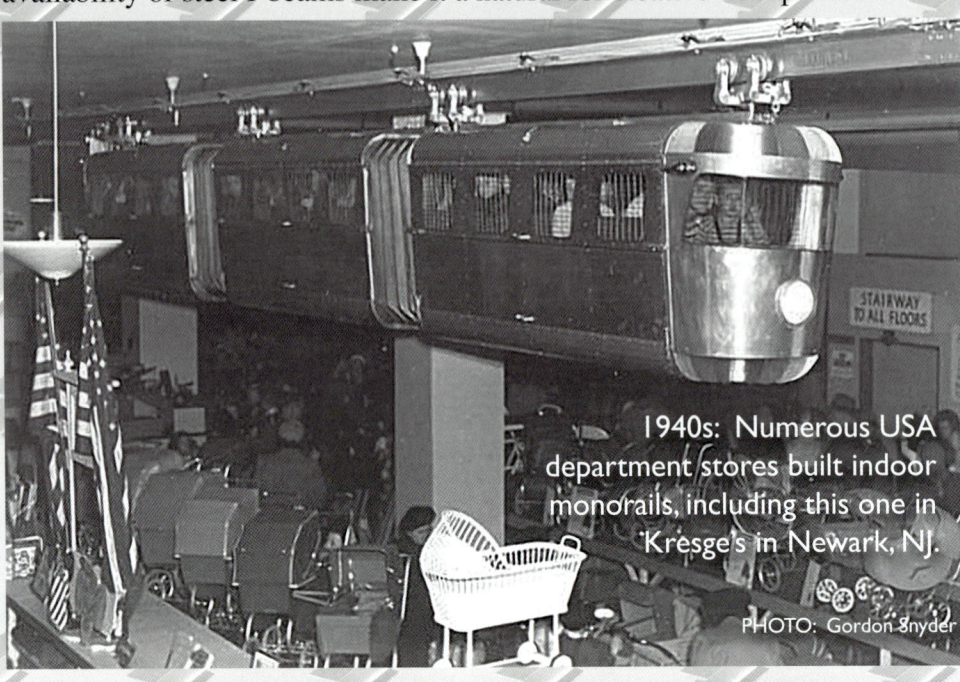

1915: Tibidado in Barcelona, Spain, built the longest lasting I-beam novelty monorail. High on a hilltop, it continues to thrill riders today.

1940s: Numerous USA department stores built indoor monorails, including this one in Kresge's in Newark, NJ.
PHOTO: Gordon Snyder

1955: Disneyland's first monorail was Peter Pan's Flight, four years before Alweg arrived in nearby Tomorrowland.
PHOTO: Author

SPECTACULAR MILE-LONG MONORAIL
Ride thrill of your life—a "bird's eye" view of the colorful fair grounds on the spectacular mile-long monorail . . . first of its kind in the West!
LOS ANGELES COUNTY FAIR
★ TOPS IN FREE GRANDSTAND ENTERTAINMENT!

1962: The Los Angeles County Fair Monorail circled the grounds until 1996.

1958: California's Pacific Ocean Park featured this Magic Carpet Ride.

1963: Miami's Seaquarium featured the USA east coast's first suspended monorail.

1968: The leaf-themed Forest Flite of Florida's Rainbow Springs

1966: Busch Gardens Van Nuys, California gave their beer factory tour via an Arrow monorail until the attraction closed in 1979. Busch Gardens Tampa in Florida featured a similar Arrow monorail from 1966 to 1999.

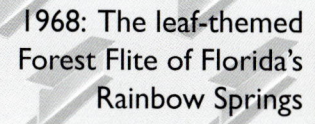

PHOTOS: Aldeia do Papai Noel

2009: Aldeia do Papai Noel, an amusement park in the hills of Gramado, Brazil used easy-to-find hardware for their little red train.

MONORAILS

1964: Steel Box Beam minirails

During the height of 20th mid-century fascination of all-things monorail, a new breed of one-track wonders began to appear. While the general public sought rides out of curiosity, not all fairs, parks and expos could afford full-scale monorails. Hence the minirail was invented, small straddle monorails on steel tracks. The beams are cheap and quick to fabricate. The trains are light but can still transport many people. After a fair they can easily be moved to other locations. Today, minirails continue to be installed where full-scale monorails don't make sense. They are still popular for international expositions, yet peoplemover-class steel beam systems have been installed at numerous non-recreation venues for transit as well.

1969: Universal Mobility Incorporation, or UMI, installed many minirails throughout the USA. This one still operates at Cal Expo in Sacramento, California.

1964: The first major minirail debuted at Expo 64 in Lausanne, Switzerland. Built by Von Roll Monorail, the company would go on to build many more monorails until its assets were acquired by AdTranz, which was later acquired by Bombardier.

Intamin Transportation began selling minirails in the 1980s. This 1992 Stuttgart Garden Expo minirail easily negotiated 20% grades uphill and downhill. Intamin's product line includes larger, faster monorails as well.

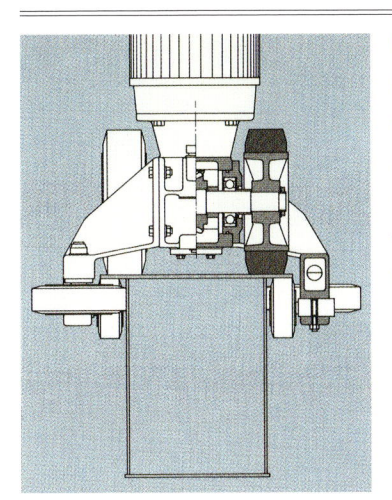

HISTORY HIGHLIGHTS

Left: Von Roll Monorail box-beam and bogie configuration. The top steel plate serves as support for load-bearing wheels and safety wheels under the lip.

1991: Newark International Airport in New Jersey has the most extensive system installed by Von Roll Monorail. Taller beams permit very long spans of track without supports. The track to the right is a spur line to the maintenance facility.

PHOTO: Author

1988: Sydney, Australia was the home to Von Roll's first Type III urban monorail. The system looped through downtown and had eight stops. The system was popular with tourists, but dismantled in 2013.

PHOTO: Author

2009: PPH Transsystem AG of Lancut, Poland developed a new steel track minirail system. Bartholet Maschinenbau AG fabricated the train and test track at their facility in Chur, Switzerland.

PHOTO: PPH Transsystem AG

MONORAILS

1975: Siemens H-Bahn

In 1972 Siemens-Duwag began development of an automated suspended monorail system, similar in configuration to the French Safege system. In 1975 a prototype track began testing at their research facility in Erglangen, Germany. H-Bahn is a medium-capacity system that uses solid rubber wheels, air suspension and cabin-sway in curves. The first public H-Bahn system opened at Dortmund University in 1984. Dortmund's system has been expanded twice since opening, linking various campus buildings and a metro station. The second H-Bahn system opened as a peoplemover at Düsseldorf International Airport in 2002. In 2011, Air Train International announced an effort to supply China with numerous monorails based on H-Bahn technology.

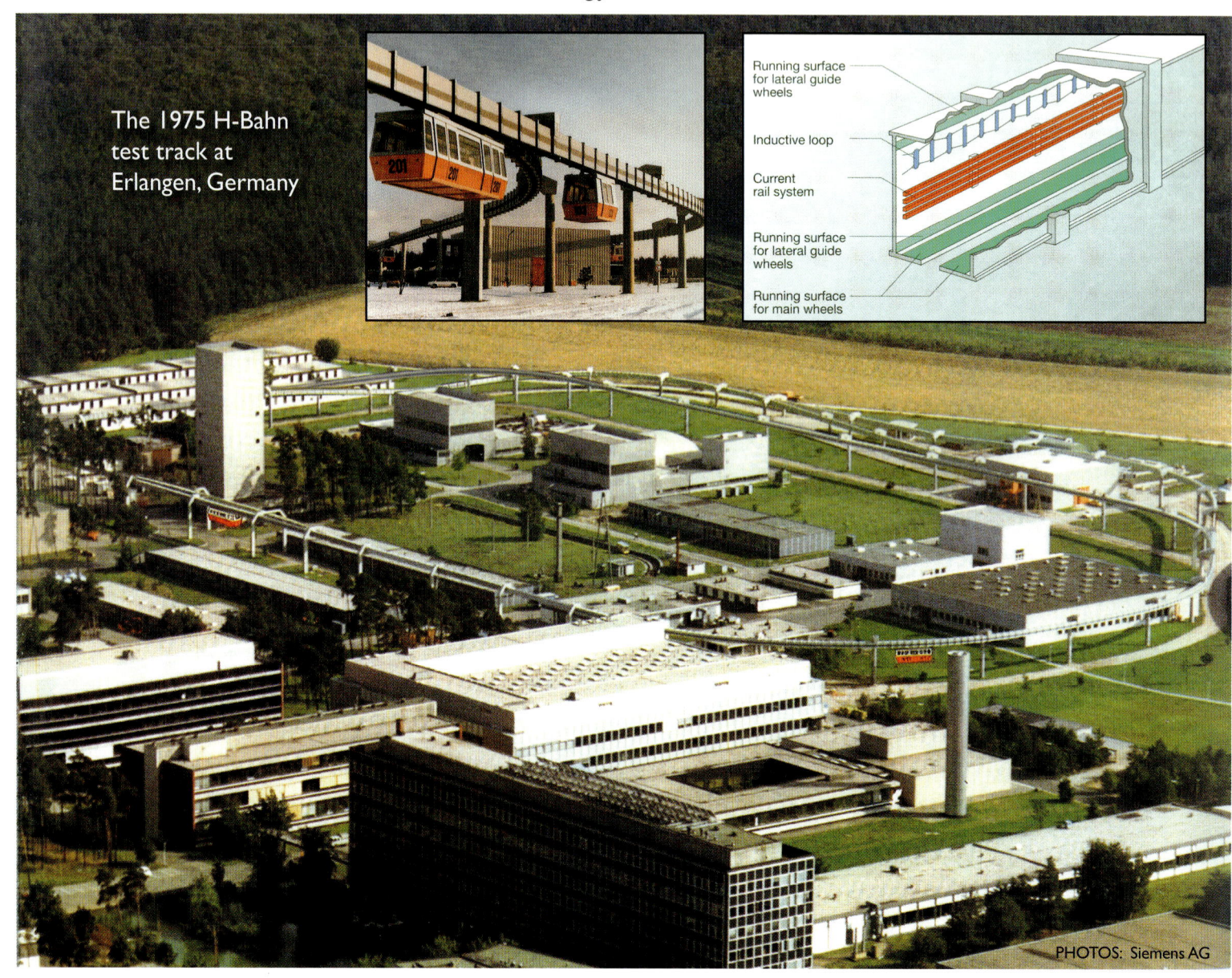

The 1975 H-Bahn test track at Erlangen, Germany

PHOTOS: Siemens AG

HISTORY HIGHLIGHTS

DIAGRAM: Siemens AG

1984: A Dortmund University H-Bahn car negotiating a switch near a campus station.

PHOTO: H-Bahn-Gesellschaft Dortmund mbH

2002: Düsseldorf International SkyTrain

PHOTO: Andreas Wiese/Düsseldorf International

77

MONORAILS

ABOVE: Eurotren Monoviga in an urban setting

1987: Eurotren Monoviga

Eurotren Monoviga was the brain child of the Spanish inventor Dr. Julio Pinto Silva. Silva's Eurotren Monoviga is an inverted-T system, similar to the 1957 design of Weldon Appelt. The load-bearing wheels ride on a lip below a central guide beam. In 1984 a 1/8th scale model was demonstrated for the Spanish Minister of Transport. In 1987 the EM-403 full scale prototype was built and tested on a 2.4-kilometer test track near Seville. Eurotren Monoviga was proposed for several locations, mostly in Spain. A high-speed version was proposed for Colorado's I-70 corridor from Denver to Aspen in the 1990s.

ABOVE: Eurotren Monoviga's test track

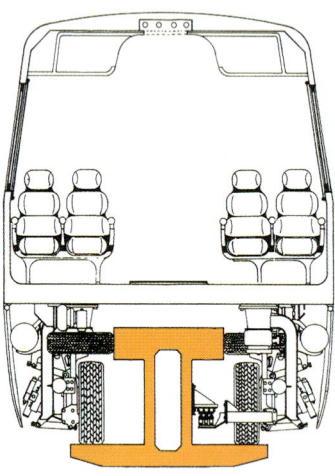

ABOVE: Inverted-T diagram

ABOVE: Guide and load tires

The EM-403 test vehicle featured linked cars with perimetral knuckle joints and no between-car walls or doors.

HISTORY HIGHLIGHTS

2002: Metrail

The innovative British design and engineering firm of Fraser-Nash brought monorail to a new level in the early 2000s with the development of hybrid monorail technology. Metrail doesn't require expensive electrical infrastructure along the alignment or track. Their hybrid-powered monorails are recharged from on-board, clean-running Wankel engines, which provide regenerative charging. Metrail features brushless AC electric motors that power each drive wheel, which allows a smaller, more compact bogie design. Cars are made of lightweight materials including carbon fiber and Kevlar.

Metrail brings cutting-edge technology to straddle beams for the 21st century, resulting in lower construction and operation costs

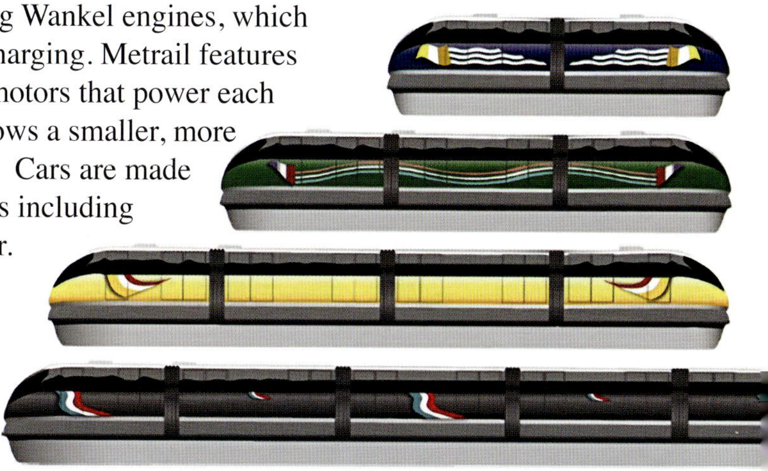

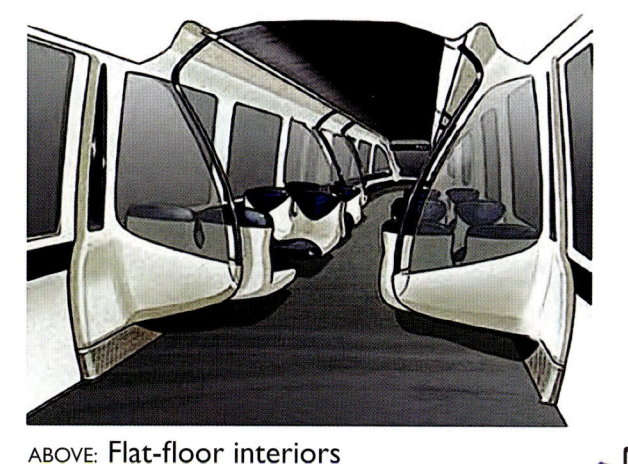

PHOTO: Author

ABOVE: Flat-floor interiors

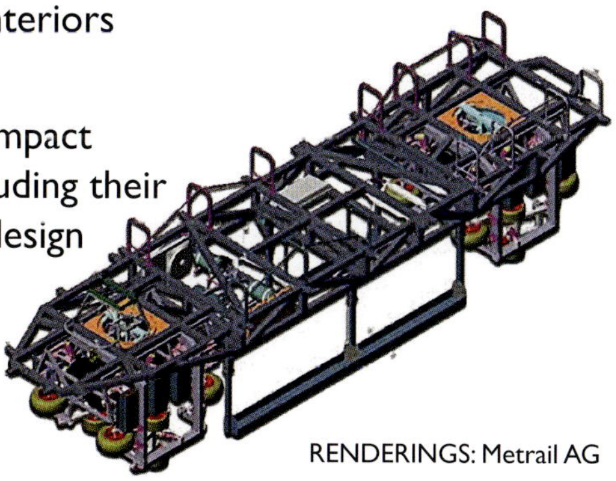

RIGHT: Metrail's compact vehicle frame including their innovative bogie design

RENDERINGS: Metrail AG

Metrail's test track in Nilai, Malaysia demonstrates their monorail's remarkable 30-meter turn radius capability

PHOTO: Author

Houston Monorail

Approved and contracted, the Houston Monorail was killed by one of monorail's great enemies...politics.

RENDERING: Bombardier Transportation

San Francisco Monorail

FACING PAGE: 1950's art rendering of a steel-wheeled, suspended monorail studied for the San Francisco bay area.

RENDERING: Gibbs & Hill Inc.

4

Could have, should have

100 years plus of missed opportunities

Highlighting some of the notable proposed, yet never-built monorail systems.

81

MONORAILS

Inventions in search of place

The history of invention is filled with tales of unfulfilled dreams and uncompleted plans. Monorail, a relatively recent invention in the history of man, is no different than any other in this regard. Yet monorail seems to have had somewhat of a curse when it comes to the large number of almost-built systems. The following pages are a sampling of monorail proposals that didn't make it to fruition.

ABOVE: The Enos Railway technology had been proven in 1887 at South Park, Minnesota (page 47). Backers of the new monorail technology managed to build a 1.2-kilometer test track, yet plans to expand into nearby St. Paul and Minneapolis were thwarted. This rendering shows how the monorail would have appeared above the horse and carriage-occupied streets.

COULD HAVE, SHOULD HAVE

ABOVE: An art rendering of a Eugen Langen Schwebebahn monorail for the City of Hamburg

LEFT: London was among the cities looking at a suspended monorail based on Langen's design. This rendering shows a monorail over one of London's main avenues.

RENDERINGS: James Pierce Fox Collection

Jannowitz Bridge Station, over the Spree River
RENDERING: Dingler's Polytechniches Journal

RENDERING: James Pierce Fox Collection

ABOVE AND RIGHT:
The Berlin Friedrichstrasse Station, built in 1878, would have been modified to connect the Schwebebahn with conventional rail lines.

RENDERING:
James Pierce Fox Collection

Berlin

Eugen Langen's design came close to fruition in Berlin. The system would have run from Gesundbrunnen in the northern part of the city to Rixdorf in the south. End-to-end travel would have taken around 22 minutes. Three-car trains were designed to carry 7,500 passengers per hour per direction. Trains could be doubled to six cars for 15,000 per hour.

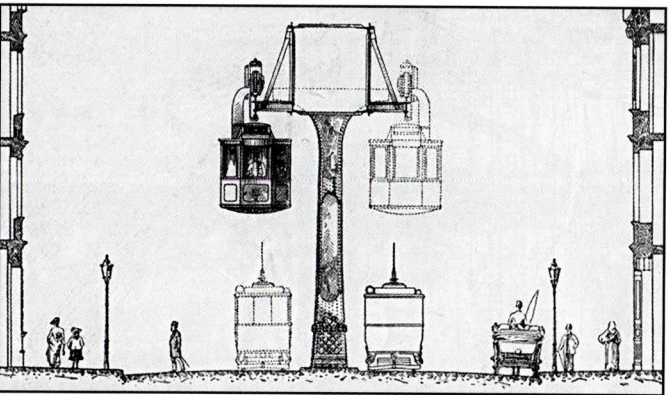

ABOVE: A three-pylon Berlin Schwebebahn track prototype was built on Brunnerstrasse.

PHOTO: James Pierce Fox Collection

LEFT: The Berlin line would have included individual pylons, as opposed to the dual supports of Wuppertal's Schwebebahn.

RENDERING: Dingler's Polytechniches Journal

85

MONORAILS

Suspended efforts in the USA

Following the opening of Wuppertal's Schwebebahn in 1901, Eugen Langen's design not only spurred proposals in Europe, but it also captured the imagination of promoters in the United States. Among proposals made based on the Schwebebahn monorail was a 5.5-kilometer line for the 1933-34 Century of Progress Fair in Chicago. It was to operate between Grant Park and the fairgrounds. It wasn't built due to difficulties obtaining funding during the Depression. Another unbuilt proposal was for 1939-1940 New York World's Fair. The 4.8-kilometer, double-tracked system was to have stations throughout the fairgrounds as well as connections with the Long Island Railroad and subway lines.

BELOW & RIGHT: **Americans took Langen's design, streamlined the trains and simplified the tracks and pylons to improve its aesthetic appeal.**

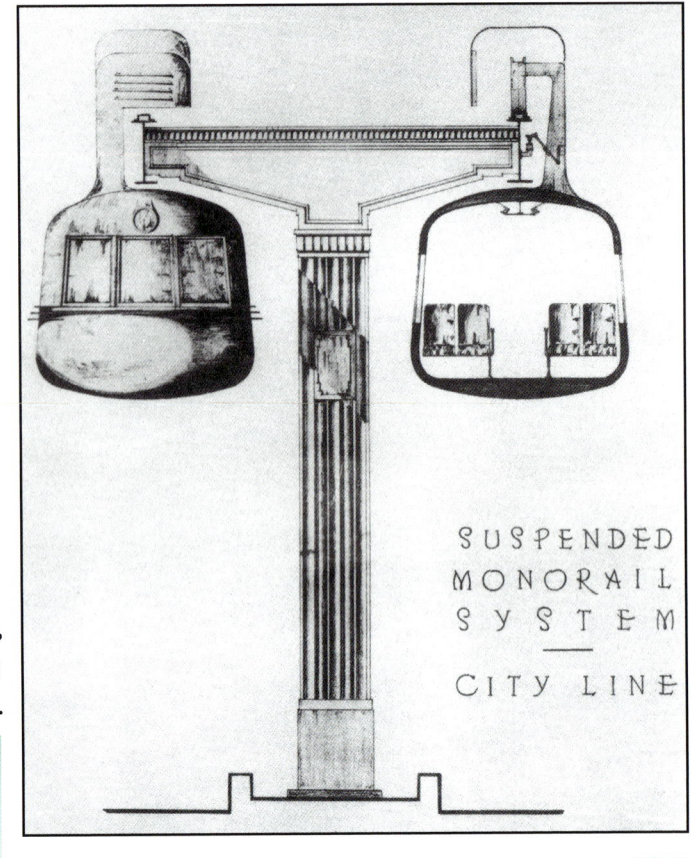

COULD HAVE, SHOULD HAVE

The suspended technology that still waits

Suspended monorails that have trains that reach over one side of the rail have a switching problem. Crossovers from side to side are impossible. Interestingly, Eugen Langen had a design that eliminated the problem before Wuppertal adopted single-rail. The split-rail monorail allowed for easy crossover switching. Others would embrace the design later in the 20th Century. Notably, the transition from interest in the Schwebebahn suspended rail to a box-beam, split-rail monorail came in the 1940s with its introduction by Gibbs & Hill Inc. for several proposals. George D. Roberts, a promoter known as Mr. Monorail, promoted the design in the USA, Europe and South America from the 1940s through the 1960s. None were built, yet the technology continues to be touted today by others.

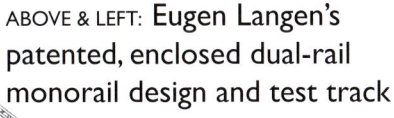

ABOVE & LEFT: Eugen Langen's patented, enclosed dual-rail monorail design and test track

ABOVE AND BELOW: Before and after renderings illustrating a change in preference to a more capable box-beam, split-rail monorail

RENDERINGS: Gibbs & Hill Inc.

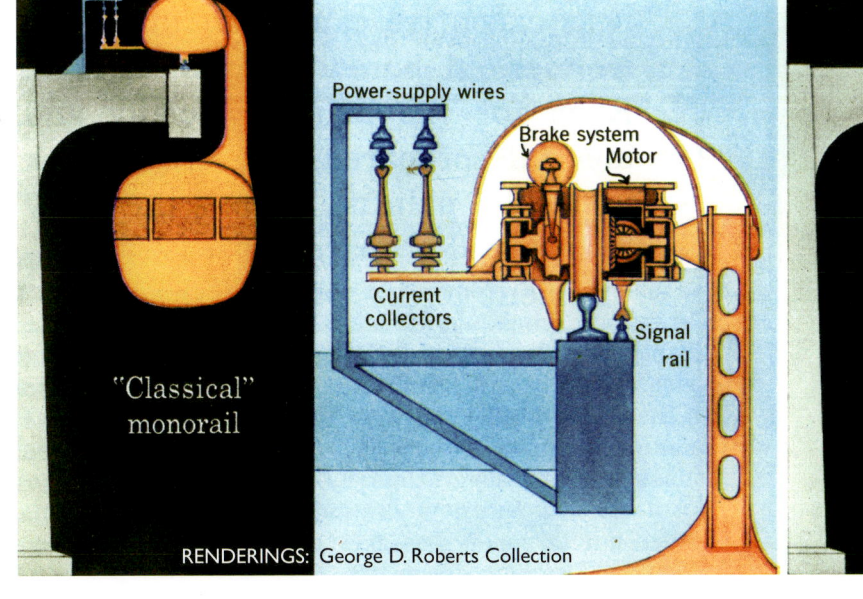

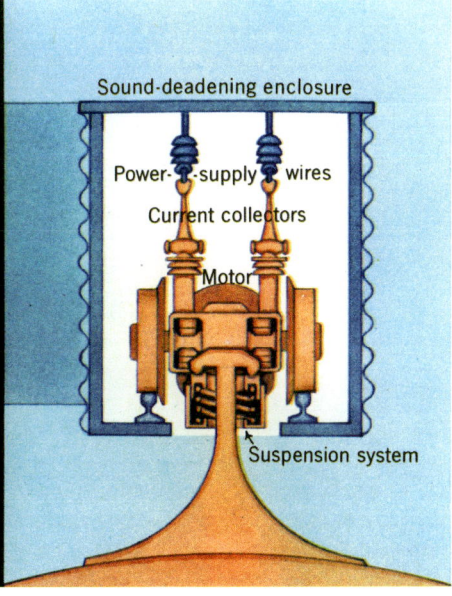

"Classical" monorail

"Split-rail" monorail

RENDERINGS: George D. Roberts Collection

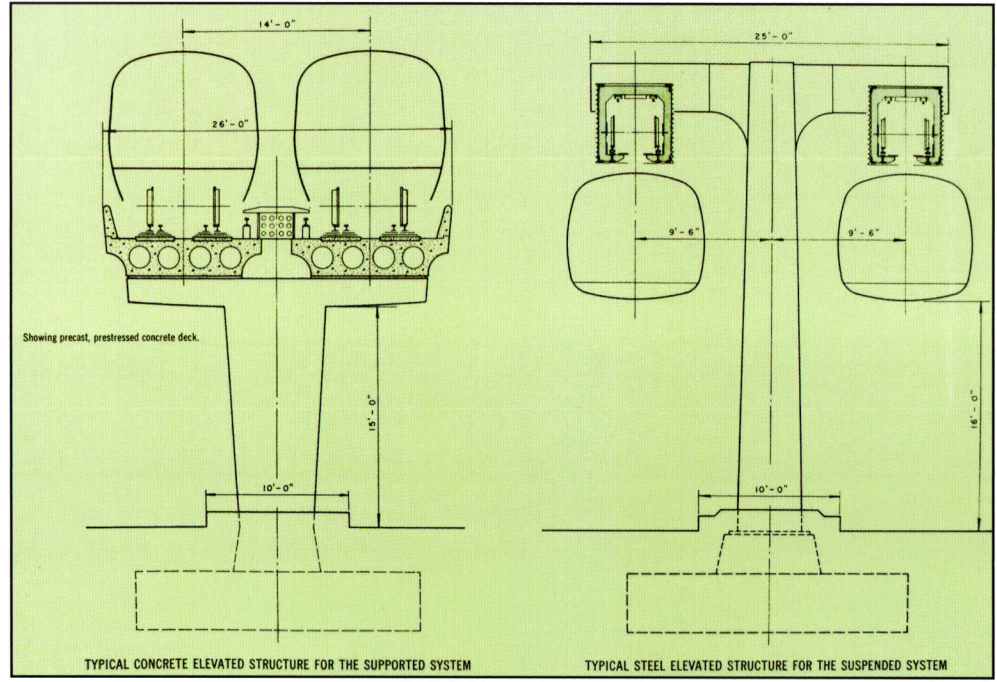

MONORAILS

San Francisco

George D. Roberts began promoting monorail in 1946. One of his major goals in the 1950s was a San Francisco Monorail System. The respected architect/engineering firm of Daniel, Mann, Johnson and Mendenhall added their talents and considerable influence to his proposals. Post-war growth was in full swing, with thousands moving to new suburb developments. Rapid transit was a hot topic, and monorail was at the top of the list of possibilities to deal with growing traffic. In 1955, engineering and design firm Parsons, Brinckerhoff, Hall and Macdonald submitted a report to the Bay Area Rapid Transit Commission, comparing monorail and conventional rail. According to Roberts, monorail lost out to subway due to a smear campaign against him and the technology, waged by the San Francisco Chronicle. At the time, the newspaper's publisher had a large interest in a major concrete company. If subway was selected over monorail, as it eventually was, concrete firms stood to make a fortune. Their efforts succeeded in preventing Roberts from selling additional monorail company stock.

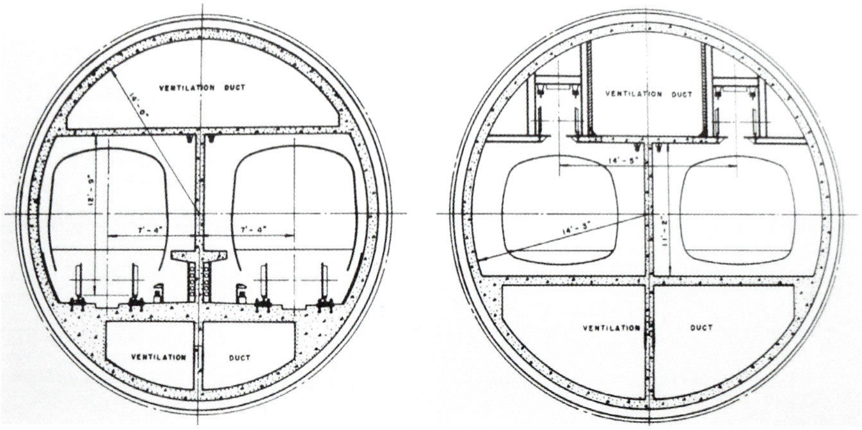

ABOVE: **Elevated conventional rail as compared to a split-rail, box-beam monorail, as shown in a 1955 report to a San Francisco rapid transit commission**

ABOVE: **Subway comparison, conventional rail vs. suspended monorail**

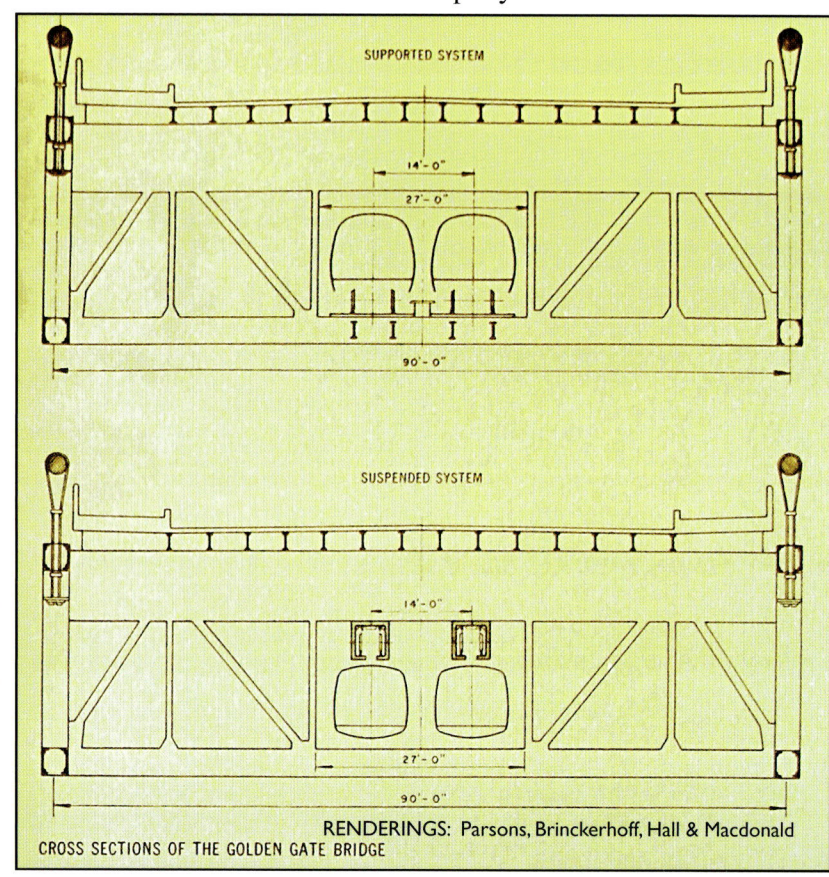

RIGHT: **Before Marin County backed out of the San Francisco bay area's effort for a regional system, rail under the road deck of the Golden Gate Bridge was planned.**

RENDERINGS: Parsons, Brinckerhoff, Hall & Macdonald

COULD HAVE, SHOULD HAVE

RENDERING: Pereira and Luckman

ABOVE: Arguably one of the most fanciful monorail renderings, this flying saucer station for the proposed San Francisco Monorail reflects the beginning of the space age and futuristic Googie architecture.

RIGHT: Enclosed dual-track, steel-rail monorail, as illustrated in the 1955 report for San Francisco. The French Safege system would later feature a similar configuration, yet with rubber tires instead of steel wheels.

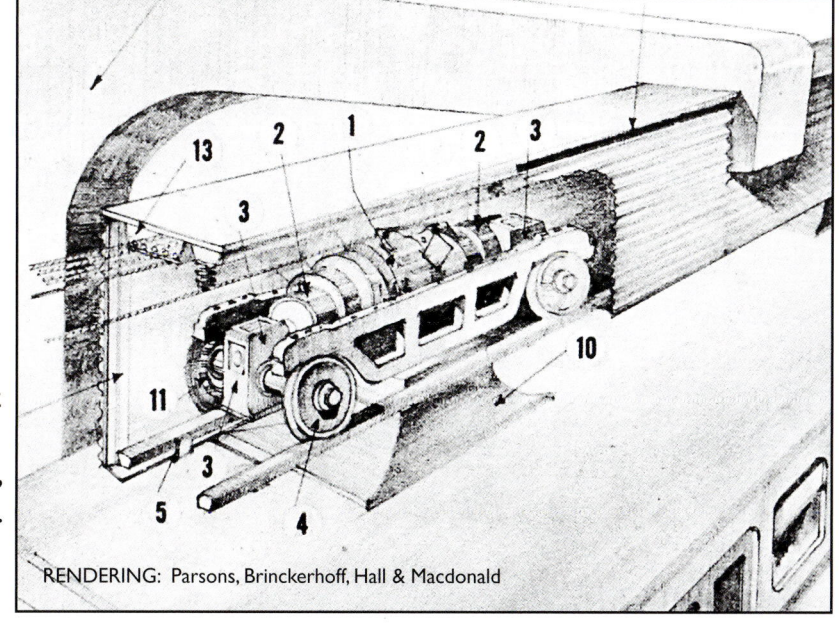

RENDERING: Parsons, Brinckerhoff, Hall & Macdonald

MONORAILS

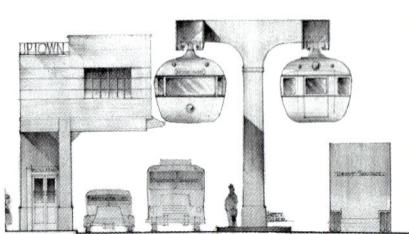

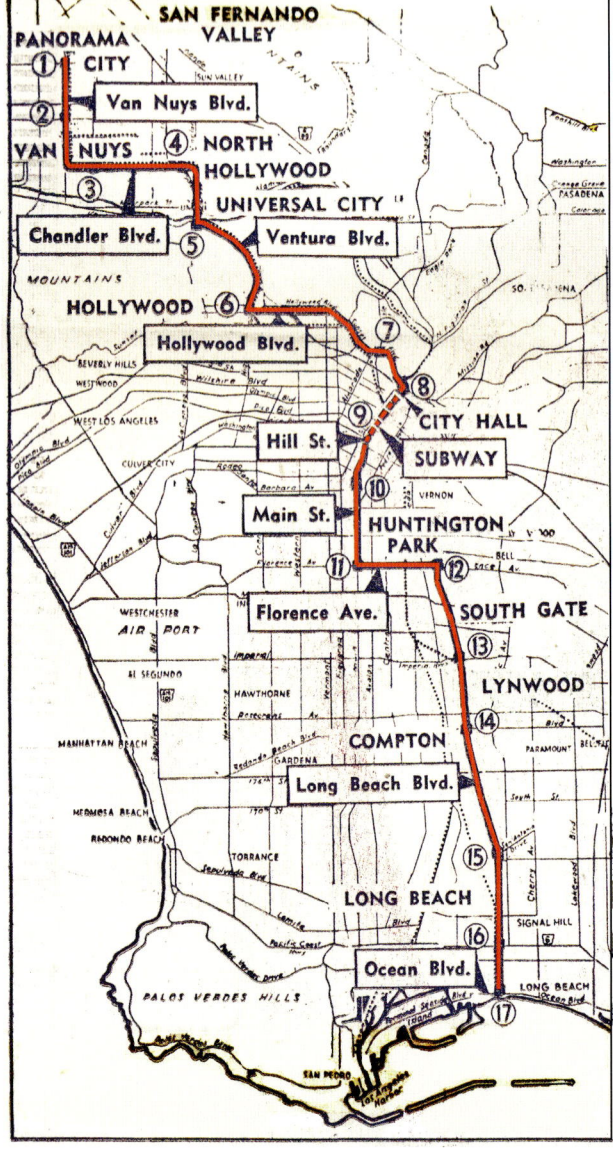

Los Angeles beginnings

George D. Roberts was instrumental in the formation of the Los Angeles Metropolitan Transit Authority (MTA) in 1951. MTA was empowered to study, construct and operate the monorail Roberts had proposed between Panorama City in the San Fernando Valley, through downtown LA, and ending in Long Beach. Newspapers ran headlines including *Monorail in Five Years*. Years of political bickering resulted instead. In Roberts's own words, "monorail became a political football." Adding to the confusion and debate, several other monorail companies made their own proposals during the 1950s and 1960s. Despite its beginnings as a monorail agency, the MTA evolved and has since only sought so-called conventional rail solutions for the area. One example is the Los Angeles to Long Beach alignment, which was first proposed as monorail but is now served by MTA's Blue Line light rail. The Blue Line has one of the worst collision records of any rail line in the USA, with over 100 pedestrian and motorist deaths since it opened in 1990. Sad, considering a collision-free monorail system was MTA's plan way back in 1951.

THIS PAGE: Art renderings and map of the monorail the Los Angeles Metropolitan Transit Authority was established to build and operate. Initially proposed as a monorail similar to Wuppertal's Schwebebahn, the design evolved into a box-beam suspended monorail.

RENDERINGS: George D. Roberts Collection

COULD HAVE, SHOULD HAVE

RIGHT AND BELOW: **Goodell Monorail** proposed a downtown–Los Angeles International Airport monorail system with their Texas-tested technology. In 1963 the MTA issued a letter of intent to build the $40-million monorail. The agreement was conditional on acquisition of right-of-way and acceptance of additional studies.

GOODELL RENDERINGS: L.C. Mitchell

BELOW: Known for being an aircraft and missile manufacturer, **Northrop** proposed their Gyro-glide monorail for LA. Northrop's train and track was similar to other suspended monorails, but featured a flywheel and generator-motor inertial drive unit.

Lockheed proposed its straddle-beam monorail for LA. Lockheed's track was concrete with steel rails on the top and both sides of the beam. Trains were supported and guided with steel wheels.

91

MONORAILS

RIGHT: **Highlighted in yellow, Alweg's 'free' monorail alignment for Los Angeles. The segmented red lines represent potential extensions.**

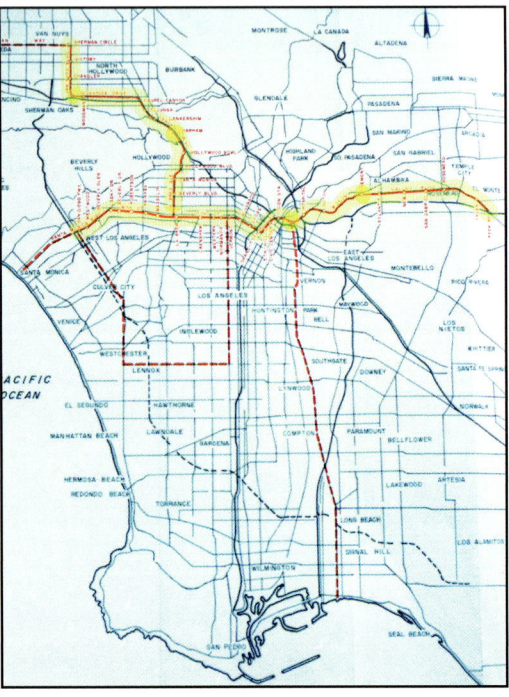

Los Angeles Alweg

Among the many proposals for Los Angeles was the most famous of all, the Alweg proposal. In 1963, Los Angeles was given an amazing offer. The Alweg USA subsidiary submitted a proposal to Los Angeles to finance and construct a 69-kilometer Alweg Monorail serving the San Fernando Valley, the Wilshire corridor, the San Bernardino corridor and downtown Los Angeles. It was a turnkey proposal in which a group would share risk, finance the construction, and turn over to the MTA the operating system. The entire system came to $105,275,000 and revenues would have paid for it. Alweg also agreed to conduct feasibility studies for expansion of the system over the entire Los Angeles area if the offer was accepted. LA supervisors rejected the offer. Decades later a portion of the same alignment was built as subway, yet costing taxpayers billions of dollars as opposed to free.

COULD HAVE, SHOULD HAVE

The Space Age had begun and architecture reflected it. These fanciful renderings by Alweg, with a train based on the wildly popular Seattle World's Fair pilot line, show open-air stations above the streets of Los Angeles.

93

MONORAILS

Alweg around the world

Including Los Angeles, Alweg GmbH made more serious monorail proposals in the 1950s and early 1960s than any other. Most were not built. Notable efforts by Alweg were made for Cologne, Frankfurt, Mexico City, São Paulo, British Columbia, Hamburg, Torino, Los Angeles, San Francisco, Detroit, London, Vienna and Tel Aviv-Jerusalem. The only major Alweg system built during the life of the company was the Tokyo-Haneda line, which Hitachi completed after acquiring rights to the technology. The fate of the Alweg GmbH was set in motion with the death of its founder, Axel L. Wenner-Gren, in November of 1961. Alweg was acquired by Krupp Corporation in 1962, and then withered and ended by 1967. Despite this, today Alweg's technology is the leading monorail technology for major systems around the world. Japan continues to build Alweg-based monorails. Outside Japan, Hitachi has sold its version of Alweg in China, Singapore, United Arab Emirates and South Korea. Malaysia reverse-engineered Seattle's Alweg system and won bids in Malaysia, India and Brazil. Ironically, one of Alweg's early target cities, São Paulo, Brazil, has once again embraced Alweg technology with several lines, the first by Bombardier Transportation. Second and third São Paulo lines are being built by Scomi Engineering.

1950s rendering of Alweg in the city

RIGHT: **Alweg rendering for Chicago**

COULD HAVE, SHOULD HAVE

Luggage being retrieved from the side of a train at Frankfurt Airport

ABOVE: Alweg's model maker, Hermann Blick, built this elaborate model of monorail crossing Wiener Platz in Cologne, Germany.

LEFT: In 1957 Alweg was chosen for São Paulo, albeit briefly. Over 50 years later the city would again embrace monorail, and this time actually build several Alweg-type lines.

BELOW: Tijuana, Mexico station concept by Mario Pani's architectural firm

RENDERING: R. Rivas C.

ABOVE: Urban settings weren't the only targets for Alweg sales. This image highlighted old and new worlds together with the Alweg 70-kilometer Tel Aviv to Jerusalem proposal.

95

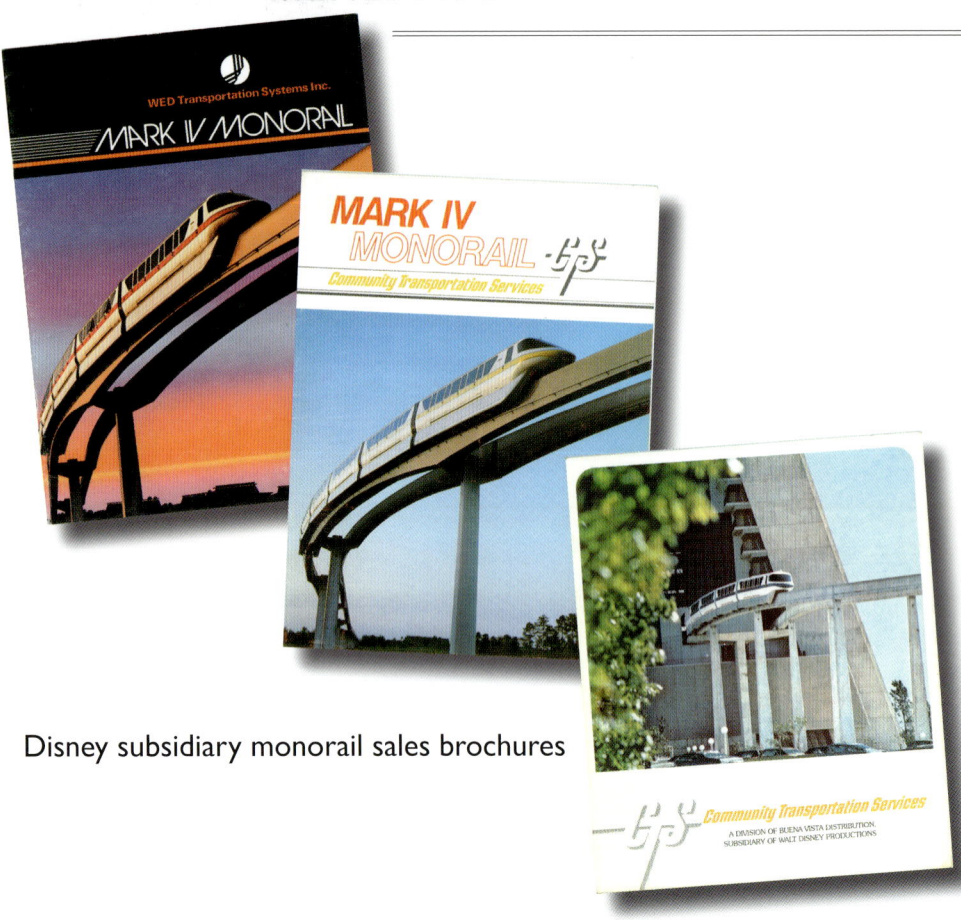

MONORAILS

Disney subsidiary monorail sales brochures

MARK IV PHOTO: Author
SKYLINE PHOTO: iStock

Alweg by Disney

Disney's Alweg-based monorails garnered a lot of attention. It's well established that Walt Disney loved to demonstrate his monorail to decision makers. After his death in 1966, his company continued to receive inquiries about them. In 1974 Disney debuted Community Transportation Services (CTS), founded "in response to numerous requests from cities, airports and shopping centers interested in applications of the company's monorail and WEDway PeopleMover systems." CTS offered expertise in all phases of transit system development including planning, design, program management, and operation and maintenance. CTS was renamed WED Transportation Systems by 1982. The company never sold any monorails, but did provide dual-rail WEDway PeopleMovers to Houston Intercontinental Airport and the US Senate Subway. Eventually Disney licensed its transportation systems to Bombardier of Canada. Bombardier's first resulting monorail contract in 1987 was for Mark VI trains for Walt Disney World Resort.

ABOVE: Before establishing its own transportation subsidiary, the Walt Disney Company had planned a 3.8-kilometer monorail loop for the 1964-65 New York World's Fair. An AMF suspended monorail was built instead (page 68).

ART: Wegematic Corporation

COULD HAVE, SHOULD HAVE

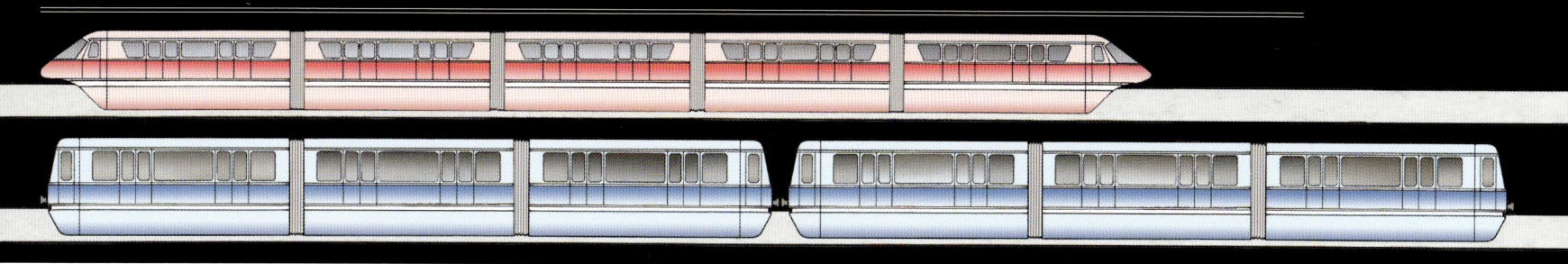

ABOVE: CTS and re-named WED Transportation Systems offered monorails larger than their Mark IV, including the 'Long Nose Model 952S' and 'Short Nose Model 1134DC'
RENDERING: Author*

RIGHT: Disney's transportation subsidiaries offered everything from small peoplemover systems to high-capacity line haul monorails. This 1970's era design for a 6-passenger vehicle matches specifications of many of today's promoted PRT systems, albeit with a less-imposing guideway.
RENDERING: Author*

BELOW: Large modular car monorails were also part of Disney PeopleMover system offerings, including this Model 811.
RENDERING: Author*
PHOTO; Pavel Shlykov/Dreamstime

*Author renderings are based on information obtained from CTS and WED Transportation marketing brochures

97

MONORAILS

Safege around the world

Safege promoted their suspended system aggressively while competitor Alweg promoted their straddle system. Initially Safege concentrated efforts for short revenue lines in the Paris area, one between Livry-Gargan and Clichy sous Bois and the other between Charenton and Criteil. These weren't built and neither were proposed lines for England, Belgium, Spain, Italy, USSR, South Africa and Australia. American Machine and Foundry (AMF) purchased licensing rights for Safege in the United States. AMF demonstrated an I-Beam suspended monorail at the 1964-65 New York World's Fair, but marketed the more-capable Safege design for many USA cities. The US Army wanted to build a ship-loading Safege system in Vietnam. AMF turned the Army down, believing the war there would be over soon. General Electric (GE) acquired the USA Safege rights from AMF in early 1967. Proposals were made to cities including San Francisco and Honolulu. GE discontinued promotion a few years later. In Japan, Mitsubishi built a Safege demonstrator line at Higashiyama Zoo in Nagoya, the first revenue-producing Safege in the world. Mitsubishi went on to build a commuter line in Shonan and the world's longest Safege system in Chiba City.

ABOVE: Artist impression of a bullet-shaped Safege train by St. Paul's Church in Hammersmith, London

COULD HAVE, SHOULD HAVE

ABOVE: Art/photo showing a Safege train bridge by Pont d'Ougrée in Liège, Belgium

ABOVE: Numerous airport connections were seen as ideal for Safege, as suggested in this rendering showing Dulles Airport in Virginia. Other airport connectors were proposed for Chicago, San Francisco, Baltimore, Tampa and London.

ABOVE AND BELOW RIGHT: Nikita Khrushchev, then-Premier of the USSR, is said to have been convinced Safege was the best new transit technology for Moscow, yet only this Russian prototype was built and a monorail postal stamp was issued.

LEFT: Artist-imagined Safege train emerging from station in El Paso, Texas

MONORAILS

H-Bahn
Siemens succeeded in building H-Bahn lines in Dortmund and Düsseldorf, but proposals for Erlangen, Germany and other cities never materialized. Siemens stopped marketing H-Bahn in 2007, yet interest continues to be shown for the technology.

Vancouver, Canada
In the 1970s, US engineer Anson S. Bilger (Bilger Monorail International) proposed a Waterfront Station to Vancouver Airport monorail. His $35-million monorail was to be an updated version of Wuppertal's Schwebebahn.

Los Angeles area keeps trying
Despite the many failed attempts during the 1940s through the 1960s, monorail remained a popular idea in Southern California. Proposals continued to be made, supported, and then defeated. To date, the only monorails coming from the area have been the creations by Hollywood for the big screen. The efforts for Los Angeles area monorails continue today.

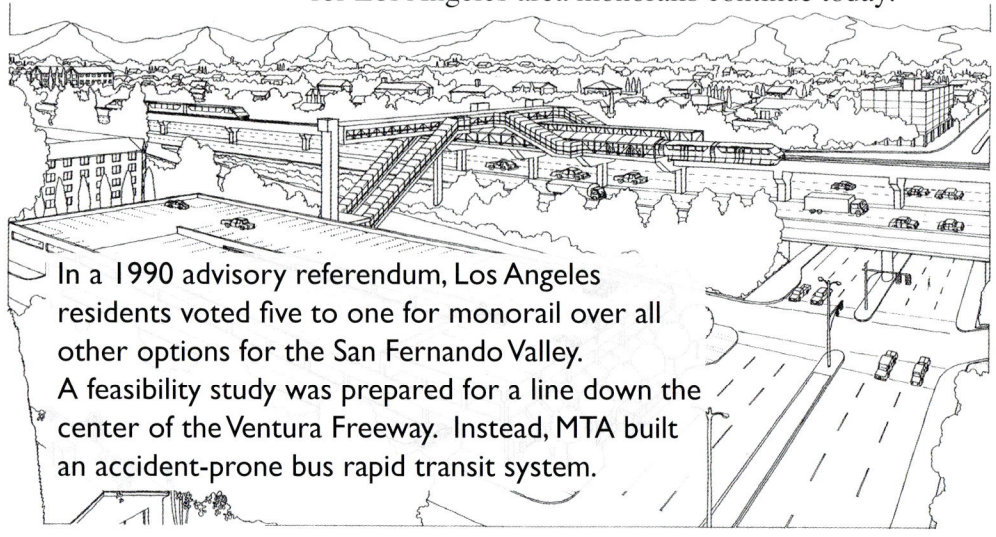

In a 1990 advisory referendum, Los Angeles residents voted five to one for monorail over all other options for the San Fernando Valley. A feasibility study was prepared for a line down the center of the Ventura Freeway. Instead, MTA built an accident-prone bus rapid transit system.

ABOVE: McDonnell Douglas Realty funded a the first leg of a planned 22-kilometer Irvine Monorail System, favored by then-Mayor Larry Agran. It was initially going to connect a nearby office building with John Wayne Airport. The first leg was to be funded by private development incentives. On a larger scale, efforts for a countywide 'monorail' were under way and supported by many cities. Irvine eventually decided to put monorail funds towards the county-wide system. Orange County changed their preference to light rail, which ended up being cancelled as well.

COULD HAVE, SHOULD HAVE

Los Angeles area keeps trying

RIGHT: In 1990, Gensler and Associates/Architects presented a city-supported feasibility study on transit options for the City of Burbank. The study recommended a monorail that would connect the three major employment and transportation centers of the city. Calling the system Burbank Metrolink, the 22-kilometer monorail would have stops at Universal City, the Media District, Burbank Center, the Golden State Area and Burbank Airport. The study found that the Metrolink would be lower in cost than that of comparable guideway systems, coming in at around $15-million per kilometer with a dual-lane system. Sources for funding of the capital costs, operation and maintenance included everyone that stood to benefit from the system. That included the city, developers of potential projects along the route, local merchants, property owners, residents and employees of area businesses. Additional funding sources could be from the County and City of Los Angeles, Burbank Airport, surrounding communities, the State of California and the Federal Government. Like most feasibility studies, it ended up being filed away.

RIGHT: In conjunction with their plans for a major transportation hub, featuring a station for high speed rail, the City of Anaheim began work in 2007 on what would be referred to as the Anaheim Rapid Connection (ARC). Years of study, public outreach and planning for ARC ended in 2012 when politicians gave up on the idea, claiming the 5.6-kilometer, five-station system would cost a whopping $700-million.

MONORAILS

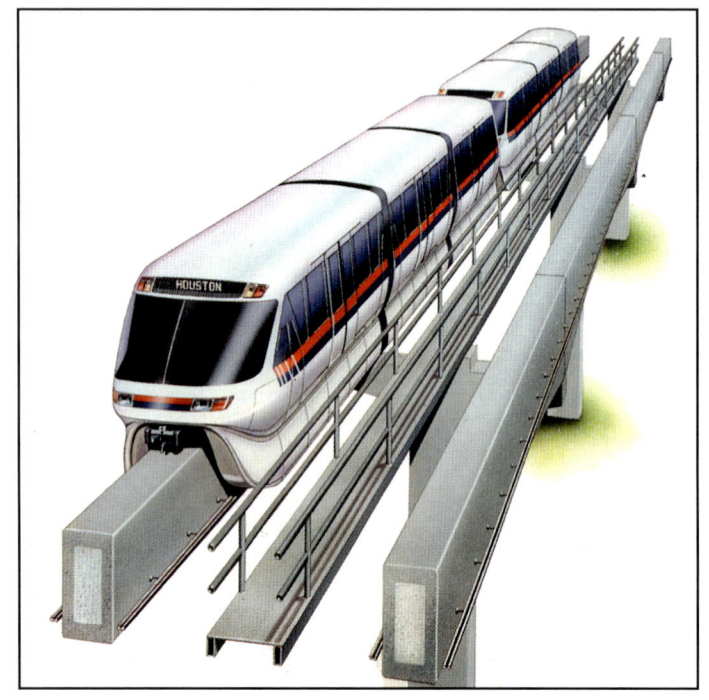

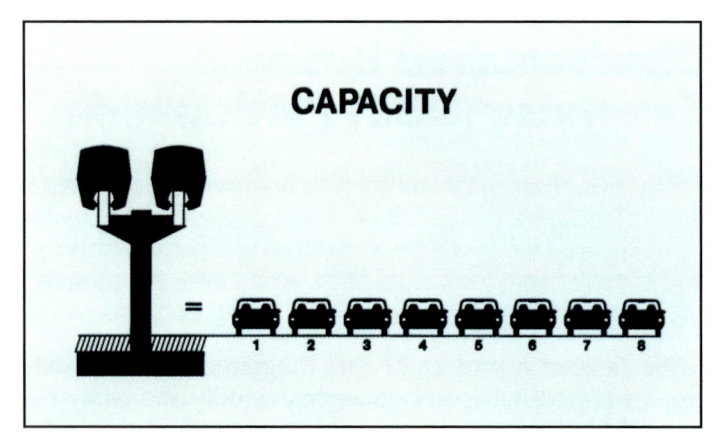

Houston, Texas

On March 28, 1991, Houston's Metropolitan Transit Authority (METRO) voted to build the first state-of-the-art urban monorail system in the USA. The Houston Monorail Team was to supply the system, members included Kiewit Construction Group and Bombardier. The initial two-line system would be 32-kilometers in length with 21 stations. It would run from downtown Houston to the southwest and west of the city. Monorail had been favored by then-Mayor Kathryn J. Whitmire. What followed the approval for monorail was a non-stop, vitriolic political campaign against it. Questions about monorail technology and alleged business improprieties filled newspaper headlines for months. Bob Lanier, a long-time rail critic, ran for mayor later that year, vowing to cancel the monorail project if elected. He won the election and did just that. The Houston Monorail project died as initial engineering was about to begin. Years later Houston revived its desire for rail, yet it built surface-running light rail instead of monorail. It was quickly nicknamed the Wham Bam Tram, as predictable mayhem between vehicles and trains became the norm. Houston's METRORail averaged seven crashes per track kilometer per year. Speaking of the troubled system, the Houston Chronicle quoted then-former Mayor Lanier as saying monorail wasn't the right choice in 1991, but indicated it might be worth a second look in Houston. "I have no objection to monorail as such, I would not rule anything out."

CAPACITY

COULD HAVE, SHOULD HAVE

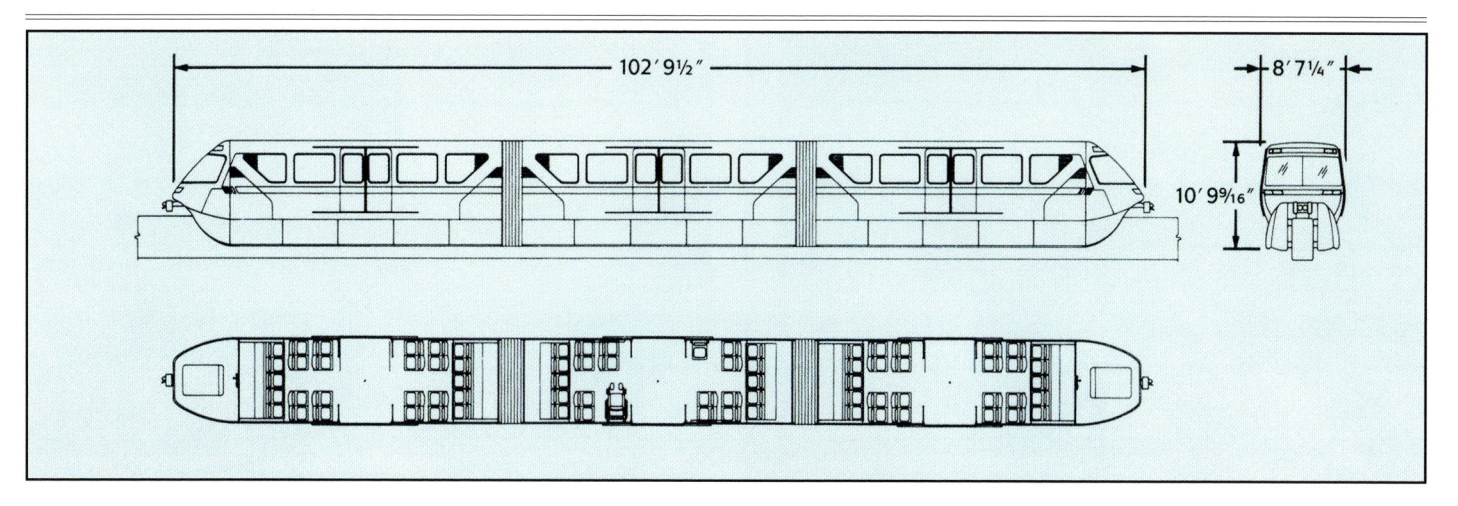

ABOVE: Bombardier's M VI, a three-car variation on the then-new Mark VI at Walt Disney World Resort, was to be the company's first large-scale urban monorail if built. Cruising at speeds of up to 88 km/h, the monorail would travel from the West Belt to downtown in less than 25 minutes. Three-car trains would only require 2/3 of the proposed platform lengths for initial operation. With expansion the ultimate capacity would have been 24,000 passengers per peak hour, per direction. Automatic couplers would allow automatically-actuated formation of multiple units, so train length could be varied throughout the day, depending on demand.

RIGHT: The M VI interior for Houston. After Houston's failure to build monorail, the first M VI system built was the Las Vegas Monorail..

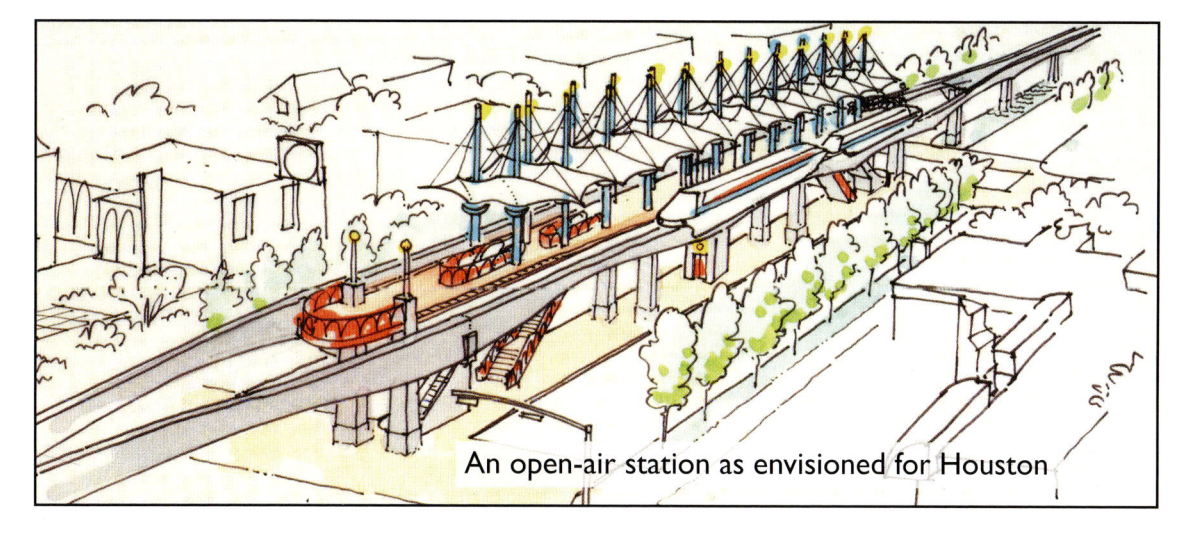

RENDERINGS: Bombardier Transportation

An open-air station as envisioned for Houston

MONORAILS

Alphen aan de Rign, Netherlands

In 1996, Holland Monorail BV was awarded the contract to build a one-kilometer shuttle between the Archeon Living Museum and Alphen aan de Rign rail station. The company was a joint venture between Grimbergn Alphen aan de Rign and Hollandin Kloos. Holland Monorail's technology was very similar to that of the Siemens H-Bahn, yet the pylons featured a unique track-through-the-keyhole design. The alignment followed canals as it departed from the rail station, then there was a stretch through a multi-story residential neighborhood before reaching the park. The system was set to open in 1998, but complaints from the residents of the area succeeded in lengthening the building permit process and eventually cancelling it. Holland Monorail had also been in discussion with other cities and officials at Schipol International Airport before folding.

RENDERING: Holland Monorail

Northern Kentucky, USA

Quest, a 1997 report prepared by a task force of many area leaders, presented a bold vision for the future of Northern Kentucky and Cincinnati, Ohio. Redevelopment, better government, better housing, better education and iconic tourist destinations were among the ideas. The idea that garnered the most attention and controversy was for a high-speed monorail between Cincinnati and the Cincinnati/Northern Kentucky Airport. Bryant 'Pete' Trenary, President of Aerorail Development Corporation, proposed to build, finance and then hand over a 53-kilometer high-speed steel monorail system, using technology similar to Safege. The offer was rejected, as was monorail in general.

RENDERING: Aerorail Development Corp.

Colorado, USA

The Colorado Intermountain Guideway Authority (CIFGA) was formed in 1998 and made up of five counties along the congested I-70 corridor between Denver and Glenwood Springs. CIFGA's proposal was for a high-speed inverted-T monorail operating at speeds of up to 160 km/h on a 258-kilometer line from Denver International Airport to Eagle County Airport near Vail. The monorail cost was the same as adding two highway lanes to the route. Governor Bill Owens chided the project as a "Disneyland ride," helping to defeat a 2001 voter initiative to build a $50-million test track. If developed, CIFGA had hopes of exporting the technology beyond Colorado.

RENDERING: CIFGA

Pinellas County, Florida

The Clearwater/St. Petersburg area has been a congested mess for decades. Since the 1980s there have been several attempts to establish a monorail system there. The most noteworthy was an effort was spearheaded by the Pinellas County Metropolitan Planning Organization (MPO). It was referred to as the Pinellas Mobility Initiative. After years of study, the MPO voted in 2005 to support the plan for 61-kilometers of guideway, starting with a 3.2-kilometer demonstrator line. Study findings concluded a demonstrator line between Clearwater and Clearwater Beach could draw as many as 3.6-million riders annually. In 2006 the MPO reversed course and halted all funds toward any rail. Mayor Frank Hibbard of Clearwater said, "Sadly, what's going to happen is all of this [monorail] will get shelved for another 10 or 15 years until the pain is so excruciating, and we have no other solutions, and the prices have tripled, and we finally say *Uncle*."

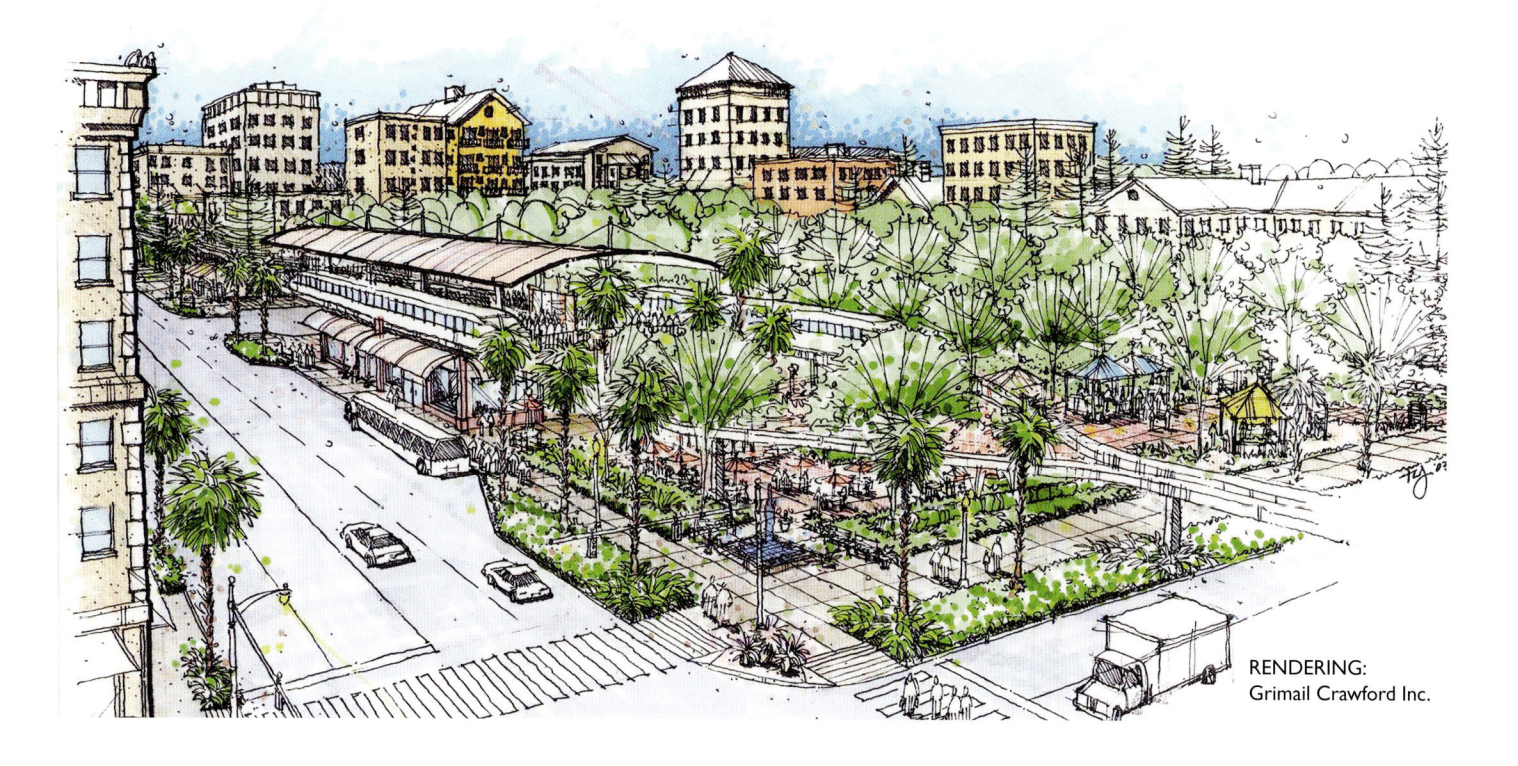

RENDERING: Grimail Crawford Inc.

MONORAILS

Seattle, Washington

Stuck in traffic, Seattle citizen Dick Falkenbury looked up and watched the 1962 Alweg monorail zip by unimpeded on its 1.5-kilometer shuttle run. That became the start an amazing grassroots effort to 'Extend the Monorail.' His successful campaign resulted in four separate election votes supporting an expanded Seattle monorail system. In 2002 the Seattle Popular Monorail Authority (SPMA) was formed to administer the design and construction of the initial 22.5-kilometer line. The Green Line would run from West Seattle through downtown and on to Crown Hill. After a dragged-out, closed-door negotiation process, the SPMA made a contract agreement with the sole-bidder, Cascadia Monorail Company. Cascadia's team included Hitachi, and Seattle would have been the company's first monorail in the Western Hemisphere. Bombardier's Team Monorail dropped out earlier because of liability requirements in the RFP. From the start, the project had its share of vocal critics, made up of major businesses downtown, residents along the route and light rail proponents. Once the Cascadia deal revealed that a financing plan would cost $9-billion in interest over fifty years, cries to halt the project grew much louder. Mayor Greg Nickels withdrew his already tepid support for the monorail, as did the city council and the city's two major newspapers. An unprecedented fifth vote was held in November of 2005 and the critics finally won, the Seattle Monorail Project was dead. In the years since the project failed, Chongqing, China has built the largest monorail system in the world. Irony of ironies: Chongqing is a sister city of Seattle.

COULD HAVE, SHOULD HAVE

ILLUSTRATION: Gus D'Angelo/Washington City Paper

ABOVE: Hitachi's train as it would have appeared crossing through Seattle Center

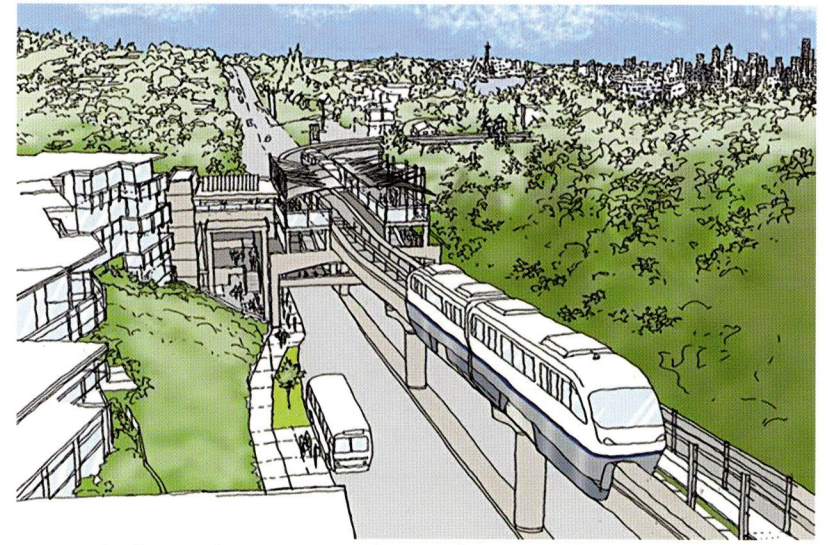

ABOVE: A Green Line station design for West Seattle

LEFT: Initial renderings for the Seattle Monorail Project included unique and sleek bi-level 'Iris' pylons, but the final design became overly bulky and controversial. Iris supports were then dropped from the plan.

ILLUSTRATION: Seattle Weekly

MONORAILS

Niagara Falls, Canada

For numerous decades the community of Niagara Falls worked toward building a monorail system. One of the first to promote the concept on the USA side of the falls was Goodell Monorail in the 1950s. That proposal failed, and later in the 1980s an effort was taken up in Canada's Niagara Falls. Visitation to the area had grown by leaps and bounds and studies showed even further growth. A monorail seemed the logical way to move people around the area without taxing the local streets. Millions of dollars were spent doing studies and acquiring land for the system, but efforts proved fruitless as the project was cancelled in 2009.

Putrajaya, Malaysia

Subway tunnels sit empty under the city's main artery, a multi-modal Putrajaya Sentral Station with track in and out of it has been built, and a large suspension bridge has monorail track that ends at each shoreline. Construction for a two-line system in Malaysia's brand new capital was well under way, but halted in 2004. The Putrajaya Monorail project is said to resume when the new city's population increases.

COULD HAVE, SHOULD HAVE

Jakarta, Indonesia

If there were an award for a project repeatedly starting and stopping, Jakarta Monorail might get the prize. With an original start in 2004, contracts have since been awarded numerous times to different entities, yet financial woes and politics have helped each effort fail. 90 abandoned concrete pillars are the only visible accomplishment of the project to date.

RENDERING: PT Jakarta Monorail

City of Arabia, UAE

In 2008 Metrail AG was awarded a monorail contract for the City of Arabia. It was Metrail's first contract for the groundbreaking hybrid monorail technology. The real estate bubble that fueled UAE projects burst in 2009, halting many projects including the City of Arabia and its monorail system.

RENDERING: Metrail AG

Tehran, Iran

In 2002 Tehran Mayor Mahmoud Ahmadinejad started a monorail project for the Iranian city. Controversy plagued the monorail from the beginning, with opponents concerned about costs and expressing concern as to whether Iran had the necessary skills to build it. Construction of the first six-kilometer, six-station line began in March of 2004, but funds to complete the line were not awarded by the state. By 2007 Ahmadinejad was President of Iran and he directed funds to complete the system. The new mayor of Tehran did not support the monorail, further endangering the project. The project was cancelled in 2009 after only 3% of its construction was complete.

LEFT AND ABOVE: **Tehran Monorail**, as envisioned by artists

ABOVE: **Short-lived Tehran construction**

Seattle Center Monorail
ABOVE: Alweg train glides beneath the Space Needle
PHOTO: Author

Walt Disney World Monorail
FACING PAGE: Mark VI monorail train approaches Disney's Contemporary Resort in Florida
PHOTO: Author

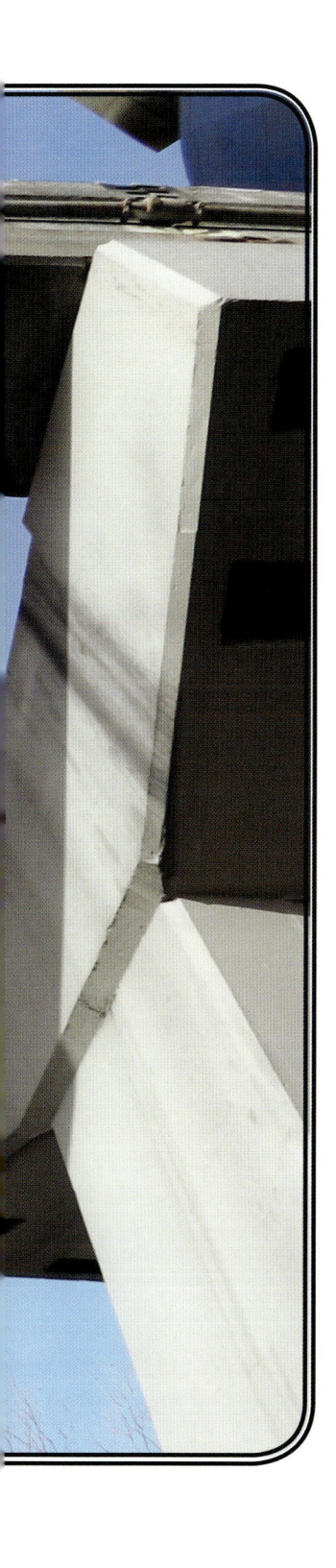

5

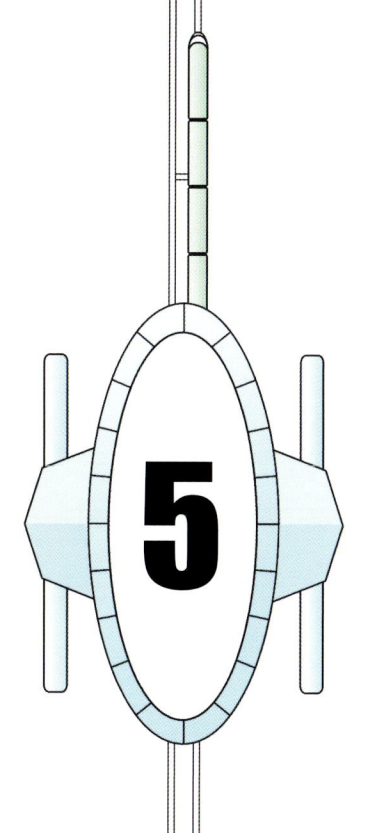

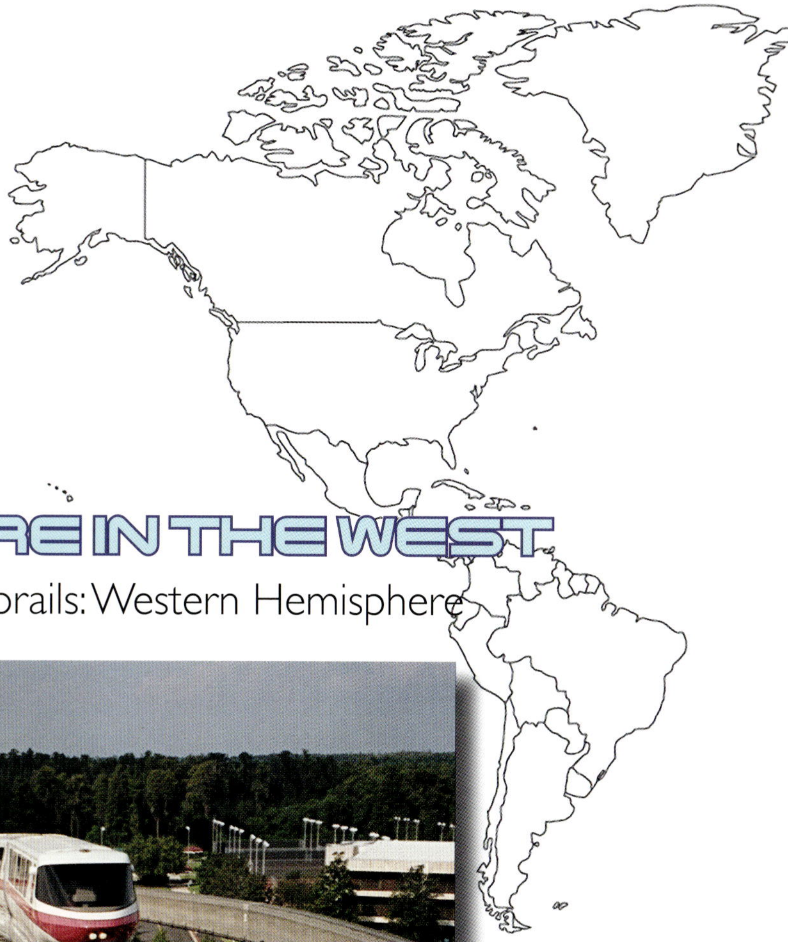

Where in the West
Today's monorails: Western Hemisphere

One of the surprising facts about monorail is the number of them currently serving in transit settings. This chapter focuses on transit monorails operating today in the Western Hemisphere, presented in the chronological order of their opening.

Disneyland Monorail
Anaheim, California, USA

Opened 1959
Extended 1961
4 km (2.5 miles)
2 stations
Single track loop

Early on in the planning of Disneyland, Walt Disney envisioned a futuristic monorail attraction in Tomorrowland. While on vacation in Europe in 1958, he visited the Alweg test facility in Fühlingen, Germany. Disney was impressed and soon after made an agreement with Alweg. To fit the scale of the park, Disney designers modified the Alweg system and opened their 5/8 scale Alweg monorail on June 14, 1959. During its first years it was the park's most popular and talked-about attraction. Millions of TV viewers first saw the monorail on Walt's Sunday show and became convinced of its future in transit. An extension was added to connect to the nearby Disneyland Hotel in 1961. Disney installed the monorail to promote it as a train of the future, yet it became somewhat typecast as an amusement park ride. Over a half century later, the monorail continues to safely carry thousands of passengers daily between Downtown Disney and Tomorrowland. Over one-billion park visitors have enjoyed the experience.

WHERE IN THE WEST

RIGHT: Pilot cab view of track as train parallels South Harbor Boulevard, just before entering Tomorrowland

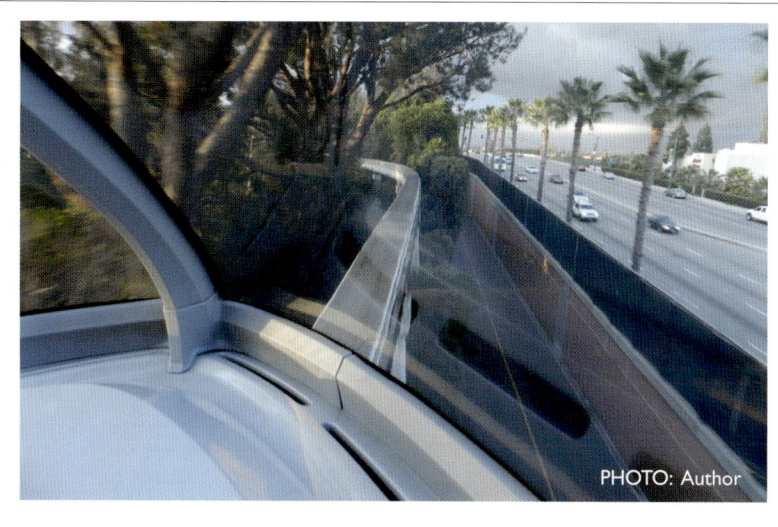

PHOTO: Author

Walt Disney wanted a thrilling, twisting and turning ride for his monorail passengers, which presented challenges for the engineers and designers of the system.

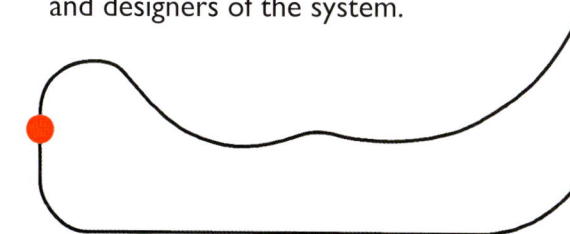

NOTE: Maps are not to scale and are for illustrative purposes only.

The 1961 extension gave Disneyland the opportunity to tout the first daily-operating monorail in the USA to cross a major street (then West Street, now named Disneyland Drive).

PHOTO: James Horecka

MONORAILS

Monorail Red cruises through Disney California Adventure. From 1961 until 1998 this stretch of track was over the original parking lot, then in February of 2001 Disney opened their second Anaheim park. The same guideway now runs through greenery in the park and a new Disney's Grand Californian Hotel & Spa on its way to Downtown Disney Station.

PHOTO: Author

WHERE IN THE WEST

If you know where to stand in Disneyland, a close look at the undercarriage is possible. You might even hear the sound of the horns while watching them pass over.

PHOTO: Author

115

MONORAILS

Seattle Center Monorail
Washington, USA

Opened 1962
1.5 km (1 mile)
2 stations
Dual-track shuttle

When it opened in conjunction with Seattle's Century 21 Exposition, the Seattle Alweg Monorail and the Space Needle were the two main icons of the world's fair. During the six-month fair, the monorail shuttled over eight-million people between downtown and the fairgrounds. Alweg spent $3.5-million to build the 1.5-kilometer line as an attention-getting demonstrator of its technology. It took only eight months of construction to complete. Revenue from ticket sales during the fair easily paid for the entire system cost. Today the monorail is owned by the City of Seattle and operated by a private contractor, Seattle Monorail Services. The historic line features the world's only surviving Alweg GmbH-built trains, each capable of carrying 450 passengers. Ridership is around two-million passengers each year. Thanks to the low cost of maintaining and operating monorail, it continues to be one of the few transit rail lines in the USA to operate at a profit. No operating funds are provided by taxpayers. All operations costs, and the profits which the City receives from the monorail, are generated through ticket sales. In 2012 Seattle celebrated its monorail's 50th anniversary. Seattle Center Monorail's legacy is that numerous countries outside the USA took notice of the technology and made use of it. In recent years Alweg-type construction has increased around the world, all traceable back to Seattle's iconic monorail.

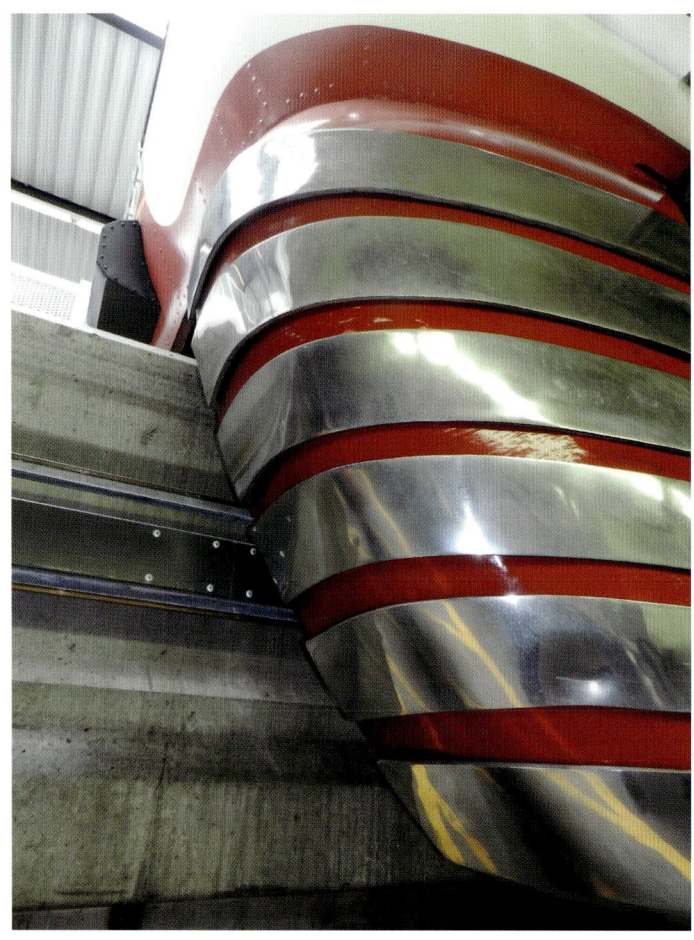

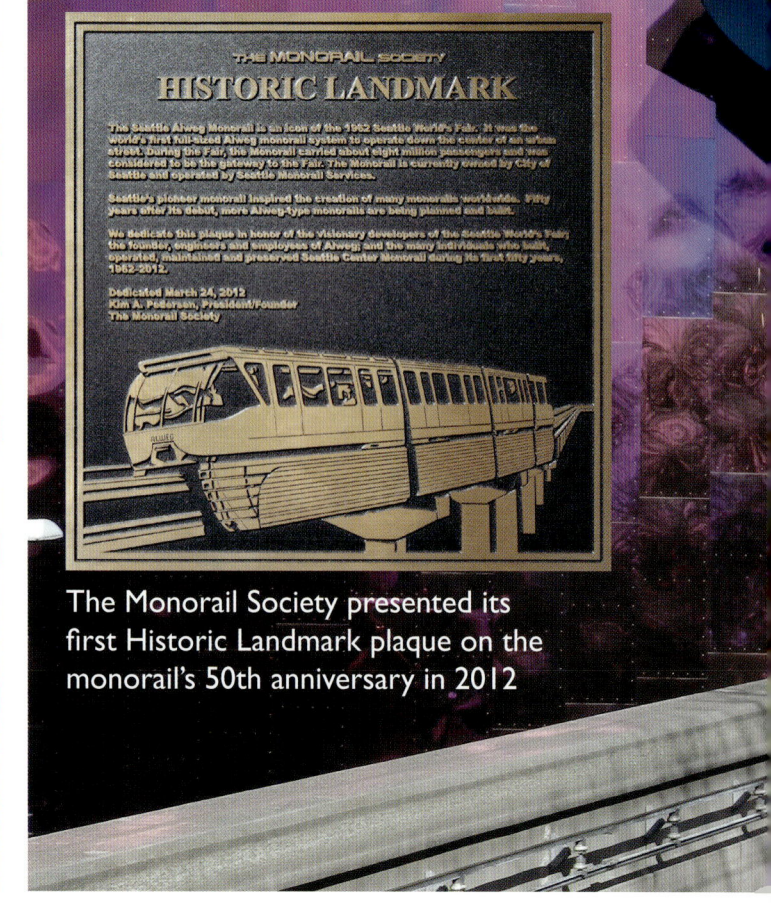

The Monorail Society presented its first Historic Landmark plaque on the monorail's 50th anniversary in 2012

WHERE IN THE WEST

Each train has travelled over one-million miles since 1962. They operate at speeds up to 72 km/h, yet were engineered for speeds up to 137 km/h if longer stretches of track existed.

PHOTOS: Author

The Blue Train at Seattle Center

117

MONORAILS

PHOTO: Keith Walls

Walt Disney World Monorail
Lake Buena Vista, Florida, USA

Opened 1971
Extended 1982
23.6 km (14.7 miles)
6 stations
Dual-track loop
Single-track loop

Using experience gained from three generations of monorail trains in Disneyland, larger Disney-designed Mark IV trains began transit service at Disney's second theme park resort in 1971. The dual-guideway loop circles the Seven Seas Lagoon and includes stations at the Ticket and Transportation Center (TTC), Disney's Contemporary Resort, Magic Kingdom theme park, Disney's Polynesian Village Resort and Disney's Grand Floridian Resort (added in 1988). When Epcot theme park opened in 1982, the Epcot loop was added along with additional trains. The Epcot loop runs from the TTC to Epcot Station. Unique to the Walt Disney World Resort system are the long stretches of track through uninhabited, forested areas, giving guests nature-scenic rides. Having accomplished nearly ten-million miles of travel with a reliability rate of 99.9% in eighteen-hour-a-day operations, in 1989 it was time to replace the original Martin Marietta/Disney Mark IVs. Bombardier, licensed by The Walt Disney Company to market the technology, provided twelve new trains. The taller Mark VI trains were the first Disney monorails to accommodate standing passengers. The Walt Disney World Resort system carries around 50-million passengers per year, which is one of the highest ridership figures for monorail in the world. When Walt Disney first introduced plans for Walt Disney World on his TV show in 1966, his map included monorail reaching all major points on the property.

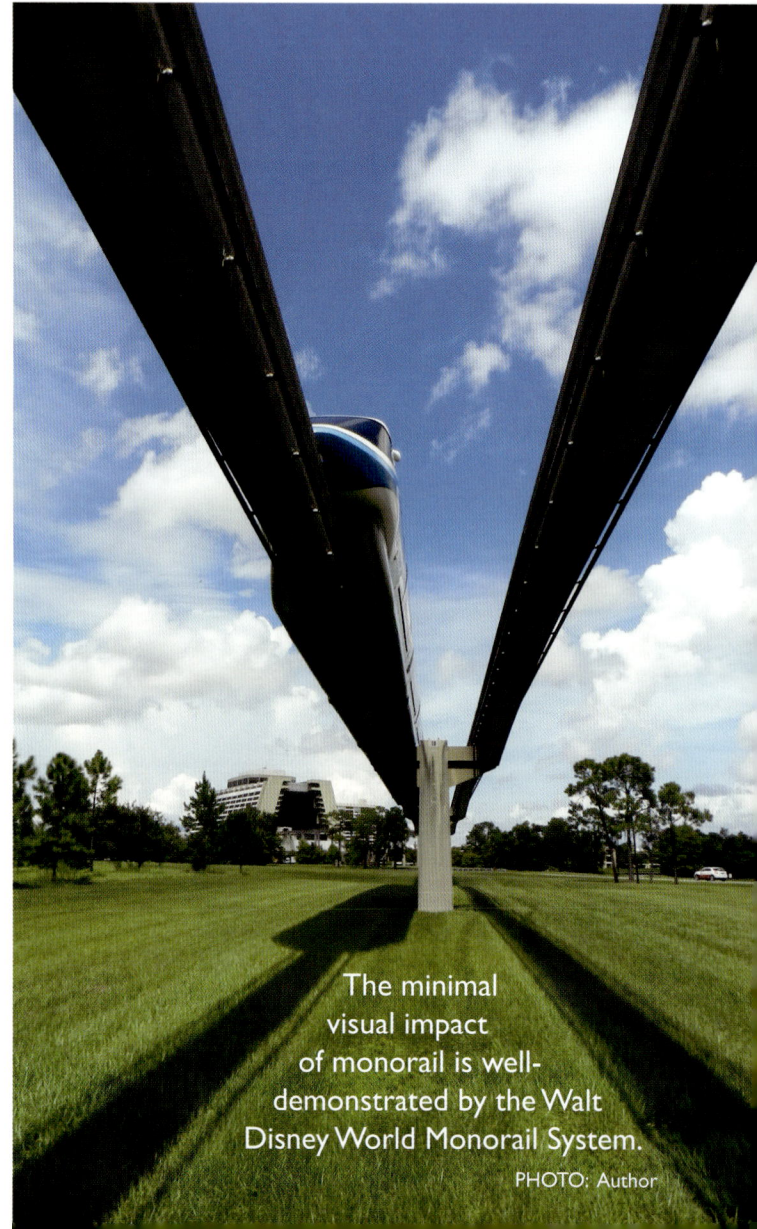

The minimal visual impact of monorail is well-demonstrated by the Walt Disney World Monorail System.
PHOTO: Author

WHERE IN THE WEST

ABOVE: Walt Disney World Monorail System was the first to incorporate gracefully-arched track. The first 1971 track was designed by ABAM Engineers, Inc., fabricated by Concrete Technology Corp. in Tacoma, Washington and delivered cross-country to Florida by rail.

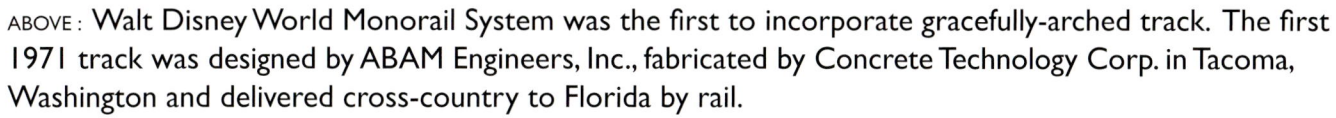

PHOTO: Keith Walls

Through the woods to Epcot

PHOTO: Author

ABOVE: Interior of Bombardier's Mark VI

PHOTO: Dale Samuelson

119

MONORAILS

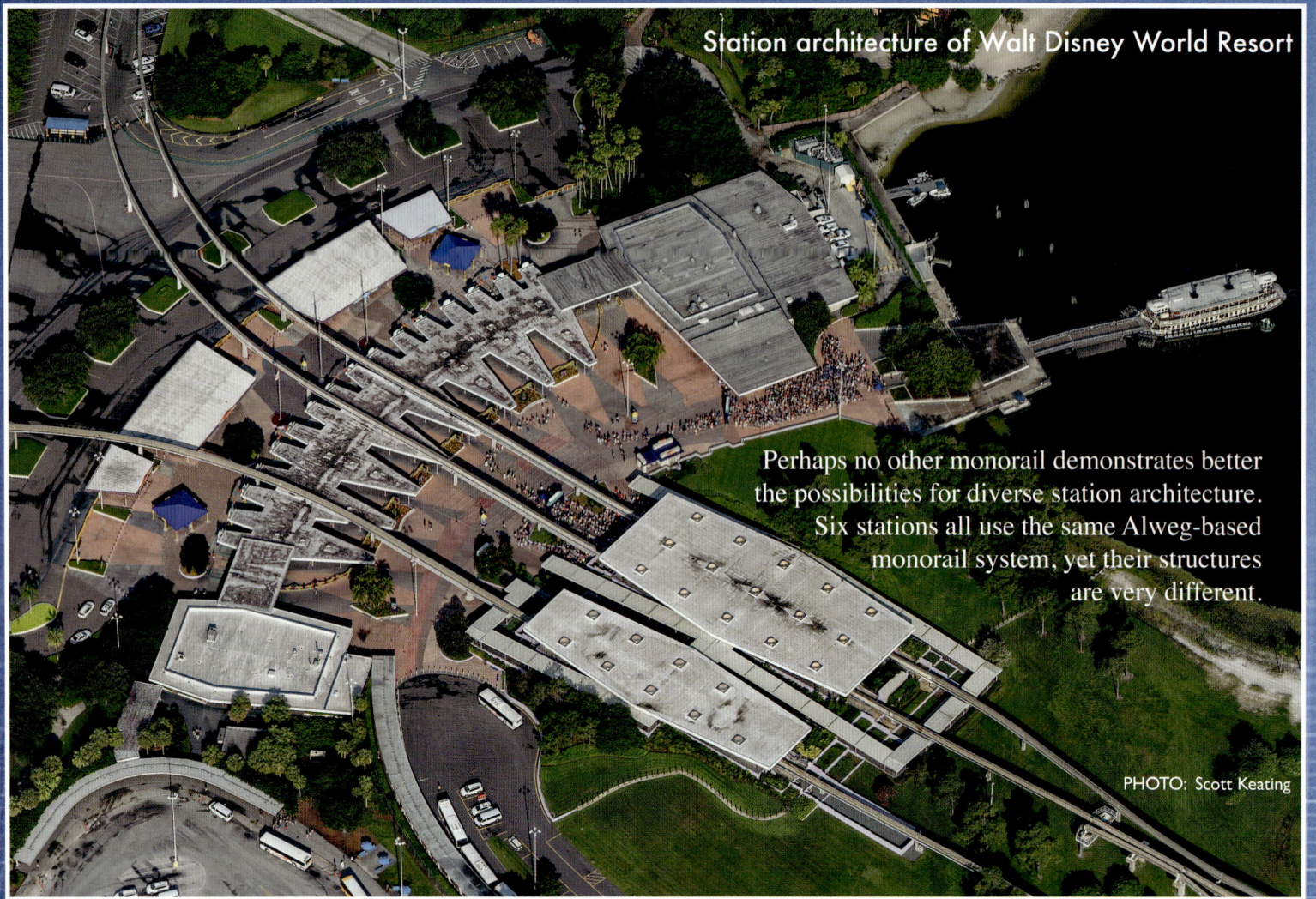

Station architecture of Walt Disney World Resort

Perhaps no other monorail demonstrates better the possibilities for diverse station architecture. Six stations all use the same Alweg-based monorail system, yet their structures are very different.

PHOTO: Scott Keating

ABOVE: The Ticket and Transportation Center (TTC) efficiently handles hundreds of thousands of guests every week. This multi-modal station allows transfers between parking lot trams, busses, ferries and is the transfer point between the Seven Seas Lagoon loop and the Epcot loop (narrower station segment at bottom with single monorail line)

The Magic Kingdom Station decor is early-20th century to match the nearby Main Street architecture. The TTC and Magic Kingdom stations are both ground-level, sitting upon low man-made hills

PHOTO: Author

WHERE IN THE WEST

RIGHT: Disney's Polynesian Village Resort Station reflects the Tiki-style resort that opened in 1971. The structure is quite simple, yet the lines match those perfectly of the hotel.

PHOTO: Author

RIGHT: The massive A-frame Disney's Contemporary Resort has one of the more remarkable monorail stations in the world. Monorail trains climb nearly 20 meters up to enter the fifth floor station platform, located inside the massive Grand Canyon Concourse.

PHOTO: Keith Walls

RIGHT: Epcot Station was added in 1982 in conjunction with the world's fair-like Epcot park.

PHOTO: Keith Walls

RIGHT: Disney's Grand Floridian Station is the newest station in the system and opened in 1988 in conjunction with the deluxe hotel opening. It was inspired by the Victorian era late 19th century beach resorts built along Florida's east coast.

PHOTO: Author

MONORAILS

Green Train in green area near Disney's Polynesian Village Resort
PHOTO: Author

WHERE IN THE WEST

Coral Train circles through gardens of Epcot
PHOTO: Author

Orange Train emerges from Disney's Contemporary Resort

PHOTO: Keith Walls

123

MONORAILS

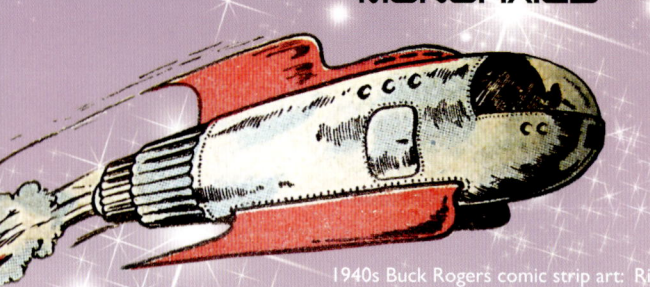

1940s Buck Rogers comic strip art: Rick Yager

The Evolution of Disney's USA Monorails

Disney monorails are arguably the world's most well-known monorails. Since the Mark I debuted at Disneyland in 1959, each new train generation has featured advancements, noticeable to those with a keen eye. One thing that has never changed is the appeal of the sleek, futuristic look, all resulting from a Buck Rogers rocket ship-inspired sketch by Disney Imagineer Bob Gurr.

MARK I: 1959-1961

LEFT: Two three-car Mark I monorail trains were built at The Walt Disney Studios with Alweg assistance. The route was a figure 8 with an outside circle excursion, all within the confines of Tomorrowland.

PHOTO: davelandweb.com collection

MARK II: 1961-1969

The Mark IIs of 1961 added one car to the original Disneyland monorails. One extremely popular feature added was the expanded bubble where lucky riders could ride up top with the pilot. The loop track was extended outside Disneyland and a second station was built at the Disneyland Hotel. An additional train brought the fleet up to three.

PHOTO: Air California

124

WHERE IN THE WEST

MARK III: 1969-1987
PHOTO: Author

LEFT: Cosmetically the Disneyland Mark III trains looked similar to their predecessors. Larger side windows were the most noticeable change. Hidden from public view were many advances with the bogie/suspension configuration. Stations were lengthened to accommodate the new five-car trains. The fleet of trains also grew to four.

MARK IV: 1971-1989
PHOTO: Karen & Patrick Engle

RIGHT: The Mark Vs of Disneyland reflected the east coast's 'Lear Jet' nose, but had rounder bodies than their larger Floridian cousins.

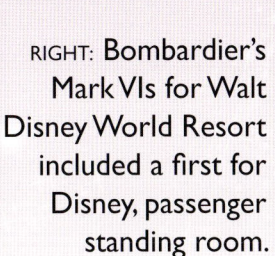

MARK V: 1987-2008
PHOTO: Author

RIGHT: Bombardier's Mark VIs for Walt Disney World Resort included a first for Disney, passenger standing room.

MARK VI: 1989-
PHOTO: Carol Pedersen

ABOVE: For Walt Disney World Resort in Florida, higher capacity trains were required. Mark IVs were larger than Disneyland's Mark IIIs, yet they still weren't enlarged to match Alweg's original transit-scale design. Bob Gurr's design talents this time resulted in a Lear Jet-inspired cab. The first ten trains were built by Martin Marietta. Two additional trains were built by Disney's WED Transportation Systems Inc. in the 1980s. The 'Lime Train' above is one of the two Disney-built Mark IVs, which later operated in Las Vegas as the MGM-Bally's Monorail.

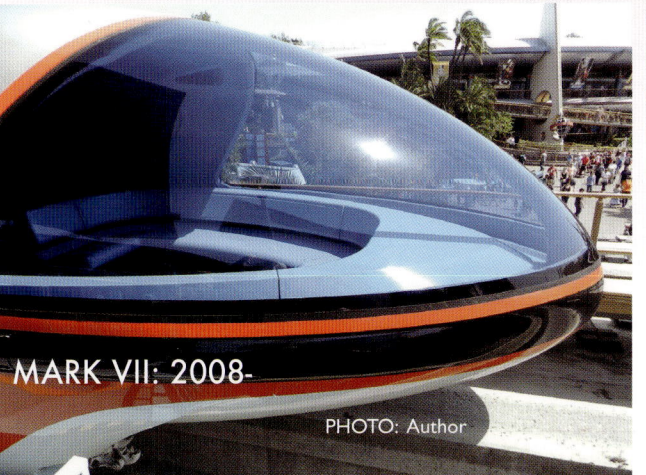

MARK VII: 2008-
PHOTO: Author

LEFT: Disneyland's newest generation, the Mark VII, includes center bench seating and a look evocative of earlier designs.

125

MONORAILS

PHOTOS: Author

Pearlridge Sky Cab
Honolulu, Hawaii, USA

Opened 1977
.4 km (.25 mile)
2 stations
shuttle

When Pearlridge Shopping Center expanded into two separate complexes in 1976, owners grappled with what to do about the watercress farm barrier between them. The solution was a monorail shuttle built by Rohr Industries, Inc. of Chula Vista, California. It carries visitors between the two building complexes, connecting Pearlridge's Uptown and Downtown facilities. Rohr used inverted-T technology for their one and only monorail. The air-conditioned 'Sky Cab' monorail shuttle opened on November 7, 1977. A one-way ride costs one dollar and is free for children under eight years old. Sky Cab is the only monorail in Hawaii.

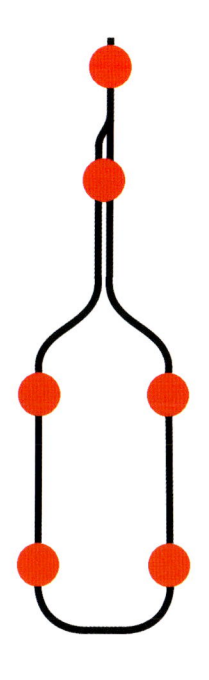

WHERE IN THE WEST

Tampa International Monorail
Tampa, Florida, USA

In the late 1980s Bombardier acquired small monorail technology from Universal Mobility Inc., which had already supplied numerous locations with their peoplemover-scale system. Bombardier's first UM Series installation was for Tampa International Airport. For less than $12-million, the airport added this automated parking lot transit system. Bombardier supplied six single-car UM III vehicles, track and a five-year extended warranty. The pinched loop system consistently provides better than 99.5% reliability. Attractive glass tile stations are located at the terminal and in the parking lot. Easy to understand graphics and TV monitors help passengers find their way to destinations. Tampa has the distinction of having the first monorail in the USA to use switches on the passenger-carrying main line. The monorail doesn't have the normal appearance of monorail as the entire guideway is built inside the parking lot and terminal structure.

Opened 1991
1 km (.7 mile)
6 stations
pinched loop

ABOVE: Bombardier's first totally automated monorail system cruises between parking lot stations.

PHOTOS: Author

RIGHT: Steel-beam track is placed on concrete floor.

LEFT: Bombardier UM III silhouette is visible through the glass tile walls of Tampa International's parking structure.

127

MONORAILS

Caption: Room for seating, standing and wheelchairs
PHOTOS: Author

Las Vegas Monorail
Las Vegas, Nevada, USA

Opened 1995
Extended 2004
6.4 km (4 miles)
7 stations
pinched loop

The Las Vegas Monorail originally opened in 1995 as the MGM/Bally's Monorail, a two-station 1.3-kilometer shuttle. The monorail made use of two mothballed Mark IV trains, purchased from Walt Disney World Resort in Florida. In 2004 the system reopened with five additional stations as the Las Vegas Monorail. Bombardier built the system and supplied nine new 4-car M-VI trains. The system is the United States' first fully-automated, line haul urban monorail rapid transit system. It connects numerous resort properties on the east side of the Strip, as well as the Las Vegas Convention Center. The nonprofit Las Vegas Monorail Company runs the system, which is the only privately owned public transportation system in the United States. The monorail utilizes no public funds to operate the system. Unlike USA government-operated conventional rail systems, revenue from ticket sales and advertising pays for all the monorail's daily operations and maintenance. In 2005 plans for expansion from the northernmost station to downtown Las Vegas were cancelled when the Federal Transit Administration decided against funding the 3.7-km extension. In 2006, Clark County commissioners granted the monorail permission to extend to McCarran International Airport. The extension plan has not progressed as of this book's printing, and neither have other extension ideas. As of 2015 the monorail had carried over 60-million passengers.

Caption: The highest track is 18 meters above grade (60')

Caption: Northbound and southbound trains at Bally's/Paris station

WHERE IN THE WEST

ABOVE: Winding through the back alleys of the Strip, the monorail quietly passes a resort pool.

PHOTOS: Author

BELOW: Bombardier improved radius performance for Las Vegas Monorail's tight 90-degree turns.

MONORAILS

ABOVE: **Von Roll train between terminals**

PHOTOS: Author

BELOW: **Newark International's Terminal C**

Airtrain Newark
Newark, New Jersey, USA

Opened 1996
4.8 km (2.9 miles)
8 stations
pinched loop

Building on its success in selling monorail to mostly to fairs, Von Roll won the contract for a peoplemover monorail at Newark International Airport. Airport planners thought ahead in their terminal designs and included space for a future peoplemover, decades before the monorail was added. The initial 1996 system served as an internal terminal/rental car/parking lot connector. Adtranz acquired Von Roll Monorail and made numerous improvements to the system, including new switches. In 2000 a 1.6-km extension to an Amtrak station on the Northeast Corridor opened. Bombardier acquired Adtranz in 2001 and no Von Roll-type monorails have been built since. The Newark International Airport AirTrain Monorail is popular for those needing a rail-connected flight to or from the Newark/New York area. Unfortunately, Von Roll monorails have a troubled history compared to other monorails. Many have closed as a result. Citing repeated service disruptions and the need for a system capable of higher ridership, in 2015 the Port Authority of New York and New Jersey voted to plan for a replacement system. The Port Authority claims the monorail system was built with only a 25-year planned lifespan.

WHERE IN THE WEST

AirTrain emerges from Terminal A.

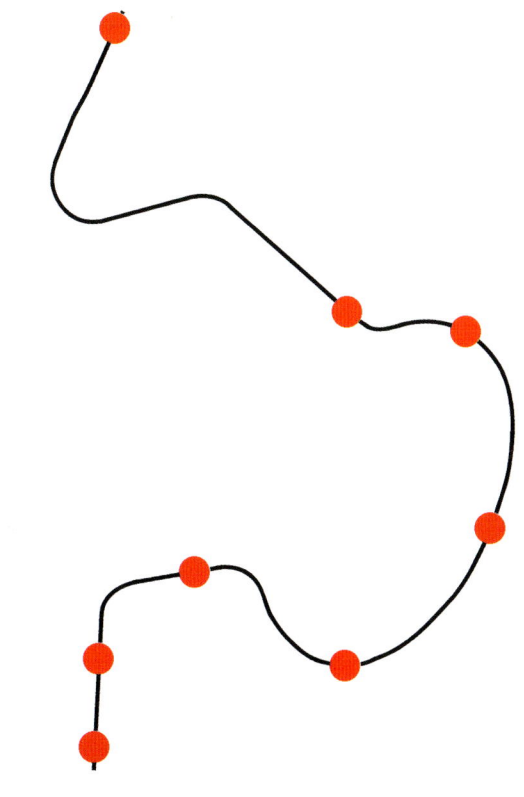

LEFT: Automated station and train doors provide safe access to the system

PHOTOS: Author

ABOVE: Crossover rotating switch platform

LEFT: New Jersey steel manufacturers benefited from construction of the monorail and stations.

131

MONORAILS

Newark International's stations are served with train arrivals every few minutes.
PHOTOS: Author

Newark Liberty Airport Station provides a popular connection between AirTrain, NJ Transit and Amtrak trains.

WHERE IN THE WEST

ABOVE: Onboard view enroute towards downtown Jacksonville

PHOTOS: David B. Simons Jr.

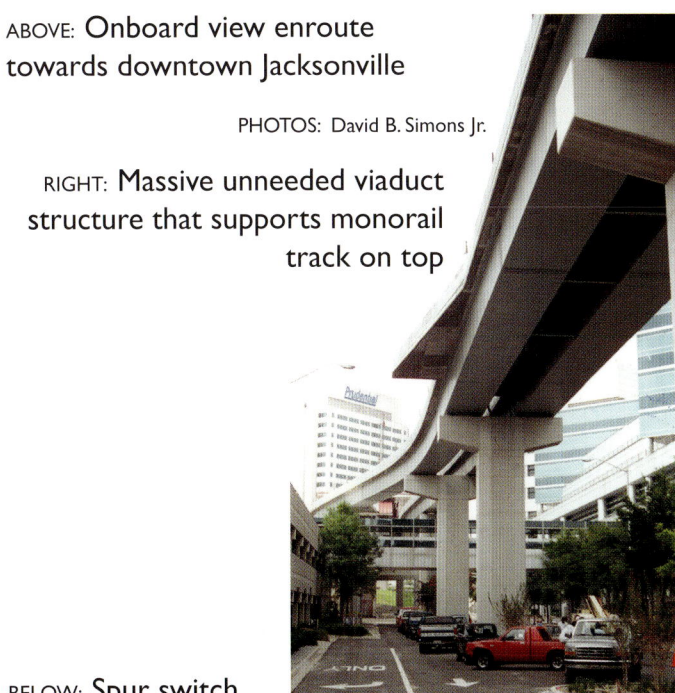

RIGHT: Massive unneeded viaduct structure that supports monorail track on top

BELOW: Spur switch

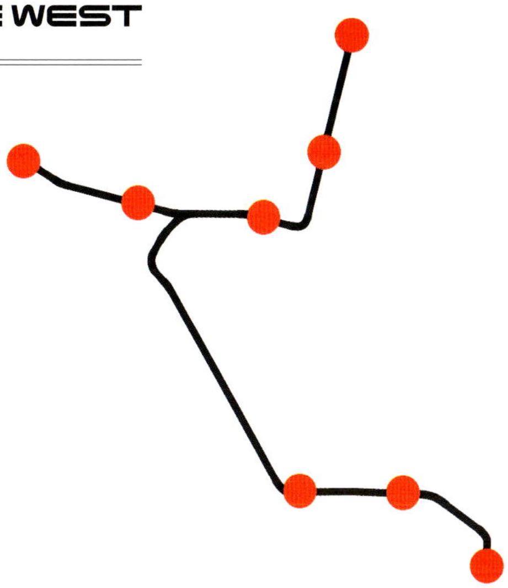

Jacksonville Skyway
Jacksonville, Florida, USA

In 1994 Bombardier was selected by the Jacksonville Transportation Authority (JTA) to replace its existing French MATRA-built peoplemover with monorail. The initial two-station segment of the Skyway monorail opened in 1997. The UM III trains are similar to their predecessors in Tampa, but run on concrete beams instead of steel. The track is placed on top of the original massive MATRA viaduct. JTA decided to forego taking advantage of monorail's small footprint track by continuing to add the unnecessary support structure for Skyway track extensions. Maximum speed of the two-car trains is 56 km/h. The system layout consists of two pinched loops that merge at a level Y-junction. Additional vehicles can be added to trains if the system grows. The monorail crosses the St. Johns River on the Acosta Bridge. The Skyway has been controversial and referred to as a 'ride to nowhere.' Extensions to make the monorail more useful have been proposed, but none have been approved. Bombardier has since changed the name UM III to Innovia Monorail 100.

Opened 1997
4.8 km (2.9 miles)
8 stations
pinched loop
spur line

133

MONORAILS

PHOTO: Sergio Mazzi

Opened 2014
25.9 km (16.1 miles)
18 stations
pinched loop

São Paulo Line 15
São Paulo, Brazil

Bombardier Transportation's first monorail system in South America includes numerous firsts for both the company and monorails in the Americas. A 2.9-kilometer demonstrator line opened in 2014. When complete, Line 15 (Expresso Tiradentes) will serve as an extension of the São Paulo Metro Line 2. It will have the capacity to transport 48,000 passengers per hour per direction (pphpd) between the Ipiranga and Cidade Tiradentes urban areas. 500,000 users per day will be able to ride the new line. Bombardier is providing 54 seven-car trains (378 cars) using their new Innovia Monorail 300 technology. The system uses Cityflo 650 automatic train control for driverless operation. A two-hour automobile journey is being reduced to approximately 50 minutes via Line 15. Parts of the monorail track have been elevated to over 15 meters to allow large trees to grow beneath the tracks. Initial trains were built at Bombardier's Pittsburgh facility in USA. Testing took place on a new test track in Kingston, Canada. Later trains were fabricated in Brazil at a plant in Hortolândia. In 2015 the Innovia Monorail 300 won a Good Design Award from Chicago Athenaem: Museum of Architecture and Design.

ABOVE AND BELOW: Over fifty years ago São Paulo contracted Alweg to build a monorail. That project failed to materialize, yet today Brazil is embarking on a monorail-building frenzy. Line 15 is the first of three contracted monorail lines in São Paulo.

PHOTO: Luke Starkenburg

WHERE IN THE WEST

Bombardier's award-winning Innovia Monorail 300 made its public debut on Line 15

PHOTO: Sergio Mazzi

Bogies are cleverly concealed between cars, leaving space for passengers to walk from car to car.

PHOTO: Luke Starkenburg

MONORAILS

São Paulo's new monorail takes up little air space, and even less ground space.

WHERE IN THE WEST

Oratório Station

PHOTO: Sergio Mazzi

PHOTO: Luke Starkenburg

Tokyo Monorail
ABOVE: A Hitachi Type 1000 monorail next to Shinkansen and Yamanote Line trains
PHOTO: Author

Düsseldorf International Airport
FACING PAGE: SkyTrain's automated Siemens monorail
PHOTO: Andreas Wiese/Düsseldorf International

6 WHERE IN THE EAST

Today's monorails: Eastern Hemisphere

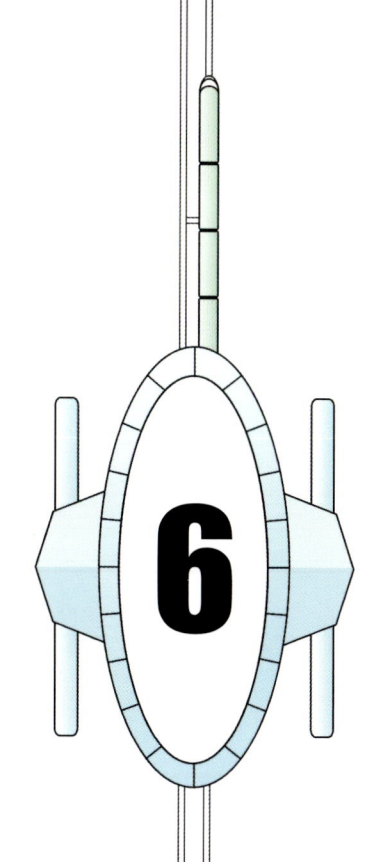

The vast majority of the world's transit monorails exist in the Eastern Hemisphere of planet Earth. This chapter presents them in the chronological order of their opening.

139

MONORAILS

PHOTO: Michael Malicke/Wuppertal Stadtwerke AG

Opened 1901
13.3 km (8.2 miles)
20 stations
pinched loop

Wuppertaler Schwebebahn
Wuppertal, Germany

The world's longest-operating transportation monorail is located in the Ruhr district of Germany. A special preview run was held for the Kaiser on October 24, 1900, with the Schwebebahn opening to the public on March 1st, 1901. During the 19th century, the towns of Barmen, Elberfeld and Vohwinkel were growing rapidly and some sort of transit system was needed. Since a good portion of the line would be above the Wupper River, massive conventional elevated rail structures were not considered to be the ideal choice. Eugen Langen, an engineer from nearby Cologne, had successfully tested a suspended steel rail monorail system. The leaders of the towns were impressed with the technology, chose it, and construction began in 1898. The original monorail cars were revolutionary in rail design as the first all-steel transit vehicles. The trains swing freely beneath the track, yet the trains never bank more than a comfortable 15 degrees. The name 'Schwebebahn' roughly translates to Suspended Railway. Top speed for the vehicles is 56 km/h. Cars operate at approximately a two and a half minute headway, and the system carries around 80,000 passengers each day.

PHOTO: Allen Ambrosini

WHERE IN THE EAST

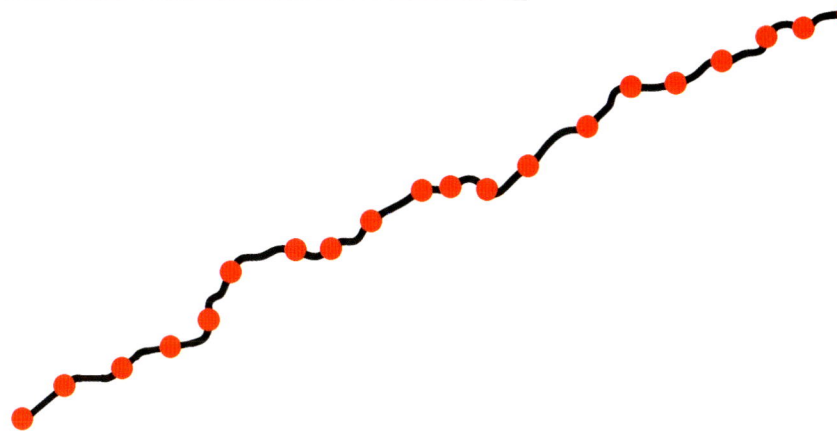

LEFT: A Schwebebahn train over the Wupper River

PHOTOS: Allen Ambrosini

BELOW: Double-flanged wheels keep trains on track

141

MONORAILS

PHOTO: Author

Opened 1964
17.8 km (11 miles)
11 stations
pinched loop

Tokyo Monorail
Tokyo, Japan

In 1960, Hitachi, Ltd. of Japan acquired rights to Alweg technology and established its Hitachi-Alweg division. Hitachi's first two lines were amusement installations at Inuyama in 1962 and Yomiuri Land in 1963. Alweg monorail technology made its biggest leap in transit history when the Toyko Monorail opened to coincide with the 1964 Summer Olympics. It was built in only 16 months and opened on September 17, 1964. For years it was the longest straddle-beam system in the world. When it first opened, the monorail only served Hamamatsuchō Station and Haneda airport. Hamamatsuchō Station is located on the heavily travelled Yamanote Line and serves as a transfer point for monorail passengers. Over the years, the area between the two terminal stations became more developed and additional stations were added. Stations have also been added at Haneda Airport as new terminals were built during airport expansion. The Tokyo Monorail serves eleven stations and operates from 5:00 AM to midnight. Airline check-in services are available at Hamamatsuchō for domestic flights. One of the busiest monorails in the world, it carried its 1.5 billionth passenger in 2007. The route is unique with long stretches of over water, one underwater tunnel and two underground tunnels. The tunnels were built at the airport to avoid conflicts with low-flying aircraft. Even with competition from a new conventional rail Keiko Rail Line, the Tokyo Monorail still carries well over 200,000 passengers each day. In 2014 plans for a north terminus extension to Tokyo Station were announced.

WHERE IN THE EAST

LEFT: In this mid-1960s postcard view, a Hitachi monorail train descends to an underwater tunnel at Haneda Airport.

LOWER LEFT: Another early postcard view shows the small footprint of an open-air station over a road.

BELOW: Portions of Tokyo Monorail feature steel pylons and steel track, useful where narrow supports and long spans are required.

PHOTO: Author

MONORAILS

ABOVE: A Type 1000 train running by one the many canals on the route

PHOTOS: Author

BELOW: Since 1964 much of the alignment's surrounding landfill islands have seen enormous development, even in close proximity to the track.

ABOVE: A narrow pedestrian corridor near Hamamatsucho Station. Landscaping and low sound levels of monorail trains minimize impact of the line on its surroundings.

WHERE IN THE EAST

ABOVE: Looking forward while approaching the longest tunnel at Haneda International Airport

ABOVE: Type 1000 trains were introduced in 1990.

LEFT: Type 2000 trains were introduced in 1997.

PHOTOS: Author

RIGHT: Tokyo Monorail riders are afforded an interesting ride, above and below ground.

145

MONORAILS

LEFT: Type 2000 and Type 1000 trains parked at the storage/maintenance facility. A ground-level switch serves five parking lanes.

BELOW LEFT: A passenger vehicle is lifted from bogies on the track.

PHOTOS: Author

BELOW: Monorail mechanics perform routine maintenance on a bogie.

WHERE IN THE EAST

ABOVE: Lush landscaping enhances the narrow alignment corridor.

PHOTOS: Author

RIGHT: Long spans over waterways are accomplished with custom steel-tracked bridges.

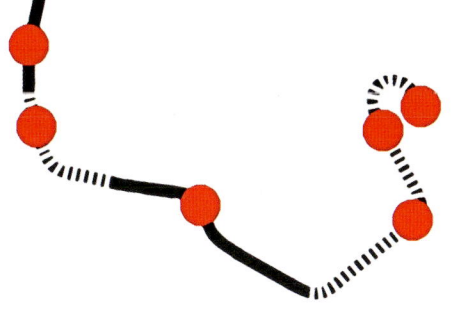

MONORAILS

Opened 1970
6.6 km (4.1 miles)
8 stations
single-track line
sidings to pass

Shonan Monorail
Kamakura, Japan

The Shonan Monorail was the first urban transit system in the world to make use of the French-developed Safege suspended monorail technology. Mitsubishi Heavy Industries, who had previously built a demonstrator Safege line at Higashiyama Park in Nagoya, built the monorail. Shonan Monorail opened on March 7, 1970. The monorail was completed in 1971 and runs between Ofuna and Enoshima stations. The line is built along one of the narrowest monorail alignments in the world; so narrow that only one track serves bi-directional service. The steel-boxed track and cylindrical steel pylons are located along narrow two-lane roads, winding through suburban and wooded areas. Two tunnels in hills add to the unique ride experience. Switches are extremely important with the Shonan system, because trains run in both directions on the single beam at all times. Passing is accomplished at four of the intermediate stations, where beams split to both sides of the platform. Timing must be perfect and it has operated this way flawlessly since its opening. From an enthusiast's point of view, the fourteen-minute monorail ride from end-to-end is one of the most enjoyable anywhere.

ABOVE LEFT & ABOVE: **Shonan Monorail's narrow two-lane road alignment**

PHOTOS: Author

BELOW: **Trains constantly pass one another on sidings at four split-track stations mid-route.**

148

WHERE IN THE EAST

LEFT: Traffic jams are no hindrance for Shonan Monorail trains as they gently sway above roadways.

LOWER LEFT: Headlights in tunnel of an approaching train just north of Enoshima Station

BELOW: The view forward is a great way to enjoy the many guideway curves and grades of up to 7.4%.

PHOTOS: Author

149

MONORAILS

Four switches in vicinity of Do-Universität S Station

PHOTOS: H-Bahn-Gesellschaft Dortmund mbH

Siemens vehicle banks as it curves through a switch

Opened 1984
3.1 km (1.9 miles)
5 stations
single-track line
spur & sidings

Dortmund H-Bahn
Dortmund, Germany

Siemens' first permanent system using their H-Bahn automated suspended monorail technology opened at Dortmund University in 1984. The initial line was one-kilometer long and connected two campuses that are separated by a valley and a major roadway. The system was so popular with students and faculty that more than five-million passengers had been carried by 1991. Additional track has since been added at both the south and north ends of the original line. A spur line and switch was added which allows passengers to transfer to an urban rail line directly below the Do-Universität station. A 1.2-km extension to a nearby science park opened in 2003. Top speed of the vehicles is 65 km/h. With a minimum frequency of 40 seconds there are 36 scheduled runs per hour. It carries more than 5,000 passengers per day. Further extensions have been considered.

WHERE IN THE EAST

Campus Nord Station in the early years of the Dortmund H-Bahn

PHOTOS: H-Bahn-Gesellschaft Dortmund mbH

The Dortmund H-Bahn in a park-like area, demonstrating that monorail fits well in a variety of environments.

MONORAILS

Opened 1985
8.8 km (5.4 miles)
13 stations
pinched loop

Kitakyushu Monorail
Kitakyushu, Japan

After the Tokyo-Haneda system of 1964, no other Alweg-type transit monorails opened in Japan until 1985 in Kitakyushu, on the island of Kyushu. After Tokyo-Haneda, the Japanese Monorail Association (JMA) was formed to establish standards for both straddle and suspended monorails. One of the new standards for straddle monorails included passenger cabins entirely above the bogies, eliminating the bogie bulge into the cabin featured on all previous Alweg monorails. While the width is close to earlier Alweg trains like Seattle and Tokyo, the Hitachi-built train interior is much more spacious, with flat floors and side-facing seats along the train walls. Later trains with this standard have incorporated more streamlined end cabins. Kitakyushu Monorail pioneered improvements in environment aesthetics with the addition of more landscaping in the road medians below the guideway. In some areas the trees that have grown up beneath it improve the appearance of the guideway. Once a year, beer and wine parties are held on the trains. Tickets must be purchased in advance of the event. Kitakyushu's 1985 opening marked a rediscovery of Alweg and inspired other systems, both in Japan and elsewhere.

Approaching Tokuriki Arashiyamaguchi Station

PHOTOS: Author

Hitachi produced the world's first Alweg-type trains with flat floors from end to end.

WHERE IN THE EAST

A ground-level road, monorail track, and above, an expressway - a tad too much?

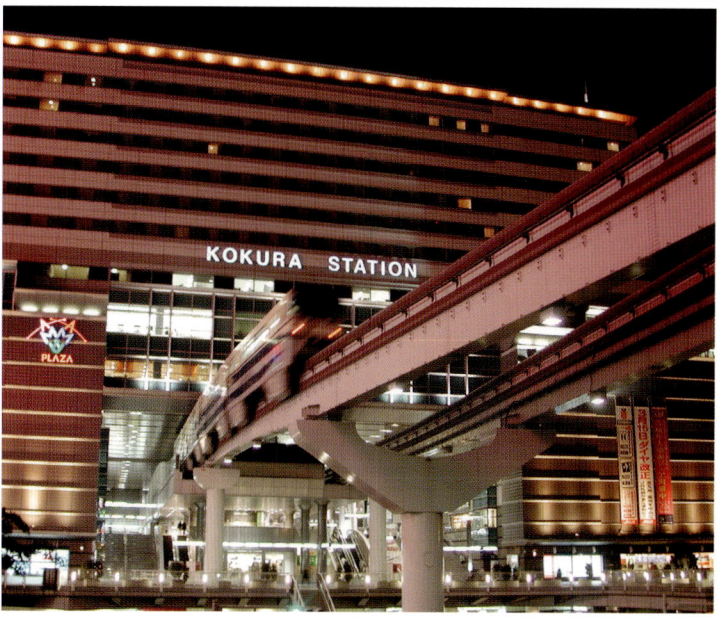

The huge multi-modal, multi-functional Kokura Station

PHOTOS: Author

Landscaped medians enhance the alignment.

Track features steel and concrete spans.

MONORAILS

A Mitsubishi Safege train glides between the trees.

PHOTOS: Author

Like Wuppertal's Schwebebahn, a portion of Chiba's monorail alignment is over a river.

Opened 1988
15.5 km (9.6 miles)
18 stations
pinched loop
spur line

Chiba Urban Monorail
Chiba City, Japan

The Chiba Urban Monorail is the longest suspended monorail system in the world. Building upon the knowledge and experience of the Shonan Monorail, the Mitsubishi Company built this dual-tracked system to connect suburbs in the Chiba Prefecture with Chiba's main rail station downtown. It is currently the world's only dual-beamed, full-scale Safege-type system, and includes a spur off the main line. One of the reasons Chiba officials selected Safege was because of the local inclement winter weather. With Safege, the running surfaces and train bogies are inside the beams, protected from the elements. Straddle monorails need either heaters in the beam, or shovels on the fronts of trains to deal with heavy snow or ice conditions. The monorail has over 45,000 passengers each day. It is owned and operated by Chiba Urban Monorail Company, which was established on March 20, 1979 with investors including Chiba Prefecture and the city of Chiba.

WHERE IN THE EAST

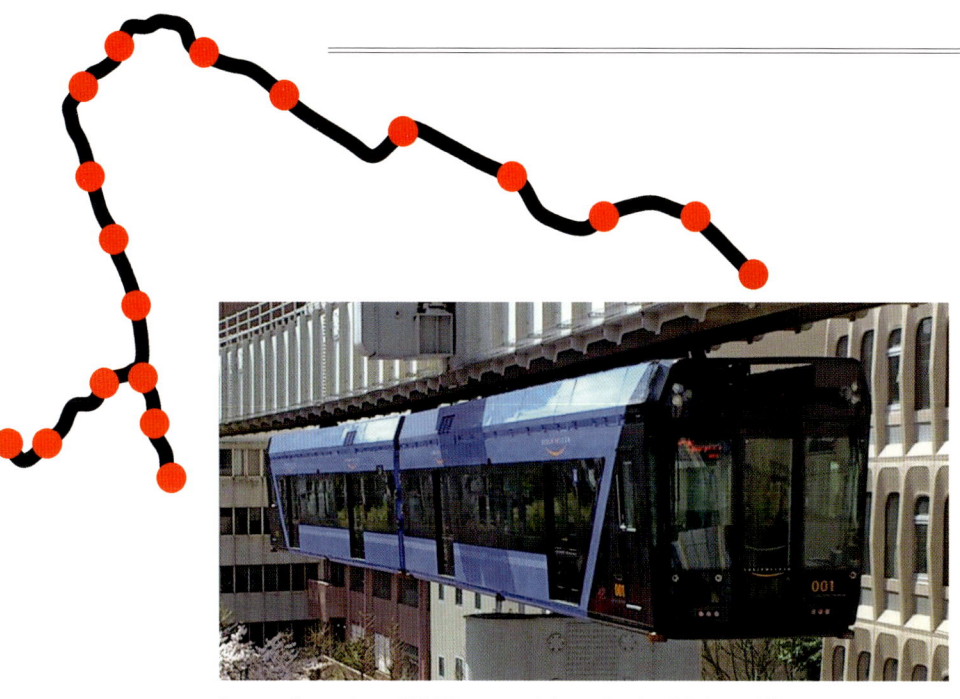

Introduced in 2012, new Mitsubishi Urban Flyer trains feature look-down windows in the floor.
PHOTO: Chiba Urban Monorail Company, Ltd.

Winding through the park at Chiba Sports Center
PHOTO: Author

Unique to Chiba, an arched bridge over a major intersection

PHOTO: Author

MONORAILS

ABOVE: Oasis Monorail crosses the Gold Coast Highway

LEFT: Looking northeast from Jupiter Casino. This water crossing features a long span between pylons.

BELOW: Oasis Shopping Centre was designed to integrate the building and monorail track structures.

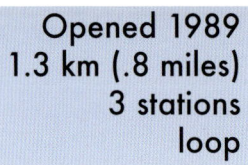

Opened 1989
1.3 km (.8 miles)
3 stations
loop

Oasis Monorail
Broadbeach, Australia

Four-car monorail trains run between the Sofitel Gold Coast Hotel, Oasis Shopping Centre and Jupiter Casino. The Von Roll Type III is actually a bit of overkill for the needs of the three-station system. However, in the late 1980's it was planned to be part of a much larger 10-kilometer system running up and down the heavily-travelled Gold Coast corridor. Funding problems and local opposition killed that proposal. Instead, light rail has been built to compete with the traffic congestion created by well over 2-million visitors to the Gold Coast each year. A unique aspect of this monorail is that the Oasis Shopping Centre was designed with the system in mind. At one point the trains quietly cruise right through the upper level in a large atrium of the mall.

WHERE IN THE EAST

LEFT: Monorail track blends in with the interior of the shopping centre.

PHOTOS: Author

BELOW: The Von Roll dual-guideway glides through a group of lorikeet-filled trees.

157

MONORAILS

ABOVE: Sometimes Hitachi's boxy trains are jazzed up with bright colors.

PHOTOS: Author

ABOVE LEFT: Yamada Station over Chogoku Expressway

BELOW: Osaka Monorail speeds past traffic on rainy day.

Opened 1990
28 km (17.4 miles)
18 stations
pinched loop
spur line

Osaka Monorail
Osaka, Japan

Metropolitan Osaka is the second largest urban area in Japan. Rail lines emanate from the center of the city to surrounding areas. The Osaka Monorail is designed to connect these outer communities with a half circle system which will eventually surround the city with over 50-kilometers of track. The first 6.6-km segment opened in northern Osaka Prefecture. The system now begins at the Osaka International Airport, heads east along a freeway, then turns south along with the freeway. It crosses a dramatic arched bridge built exclusively for the monorail. A 6.8-km spur line to the north was added which connects the system to a university and a new community, all planned with the monorail corridor in mind. The Hitachi four-car trains draw 1500 volts of direct current from the bus bars that run along the side of the guideways. In 1995, the disastrous earthquake of nearby Kobe proved to be a test for Osaka Monorail. It withstood the violent quake and proved to be a vital transit link in the area as traffic on the parallel freeway became jammed with evacuees. Osaka Monorail has over 100,000 daily boardings. A 9-km extension to the south is planned.

WHERE IN THE EAST

Unique single-arch bridge with steel guideway over Kinki Expressway

PHOTOS: Author

A multi-arched monorail-only bridge crosses Yodo River.

Osaka Monorail was the longest in the world until it was surpassed by Chongqing in 2011.
PHOTO: Luke Starkenburg

RIGHT: The small footprint of a monorail alignment is evident in comparison to this expressway.

PHOTO: Author

WHERE IN THE EAST

The Saito Line branch switches

PHOTOS: Author

Storage/Maintenance Facility and its many switches

White-gloved Osaka Monorail operator

MONORAILS

Opened 1998
16 km (9.9 miles)
19 stations
pinched loop

Tama Monorail
Tama, Japan

Another Hitachi system in the Western Tokyo suburbs added to Japan's growing list of monorails in 1998. The north-south Tama Monorail line runs between Higashiyamato and Tama via Tachikawa. A ride from end to end takes about 36 minutes. It was the first complete Hitachi monorail system built with VVVF Control equipment (variable voltage, variable frequency). Four-car Type 1000 trains operate on 1500 volts DC. Five of the stations are located where passengers can transfer between monorail and other rail lines. The corridor is an interesting one with the tracks crossing the Tamagawa River, following major roads, climbing and descending 6% grades, and in one segment, the guideway dips below grade and negotiates a hill via tunnel. The system carries over 120,000 passengers each day.

PHOTOS: Author

WHERE IN THE EAST

ABOVE: Tama Monorail and a station bicycle parking lot

PHOTOS: Author

RIGHT: Triple-tunnel for monorails and automobiles through top of a hill

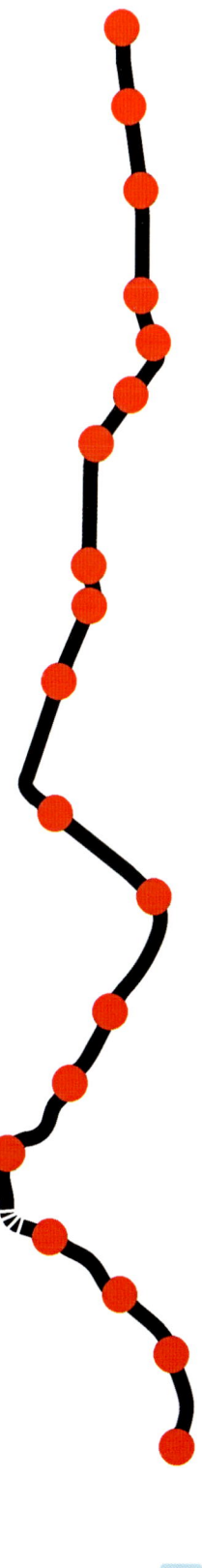

163

MONORAILS

Opened 1998
3.8 km (2.4 miles)
7 stations
loop

Happy Line Monorail
Shenzhen, China

In 1993 the Window of the World amusement park installed a small three-station Intamin monorail system. Because of the success of this monorail, a larger Intamin loop system was built for downtown Shenzhen. The Happy Line Monorail connects numerous attractions in China's first Special Economic Zone. Stops include Window of the World theme park, China Folk Culture Village, Happy Valley Amusement Park and Splendid China. The system has five of the P28/24 class trains operating on a single-track loop. The box beam guideway is 500mm wide and 700mm tall. The maximum grade is at 10%, but the Intamin trains are capable of an negotiating an amazing 20% gradient if needed. The three-car train can carry 24 seated passengers. The typical span between columns is 15 meters, but spans can be up to 24 meters.

PHOTOS: Intamin Transportation Ltd.

WHERE IN THE EAST

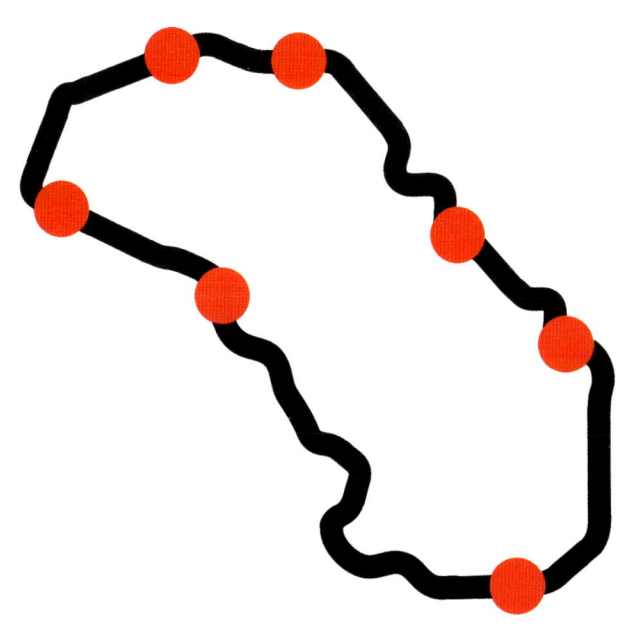

PHOTO: ImagineChina

LEFT AND BELOW: **Intamin P8/24** trains cruise through and above a variety of wooded and urban environments on Shenzhen's Happy Line

PHOTO: SINA Corporation

MONORAILS

ABOVE: **Tokyo Disneyland Station at day**

PHOTOS: Author

BELOW: **Spacious Hitachi walk-through interior**

Opened 2001
5 km (3.1 miles)
4 stations
loop

Disney Resort Line
Urayasu, Japan

The first Disney resort monorail to go without a 'Mark' designation (page 124) is also the company's first and only monorail outside of the United States. With the great success of Tokyo Disneyland, the park owners at Oriental Land Company expanded the resort area with a second theme park, Tokyo DisneySea. A monorail was built to connect the two theme parks, as well as on-property hotels and Maihama Station on the JR Keiyō Line. The Tokyo Disney Resort Line trains are much bigger than any previous Disney Monorail, complete with walk-through trains and much higher capacity capability. They were built by Hitachi, yet decorated with fanciful Mickey Mouse ear windows and new, rounded driver cabs. Similar cab designs appeared on later Hitachi monorail trains elsewhere. The system is automated, but there are attendants onboard. All four stations are on the private property of Oriental Land.

WHERE IN THE EAST

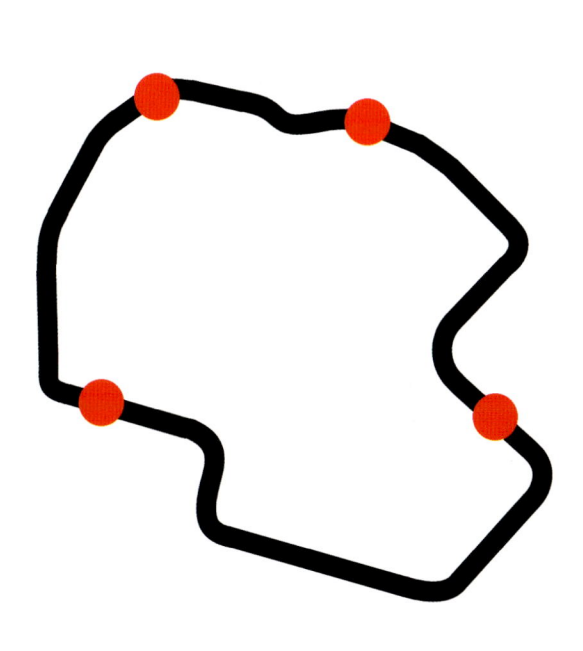

PHOTO: Chris Calabrese/tdrfan.com

Bayside Station serves six separate resort hotels.

PHOTO: Author

RIGHT: Tokyo Disneyland Station at night

PHOTO: Author

167

MONORAILS

ABOVE: SkyTrain approaching terminal area of Düsseldorf International Airport

BELOW: The intermodal station connects major rail lines with the airport via SkyTrain monorail.

PHOTO: Alan Spence

PHOTO: Andreas Wiese/Düsseldorf International

Düsseldorf SkyTrain
Düsseldorf, Germany

Opened 2002
2.5 km (1.5 miles)
4 stations
pinched loop

Siemens built their second public monorail system for Düsseldorf International Airport. The monorail is based upon the same Siemens H-Bahn technology used at Dortmund University, yet it was the first dual-guideway line for the technology. Built to drastically reduce the amount of automobile traffic to the airport, the monorail line connects the airport terminal with a rail station on a heavily-traveled Düsseldorf-Duisburg line. A parking lot station is included along the route. Like Dortmund, the system is totally automated. Five two-car trains operate around ten meters above the ground. Traveling at a top speed of 50 km/h, end to end transit time is around six minutes. Trains depart each station every 3½ to 7 minutes, depending on the time of day and traffic requirements.

WHERE IN THE EAST

LEFT SkyTrain glides through a monorail-exclusive corridor in the airport's curved terminal structure. Cabins feature large windows and plenty of space for luggage.

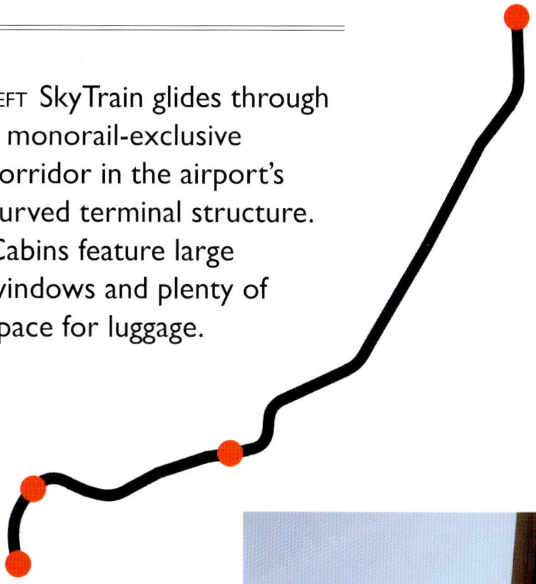

PHOTO: Andreas Wiese/Düsseldorf International

SkyTrain monorail track takes up minimal ground and air space as it winds its way to the airport terminal facility.
PHOTO: Matt Wegener

PHOTO: Peter Lovás/Dreamstime

169

MONORAILS

As with other Hitachi-built monorails, Okinawa's system has a combination of steel and concrete pylons and track.

PHOTOS: Author

Opened 2003
12.8 km (7.9 miles)
15 stations
pinched loop

Okinawa Monorail
Naha, Japan

The Okinawa Urban Monorail was the first rail system built on the island of Okinawa since World War II. Named Yui Rail as a result of a public competition, the Naha dual-beamed line connects city points with Naha Airport. From the airport, the line runs northeast through the city center. The guideway currently terminates near Shuri Castle, but work has begun on a 4.1-kilometer extension to Uranishi. Including the thirteen stops along the route, end to end journey time is around a half hour. The two-car Hitachi trains run every six minutes during peak periods. Following a precedent set over a century earlier in Wuppertal, part of the line follows along a river channel. The line also negotiates some large hills with heights between 8 to 20 meters above the ground.

Monorail speeds along guideway, unimpeded by traffic jams below.

WHERE IN THE EAST

ABOVE: Kencho-mae Station is a unique curved station squeezed between buildings and a canal in downtown Naha.

PHOTOS: Author

RIGHT: Okinawa Monorail's storage and maintenance facility, with Naha International Airport in the distance

171

Opened 2003
8.6 km (5.3 miles)
11 stations
pinched loop

PHOTO: David M. Ice

PHOTO: Author

KL Monorail
Kuala Lumpur, Malaysia

KL Monorail started out in 1997 with the contract awarded to Hitachi, but the project was halted due to the East Asian financial crisis. Malaysian bus manufacturer, MTrans Holdings, took over the project in 1998 and completed the system. The train technology was reverse-engineered from Seattle's Alweg blueprints. Scomi Engineering Bhd acquired MTrans in 2006. Scomi has since aggressively pursued opportunities to build more monorails based on the technology developed for KL Monorail. They have been successful in winning several bids in India and Brazil. The system currently carries over 20-million passengers each year. On July 29, 2009, KL Monorail carried its 100 millionth passenger. To increase capacity, Scomi began replacing all ten original two-car trains with four-car trains in 2014.

WHERE IN THE EAST

ABOVE AND RIGHT: KL Monorail stations are covered with artfully-designed canvas roofs. Economical to build, they are strong enough to keep passengers protected from the tropical Malaysian sun and monsoon rains.

PHOTO: Author

PHOTO: Author

One of KL Monorail's new four-car Scomi Sutra trains passing Al Bukhary Mosque

PHOTO: Nicholas Lim

ABOVE: Along the Klang River in the Brickfields district

PHOTO: Author

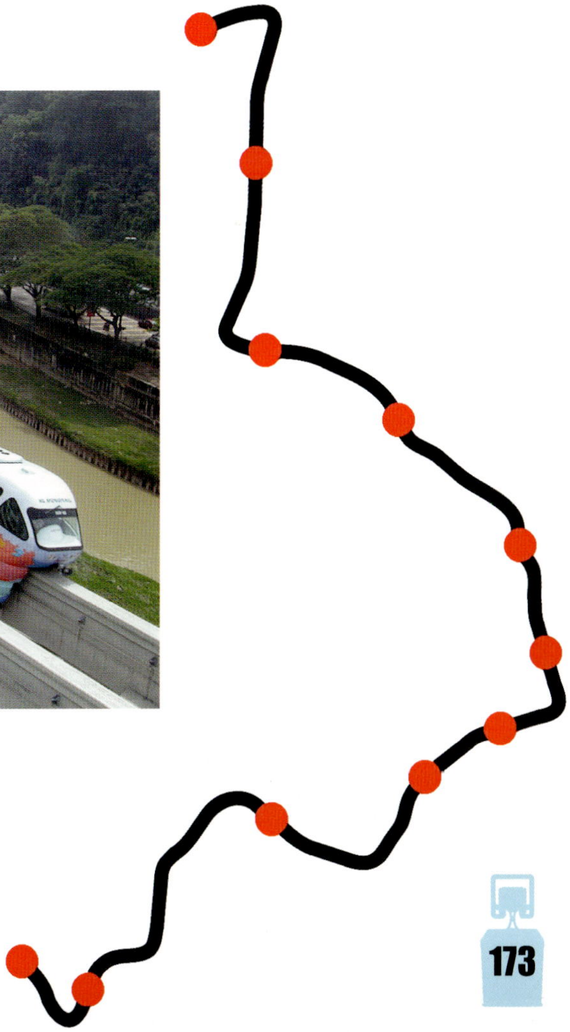

173

MONORAILS

Opened 2004
4.7 km (2.9 miles)
6 stations
pinched loop

Moscow Monorail
Moscow, Russia

Faced with growing auto traffic jams in northeastern Moscow, planning for a monorail began in 1998. Monorail was selected after studies showed construction would be five to seven times cheaper than building another underground Metro line. The Moscow Monorail is based on Swiss Intamin technology, yet it includes numerous modifications designed by the Moscow Institute of Thermal Technology. Changes were made to primarily deal with Moscow's harsh winter conditions. The drive system was changed to a linear motor in the guideway, making the system the world's first linear motor straddle monorail. The line connects Timiryazevskaya multi-modal station with Ulitsa Sergeya Eisensteina Station. Stops include Telesentr Station and Vystavochny Tsentr Station. Instead of switches at the terminal stations, teardrop loops turn trains around to head back on the other side of the dual-guideway.

PHOTO: Konstantin Ventzlavovich

PHOTO: Igor Grochev

Moscow Monorail at Ostankino Tower

WHERE IN THE EAST

PHOTO: A. Savin

PHOTO: Konstantin Ventzlavovich

Moscow's six-car trains are equipped with air-conditioning, heating, audio and visual passenger information systems, automatic door operation, and allow handicapped access. The system is designed to run in a fully-automated mode.

PHOTO: Anton A. Chigrai

175

MONORAILS

Opened 2005
80.0 km (49.7 miles)
59 stations
pinched loop

Chongqing Monorail
Chongqing, China

China's first Alweg-type monorail system opened on June 18, 2005 in Chongqing. Hitachi manufactured the first two prototype trains, along with electrical equipment and other infrastructure technology including switch hardware. All following trains were built by Changchun Railway Vehicles Co. Ltd. in technical cooperation with Hitachi. Since opening, an aggressive expansion plan has made the monorail a record breaker on several fronts. The first segment of Line 1 begins as a subway under downtown Chongqing. It then runs west elevated along the southern bank of the Jialing River, turning south into the city's southwestern suburbs and ending in the Daduokou district. In September of 2011, Line 3 opened (Chongqing's Line 2 is conventional subway), adding over 17 kilometers to the system and making it the longest monorail system in the world, surpassing the previous record holder of Osaka. In December of 2011, Line 3's extension to Jiangbei Airport opened. One year later, Line 3 was extended farther to the south, making it the longest monorail line in the world at 55.5 kilometers. The Chongqing Monorail is also the only urban monorail system in the world with an X-shaped crossover intersection point. Line 3 features the two longest and highest monorail bridges in the world. The connection of Lines 1 & 3 at Yudong in 2014 have ensured the system's world records for the foreseeable future.

PHOTO: ImagineChina

WHERE IN THE EAST

ABOVE: A Chinese-built train approaches one of many tunnels built for the system. Because of the hilly nature of the city, the system has the most monorail tunnels as well as the longest monorail tunnels in the world.

PHOTOS: ImagineChina

LEFT: The Jialing River on a hazy Chongqing day

MONORAILS

ABOVE AND RIGHT: A new span specifically for Line 3 was added across Jialing River. Chongqing has the tallest and longest monorail bridges in the world.

PHOTOS: ImagineChina

WHERE IN THE EAST

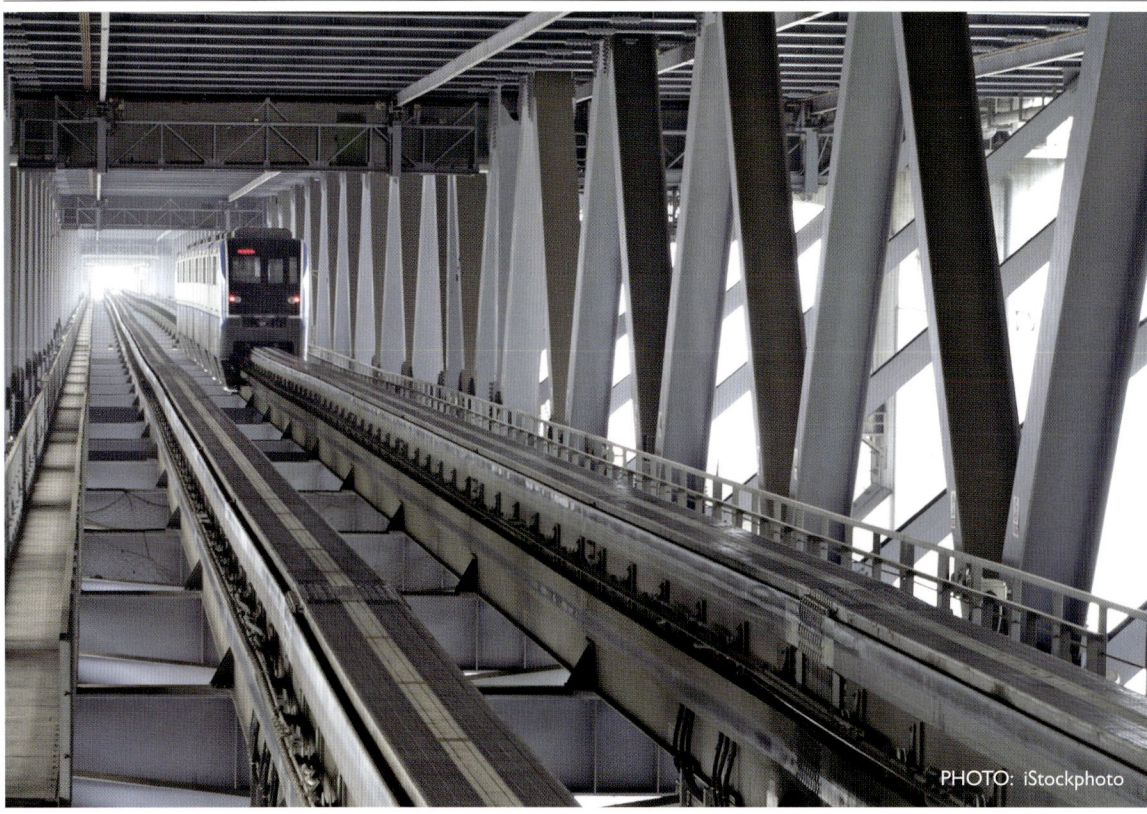

ABOVE AND BELOW: Caiyuanba Changjiang Bridge across the Yangtze River features a lower level devoted entirely to Chongqing Monorail.

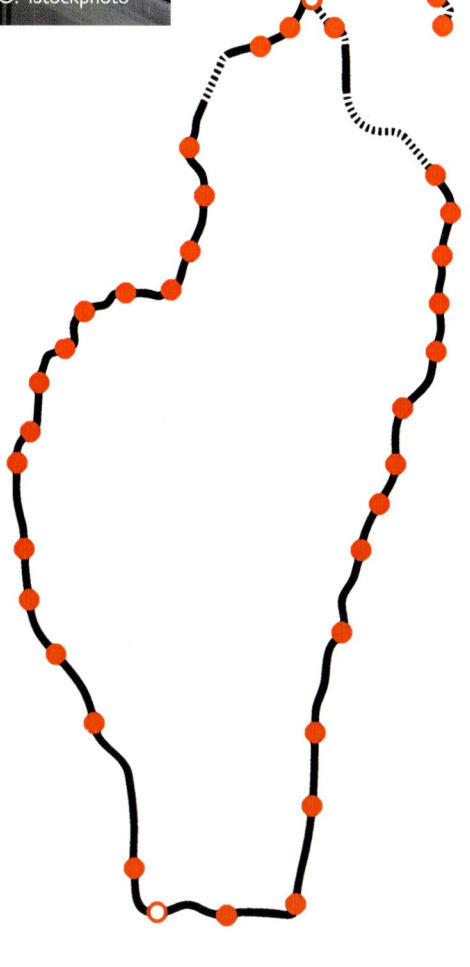

179

MONORAILS

Opened 2007
2.1 km (1.3 miles)
4 stations
pinched loop

Sentosa Express
Sentosa, Singapore

Noting that smaller communities were expressing interest in monorail systems, in the early 2000s Japan's Hitachi Ltd. designed a new Hitachi Small classification of monorails. The smaller monorails are lighter in weight and have the ability to negotiate tight 40-meter radius turns. They also require smaller guideways and supports, making them more economic to install. The first Hitachi Small to be built went to Sentosa Development Corporation (SDC) for the colorful Sentosa Express monorail in Singapore, at a cost of US $78-million. The 2.1 kilometer, double-track line links the main island of Singapore and the resort destination of Sentosa Island. There are gateway stations at World Trade Centre's Harbour Front MRT Station and Central Beach on Sentosa. The Sentosa Express takes advantage of the Hitachi Small tight turn radius capability near its northernmost station, with a 90-degree turn.

PHOTO: Shaun Williams

Monorail crosses hill on Sentosa Island at ground level

PHOTO: David Kamada

WHERE IN THE EAST

Central Beach Station
PHOTO: iStockphoto

Hitachi Small trains feature an articulated bogie between cars
PHOTO: David Kamada

MONORAILS

The Middle East's first monorail crosses a waterway of Palm Jumeirah.
PHOTO: iStockphoto

Opened 2009
5.4 km (3.3 miles)
4 stations
pinched loop

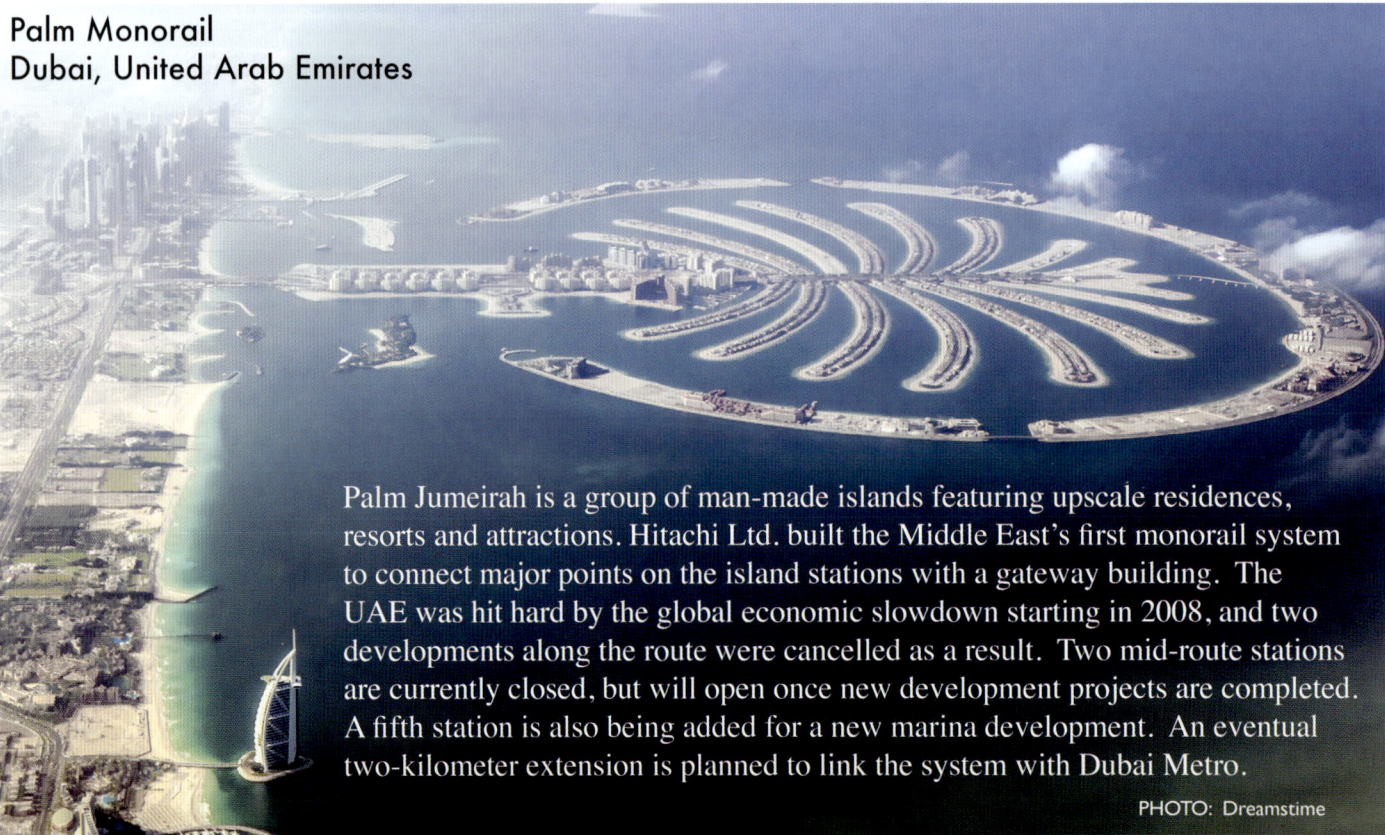

Palm Monorail
Dubai, United Arab Emirates

Palm Jumeirah is a group of man-made islands featuring upscale residences, resorts and attractions. Hitachi Ltd. built the Middle East's first monorail system to connect major points on the island stations with a gateway building. The UAE was hit hard by the global economic slowdown starting in 2008, and two developments along the route were cancelled as a result. Two mid-route stations are currently closed, but will open once new development projects are completed. A fifth station is also being added for a new marina development. An eventual two-kilometer extension is planned to link the system with Dubai Metro.

PHOTO: Dreamstime

WHERE IN THE EAST

RIGHT: Atlantis Station is the northern terminus.

BELOW: Atlantis-The Palm Resort

MONORAILS

PHOTO: Luke Starkenburg

Opened 2014
19.5 km (12.1 miles)
18 stations
pinched loop

Mumbai Monorail
Mumbai, India

Scomi's first contracted monorail outside of Malaysia is Mumbai Monorail. The Mumbai Metropolitan Region Development Authority (MMRDA) approved a contract submitted by L&T-Scomi for the US $545-million system. Construction began in January of 2009. Despite the enormous challenges with narrow routes and busy traffic below, the first 8.8-kilometers opened in 2014. The second phase to Jacob Circle was due to open by 2016. The four-car Sutra model trains were fabricated at Scomi's Malaysian factory and shipped to Mumbai. Sutra is designed to comply with international standards in quality, reliability and safety. It is an advanced version of Scomi's first train; developed for Kuala Lumpur and based on Seattle's Alweg trains. The trains have a top speed of 80 km/h and a capacity of 500 passengers. The system was implemented on a build-operate-transfer (BOT) basis. Other Indian cities are planning monorail as well.

Mumbai Monorail was constructed along a challenging corridor of narrow streets.

PHOTO: Luke Starkenburg

WHERE IN THE EAST

A blue train approaching Bharat Petroleum Station

PHOTO: Danish Siddiqui/Reuters/Corbis

When it opened on February 2, 2014, Mumbaikers showed their enthusiasm by cheering the arrival and departure of each new train.

PHOTO: Luke Starkenburg

MONORAILS

Monorail's go-almost-anywhere capability is demonstrated in Mumbai.

PHOTO: Luke Starkenburg

PHOTO: Luke Starkenburg

WHERE IN THE EAST

ABOVE: Brightly colored trains serve the low-rise and high-rise suburban neighborhoods of Mumbai.

LEFT: Chumbur Station is the northern terminus of Mumbai Monorail. Scomi Sutra monorail trains load and unload in the station, while heavy city traffic passes below.

187

MONORAILS

ABOVE: **Monorail track harmony with greenery**

PHOTOS: Intamin Transportation Ltd.

BELOW: **Swiss technology in China**

Opened 2015
9.6 km (5.9 miles)
11 stations
loop

Xi'an Monorail
Xi'an, China

Xi'an is one of the most populous metropolitan areas in inland China. Over eight million people live in the city with over 3,100 years of history. Intamin Transportation Ltd. installed a single-lane loop model P8 monorail in the Qujiang tourist district. Each of the three trains has a capacity of 48 seated passengers, hence the designation P8/48. The maximum recommended speed is 12 meters per second. Typical spans between pylons are 15 meters, but special spans of up to 24 meters are possible. The monorail opened to the public on January 16, 2015.

WHERE IN THE EAST

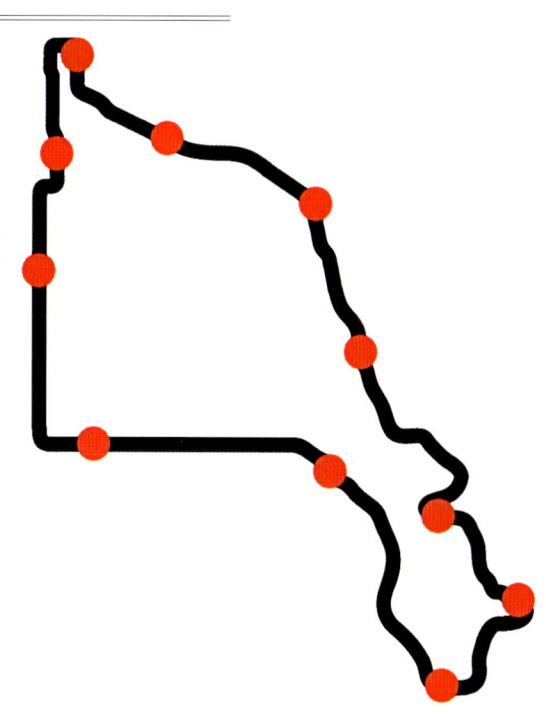

Stations and pylons are creatively designed to match historic Chinese architecture.

PHOTOS: Intamin Transportation Ltd.

MONORAILS

Opened 2015
24 km (14.9 miles)
30 stations
pinched loop

Daegu Sky Rail
Daegu, South Korea

Per a contract signed in 2008, Hitachi provided its monorail technology for Daegu, the fourth largest city in South Korea. Construction began in 2009 and the system opened on April 23, 2015. The 24-kilometer system connects southeastern and northwestern sections of the city. Two transfer stations allow access to subway Lines 1 & 2. The monorail has two storage/maintenance depots. The line features two large, specially built water-crossing bridges and one cable-stayed intersection bridge. It is completely automated and incorporates new technologies, including an onboard fire fighting system and deployable emergency egress spiral chutes. Train windows have 'mist glass' with liquid crystal screens that automatically block passenger views for the privacy of residents in selected areas along the alignment. A new signaling system allows shorter intervals between trains than previous monorails. Daegu Sky Rail is Korea's first major monorail system.

ABOVE: A unique cable-stayed intersection bridge and Manpyeong Station just beyond add artistic lines to the City of Daegu.

BELOW: Wide, flat-floored trains with side seating provide plenty of room for passengers

WHERE IN THE EAST

ABOVE: Arguably the world's best-looking Hitachi-technology trains, Daegu's monorail design was chosen by citizens. This is the northern maintenance/storage facility, just north of the terminus Chilgok KNU Medical Center Station.

BELOW AND RIGHT: The northernmost segment of monorail follows Palgeo Creek, where thousands of apartment residents are within walking distance of Sky Rail stations.

PHOTO: Hitachi Transportation

PHOTO: Author

PHOTO: Carol Pedersen

MONORAILS

ABOVE: Daegu's monorail-only bridge across Guemho River, designed and built by Hyundai Engineering & Construction

New linear parks with lush landscaping beautify the route, including this river channel along Dongdaegu-ro.

PHOTO: Author

WHERE IN THE EAST

BELOW: **Monorail bridge over Sincheon River**

BELOW: **Conflicts with traffic? No.**

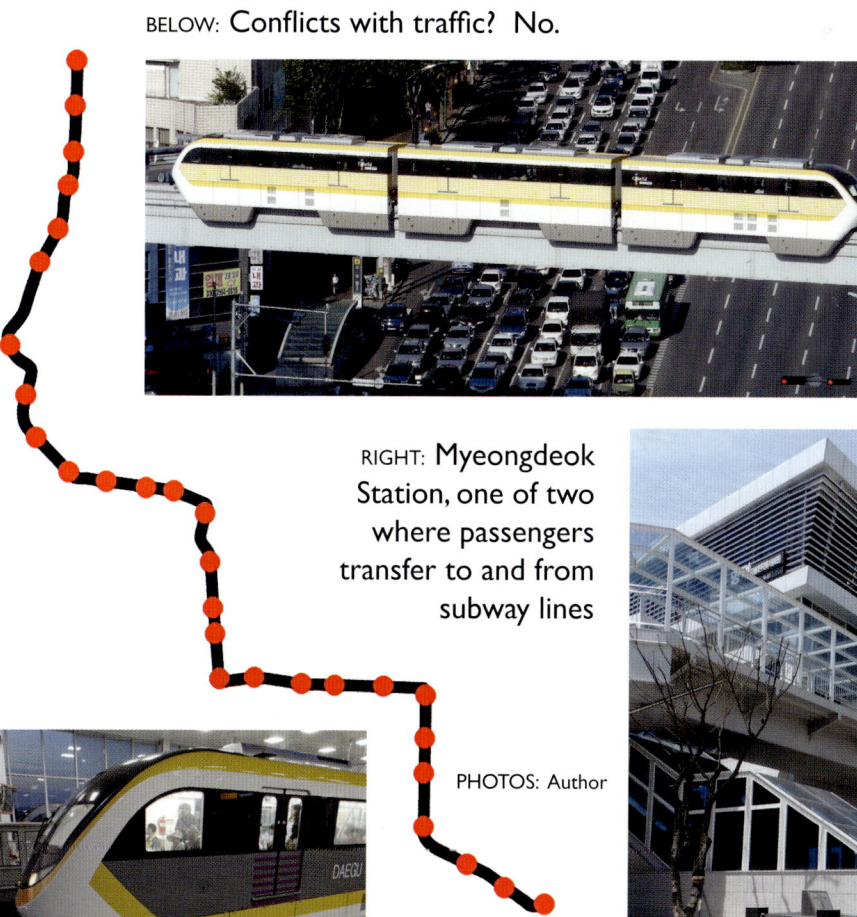

RIGHT: **Myeongdeok Station, one of two where passengers transfer to and from subway lines**

PHOTOS: Author

São Paulo Line 15
Construction of South America's first major monorail system. Despite challenging terrain, track was installed at the rate of one kilometer per month.

PHOTO: Sergio Mazzi

MGM-Bally's Monorail
FACING PAGE: A freshly cast monorail beam is lifted from its form, miles away from its final destination.

PHOTO: Author

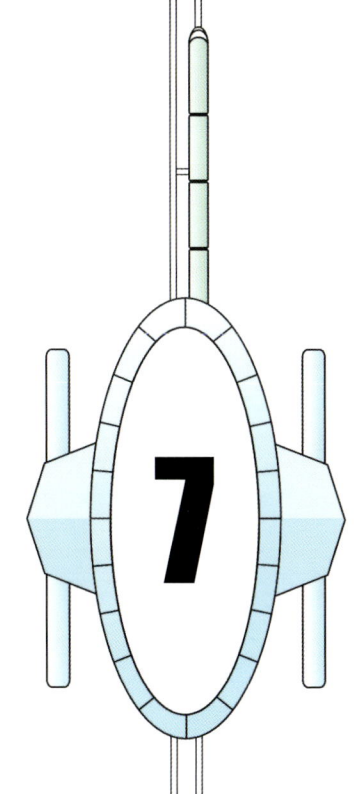

7 How to build monorail
In ten easy steps

Monorail has advantages in construction over conventional rail. To best illustrate this critical part of a monorail's life, this chapter follows the construction of Las Vegas Monorail through a photographic essay.

195

MONORAILS

Build Subway?

Before building our monorail, let's briefly review other options. Subways are loved by the people that design and build them. Whether digging tunnels with boring machines or using the disruptive cut and cover method, both methods take a lot of time, materials, labor and most of all, money. Be patient, your train won't be carrying you through the dark for quite a while.

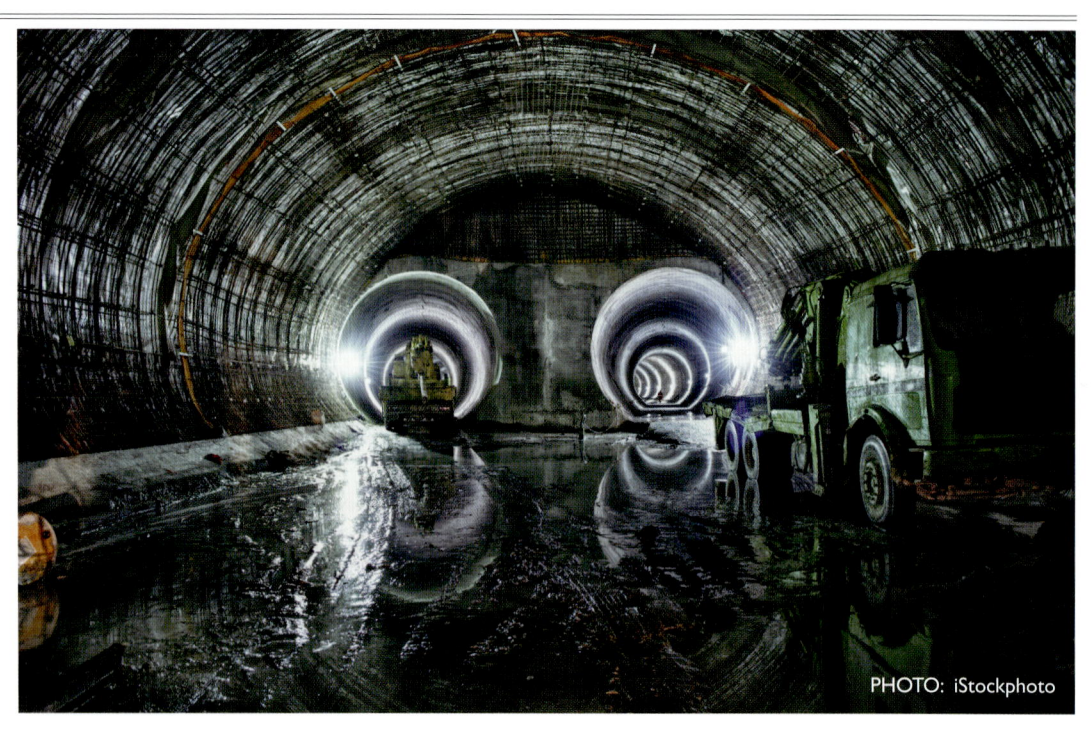

PHOTO: iStockphoto

Build Light Rail?

Light rail has enjoyed a surge of popularity in recent decades. The allure of rail within a few steps of the sidewalk has enticed many communities to build it. Notwithstanding negatives with safety and speed pointed out in Chapter Two, construction also has its problems when compared to monorail. While monorail requires holes to be dug for supports every 30 meters or so, surface light rail requires re-construction of the entire street. Underground utilities must be re-routed, and the subsurface support must be thickened to carry the weight of light rail trains, which are not light in weight. Light rail, like subway, takes a lot longer to build than monorail.

RIGHT Elevated light rail construction requires a massive amount of materials.

PHOTO: Ian Piggott

ABOVE: Light rail construction is disruptive and requires more time. Nearby businesses don't always survive.

PHOTO: Author

HOW TO BUILD MONORAIL

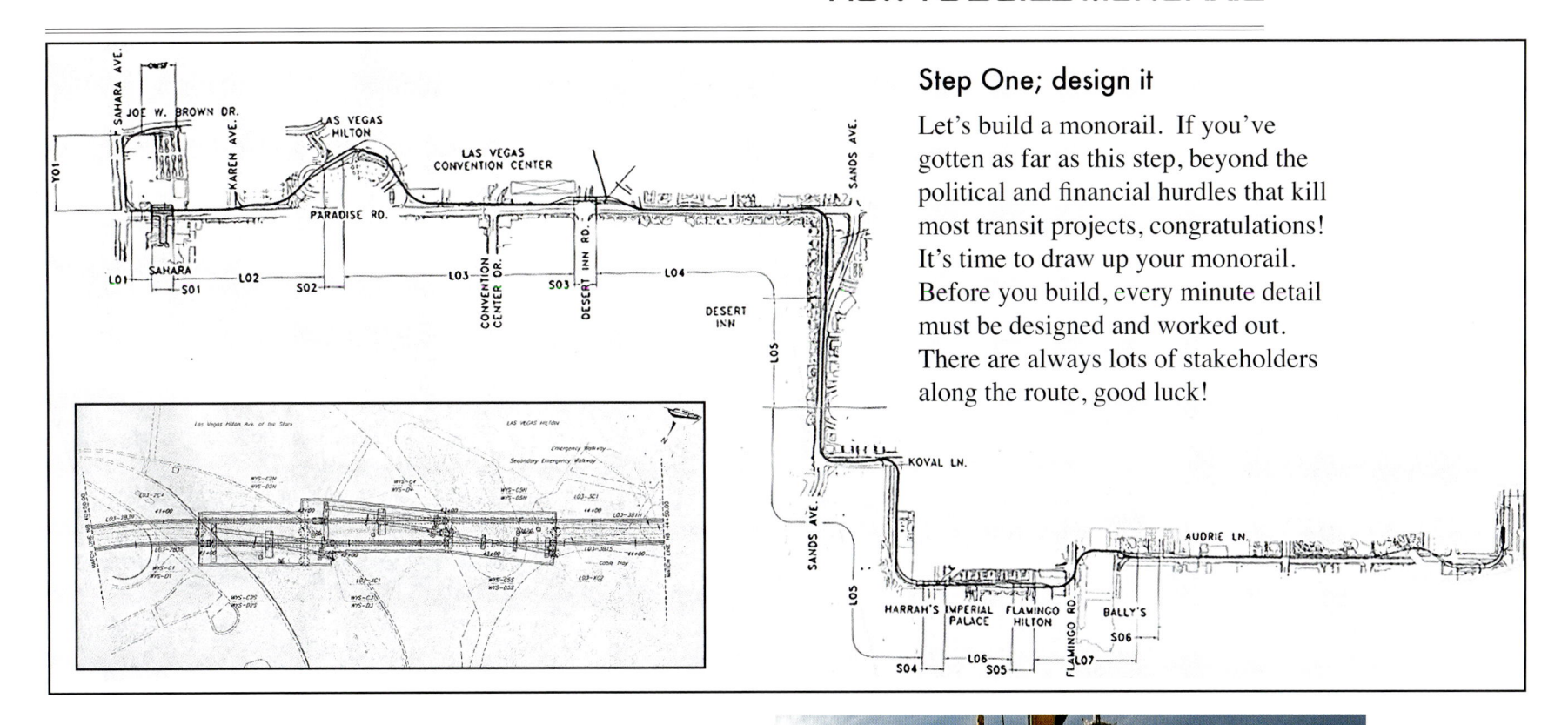

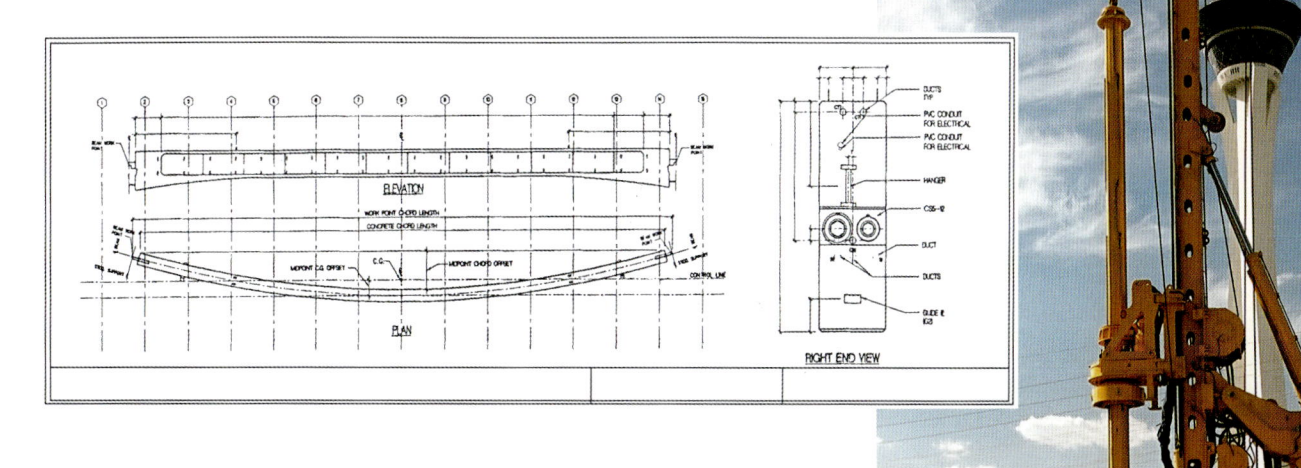

Step One; design it

Let's build a monorail. If you've gotten as far as this step, beyond the political and financial hurdles that kill most transit projects, congratulations! It's time to draw up your monorail. Before you build, every minute detail must be designed and worked out. There are always lots of stakeholders along the route, good luck!

Step Two; dig it

Ready to go? It's a big deal, so a groundbreaking ceremony is certainly in order. Have the right people make some speeches, show off some completed monorail art renderings, then dig a hole for your first pylon using a gold-painted drill bit. Applause, applause, you are on your way. Take lots of pictures, because construction time will go by quickly compared to the types of rail other cities are building.

PHOTO: Keith Walls

MONORAILS

Step Three; pylons

Drop pre-prepared rebar columns into your freshly drilled holes and your project is officially above ground. Reusable steel forms wrap around the rebar, and when firmly clamped into vertical position, concrete is poured in from the top. For taller pylons, work your way up with several different pours. Once they are ready, place more forms at the top of pylons to form the T-shape, which will support dual-directional operation. Some supports will vary in shape, such as inverted L-pylons for cantilevers. Inverted U-shaped bents may also be required for some crossover areas.

PHOTO: Author

ABOVE LEFT: **Rebar towers in holes**

PHOTO: Carter & Burgess, Inc.

LEFT: **Right to left; rebar, rebar with form, finished concrete pylon**

LEFT AND BELOW: **T-tops are added to pylons, and they include rebar to attach to track segments.**

PHOTO: Rosie Jones

PHOTO: Karl Buiter

HOW TO BUILD MONORAIL

Step Four; track fabrication

The beauty of monorail track is that it requires little space and is comparatively lightweight. Because of this, track is fabricated in a construction yard far from the hustle and bustle of the monorail alignment. Forms for straight track are reused time and time again with minor variations for length, while adjustable forms allow a wide variety of curved and superelevated beams. Track segments are fabricated at a speedy pace. Modern technology has improved on beam production quality in the last fifty years. Beams for São Paulo's Line 15 monorail had extremely tight tolerances of +/-2 mm in a 1.5-meter straight edge, 3 mm in width at any location and +4/-8 mm in any 11.6-meter length. Tight tolerances help achieve smooth track and improve ride quality.

ABOVE RIGHT: **Rebar is shaped by workers prior to being placed in forms.**

RIGHT: **Adjustable form for superelevated track**

BELOW AND BELOW RIGHT: **A new curved piece of track is lifted from the form, then transported to storage until it's needed at the monorail project site.**

PHOTO: Carlos Banchik

PHOTO: Carlos Banchik

PHOTO: John Flores

PHOTO: John Flores

199

MONORAILS

Step Five; track installation

Track delivery can be whenever necessary. If the location for the track is in an area of high-congestion traffic, delivery and lifting into place can be carried out in the middle of the night or on weekends. Monorail beam placement is done at an astonishingly quick pace, with beams lifted into place in a matter of minutes. A variety of lift processes are used, depending on the shape of the track and the location it needs to be lifted into.

ABOVE LEFT: **Beams ready for transportation at fabrication yard**

ABOVE RIGHT: **A track section is trucked to monorail site on special semi-truck trailer rig.**

RIGHT: **A relatively small crew is needed to lift track segments into place and secure them**

HOW TO BUILD MONORAIL

LEFT: Track segments being lifted into place on tall pylons by the Las Vegas Convention Center. This area of track climbs to over 18 meters to cross over a pedestrian bridge.

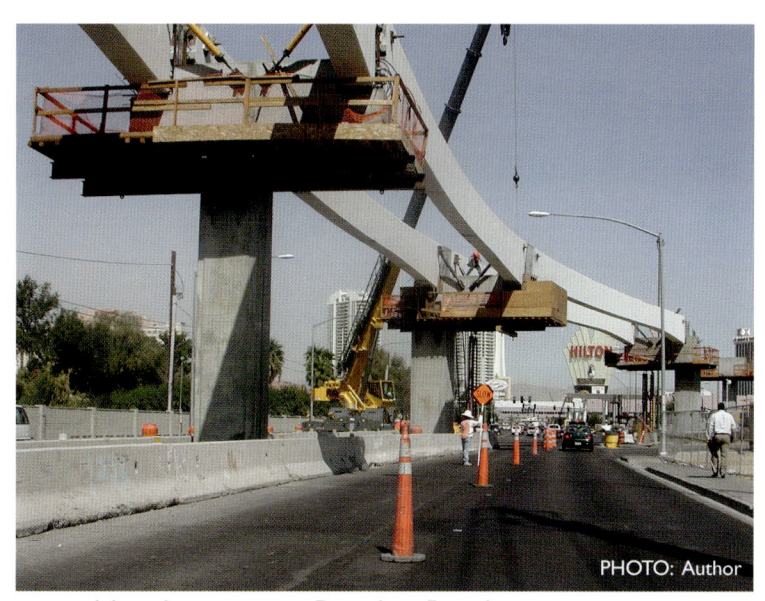

ABOVE: New beams on a Paradise Road crossover

LEFT: To avoid adding to congestion, beams along Paradise Road were lifted into place on weekends. The entire half-kilometer of straight track was put into place in only three Sundays.

MONORAILS

Step Six; connect track

Once the beams are temporarily secured in place, strands of high strength steel cable are placed in ducts to connect several beams together. Forms are placed over gaps between beams and concrete pours in place tie them together. Once the concrete gains strength, the post-tensioning cables are stressed. Post-tensioning increases structural integrity and durability, as well as reducing the amount of material needed for construction. Twin pylons are built where one post-tensioned segment meets another, to allow for expansion and contraction during different climate conditions.

LEFT: **Forms in place, ready for concrete fill-in between beam segments.**

PHOTOS: David M. Ice

A track expansion joint above twin pylons, forms have been removed and concrete is curing

HOW TO BUILD MONORAIL

Step Seven; stations and stuff

Track is only one aspect of construction. Elements such as passenger stations, electrical sub-stations, switches, the control center and a storage and maintenance facilities must also be built.

RIGHT: Steel structure for a cantilevered station takes shape.

BELOW RIGHT: Think ahead. Include switches for future expansion, as this platform was built at the Westgate Las Vegas (formerly Hilton) for an eventual extension to the west side of The Strip.

PHOTOS: Author

BELOW: This terminal station features a crossover switch to accomodate journey direction reversal.

MONORAILS

Step Eight; finish up

There are many final details to finish your work. Track needs power, so put busbars in place. Add emergency walkways, if desired. Train cars usually arrive from distant factories shortly before segments of the guideway are ready for testing. Lift them off their truck beds, put them on the beam, and roll them into the shop. Connect the cars into trains and prepare to test them.

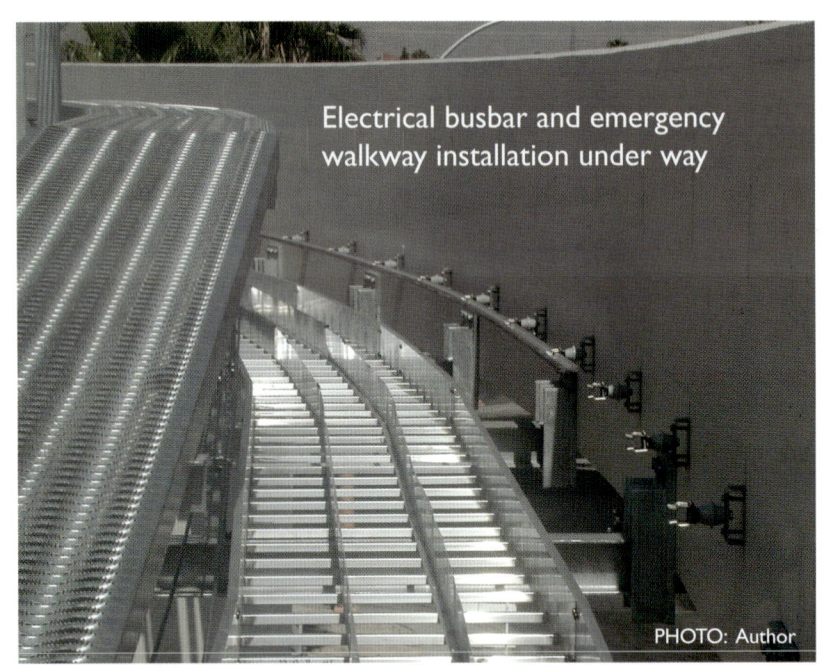

Electrical busbar and emergency walkway installation under way

PHOTO: Author

ABOVE: **Easy-to-build mobile platform for track work, including busbar installation and guideway fine-tuning**

BELOW: **Train vehicles are trucked in from assembly plants, lifted into place and rolled into the storage/maintenance facility for integration with each other.**

PHOTO: David M. Ice

PHOTO: John Flores

PHOTO: John Fl

HOW TO BUILD MONORAIL

Step Nine; test

Nobody wants to throw passengers onto an untested system and push start, so put your newly completed system through rigorous testing. Simulations of revenue operations include water-filled tanks onboard trains to simulate the weight of passengers. Software glitches will almost always be found and need fixing, so now is the time.

PHOTO: Author

July 14, 2004; the exclusive VIP celebration for the new Las Vegas Monorail

Step Ten; Grand Opening!

Throw yourself a VIP party and break out the champagne! While you're at it, get your Public Relations folks to work publicizing the completion of your new creation. When the magic moment has arrived, welcome the first passengers onboard. Congratulations!

PHOTO: Author

MONORAILS

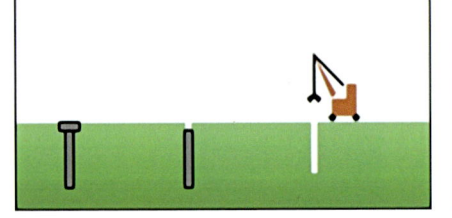

What about suspended monorail construction?

Suspended monorails are virtually identical to straddle monorails as far as the construction process. Beams and pylons are fabricated offsite and erected after transportation to the monorail alignment. Keep it simple!

Goodell Monorail Houston test track construction in 1956

Safege test track

ABOVE: Simplified illustration of the speedy H-Bahn construction sequence

H-BAHN PHOTOS: Siemens AG

RIGHT: Construction site of H-Bahn test track in Erlangen, Germany

HOW TO BUILD MONORAIL

Should we worry about earthquakes?

Modern monorails have survived many earthquakes in the past 50 years, but perhaps these early tests of a Goodell Monorail pylon and track will give you more comfort? Keep in mind that engineering has advanced even further since these photos were taken.

Axel Lennart Wenner-Gren
The founder of Alweg GmbH drives his test train.
PHOTO: Author collection

Just build it!
FACING PAGE: Monorailists Keith Walls and Rodney Rutherford campaign in the streets during a Seattle election.
PHOTO: Author

8 Monorailists

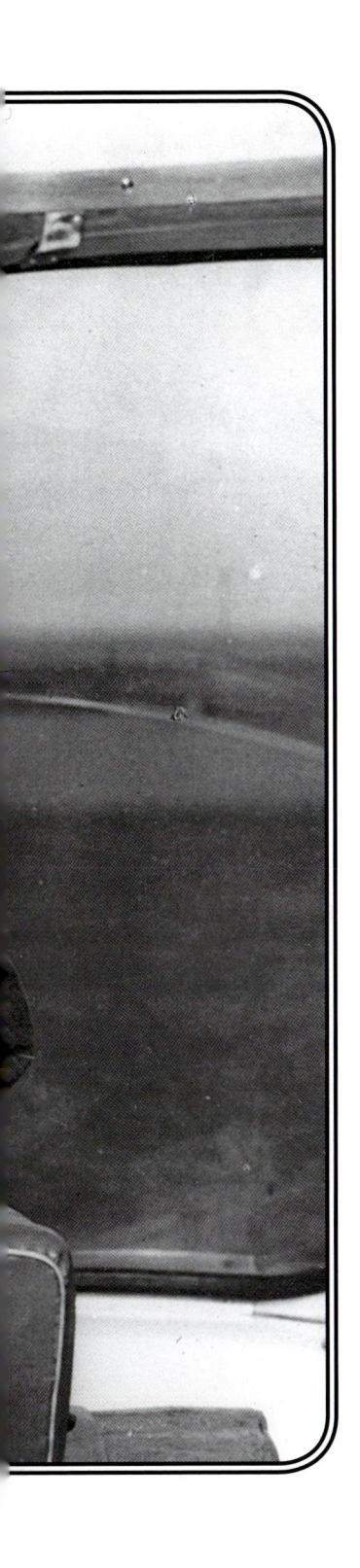

Promoters, believers and fans

The most important element of monorail advancement is the people that believe in them and promote them. Far too often the title 'kook' is bestowed upon them, but when their dreams come true they get an upgrade to 'visionary.'

MONORAILS

The history of monorails includes a fascinating variety of unique technologies. The individuals that have invented, promoted and marveled at those single-track technologies are just as interesting. Monorailists number in the thousands, and this chapter endeavors to share only a sampling of the diverse characters in the world of monorails.

Joe Vincent Meigs

The most futuristic prototype monorail of the 1800s belonged to Joe V. Meigs. Captain Meigs had distinguished himself in the Civil War by organizing and commanding the first black artillery group. After the war, Meigs invented and demonstrated his monorail in Cambridge, Massachusetts. For years he appeared before committees of the legislature arguing for his system and was familiar to everyone in Boston. His 1907 Boston Globe obituary stated, "He was modest and quiet, but energetic, with a great knowledge of rail-roading details and the possibilities of quick transportation over short distances."

Louis Brennan

Louis Brennan started out as a watchmaker in Australia. In 1874 he invented the concept of a steerable torpedo, selling his patent for the device for a large sum of money. From 1896 to 1907 he was a consulting engineer for the Brennan Torpedo Company. In 1903 he patented a gyroscopically stabilized monorail. He first demonstrated it with a scale model, then a full-sized vehicle carried 40 passengers at Gillingham, England. The prototype operated flawlessly, and Brennan subsequently demonstrated it to the military, scientists and engineers. In the 1920s Brennan went on to work on the invention of a never-built helicopter for the Royal Aircraft Establishment. In 1932, the transportation innovator died as the result of being hit by an automobile in Montreaux, Switzerland.

Eugen Langen

As shown in Chapter Three, monorail history began in the early 1800s. Standing out from the others, Eugen Langen's suspended railway in Wuppertal, Germany was to become the longest-operating monorail in the world.

Born in 1833, Langen was an engineer and inventor, spending much of his adult life working in cooperation with Nikolaus August Otto. Their company made improvements to the gasoline engine, winning them the Grand Prize at the 1867 Paris World Exhibition.

Langen invented a single-tracked suspended railway targeted for Berlin, but it was the cities of Barmen, Elberfeld and Vohwinkel that built his monorail between 1987 and 1903. Years later those cities merged to become Wuppertal. Sadly, he didn't live long enough to see his Schwebebahn built. Langen died in 1895, five years before the Kaiserwagen carried its namesake for a first ride in 1900. Fortunately he had just sold his monorail invention rights to Continentale Gessellschaft für Elecktrische Unternehmungen, who had agreed to build a prototype, setting the technology in motion.

Langen's creation continues to operate, well over a century after Kaiser Friedrich Wilhelm II first rode it.

MONORAILS

George D. Roberts

While the first fifty years of the 20th Century had numerous monorail proposals, George D. Roberts brought a new level of attention to the technology starting in 1946. As the President of Monorail Engineering & Construction Corporation, Roberts worked on plans for Los Angeles, San Francisco, Detroit, Caracas and others from the 1940s to the 1960s. Roberts enlisted support through the issuance of stocks and by making professional alliances. He formed the London-based International Monorail Limited to promote monorail on a worldwide basis. The press often referred to Roberts as Mr. Monorail. Roberts began his efforts suggesting technology based on Wuppertal's Schwebebahn, but later switched to a steel-wheeled Safege monorail as the best option. A 1958 revolution ended the Caracas Monorail project, but Roberts attributed most monorail promotion difficulties to oil companies as well as bus and conventional rail interests.

Subway in the Sky!

Commuters in Los Angeles soon may rush to work by this monorail overhead transit system, unhampered by street level traffic. Super-streamlined 100-passenger cars can travel safely at speeds up to 100 miles an hour. The 44-mile run through metropolitan Los Angeles will cut the present commuting time in half.

ABOVE: Ironically, a 1953 Continental Oil ad featured the Roberts Los Angeles proposal.

BELOW: A 1951 monorail stock certificate

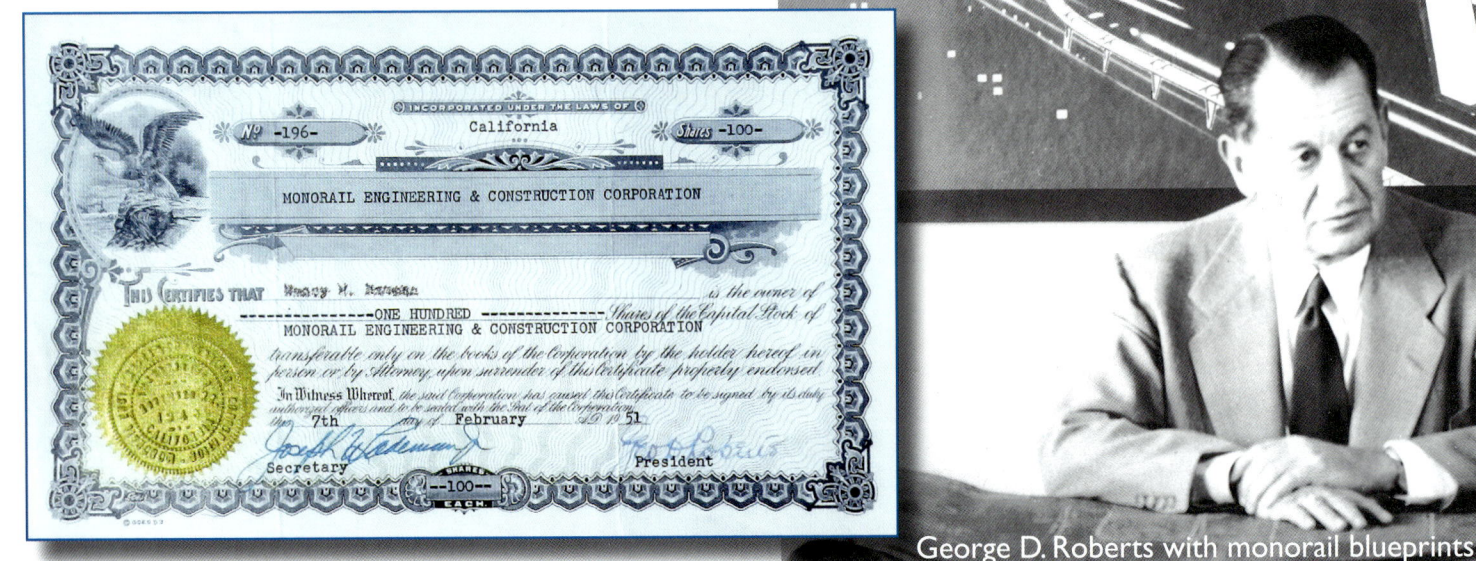

George D. Roberts with monorail blueprints

212

MONORAILISTS

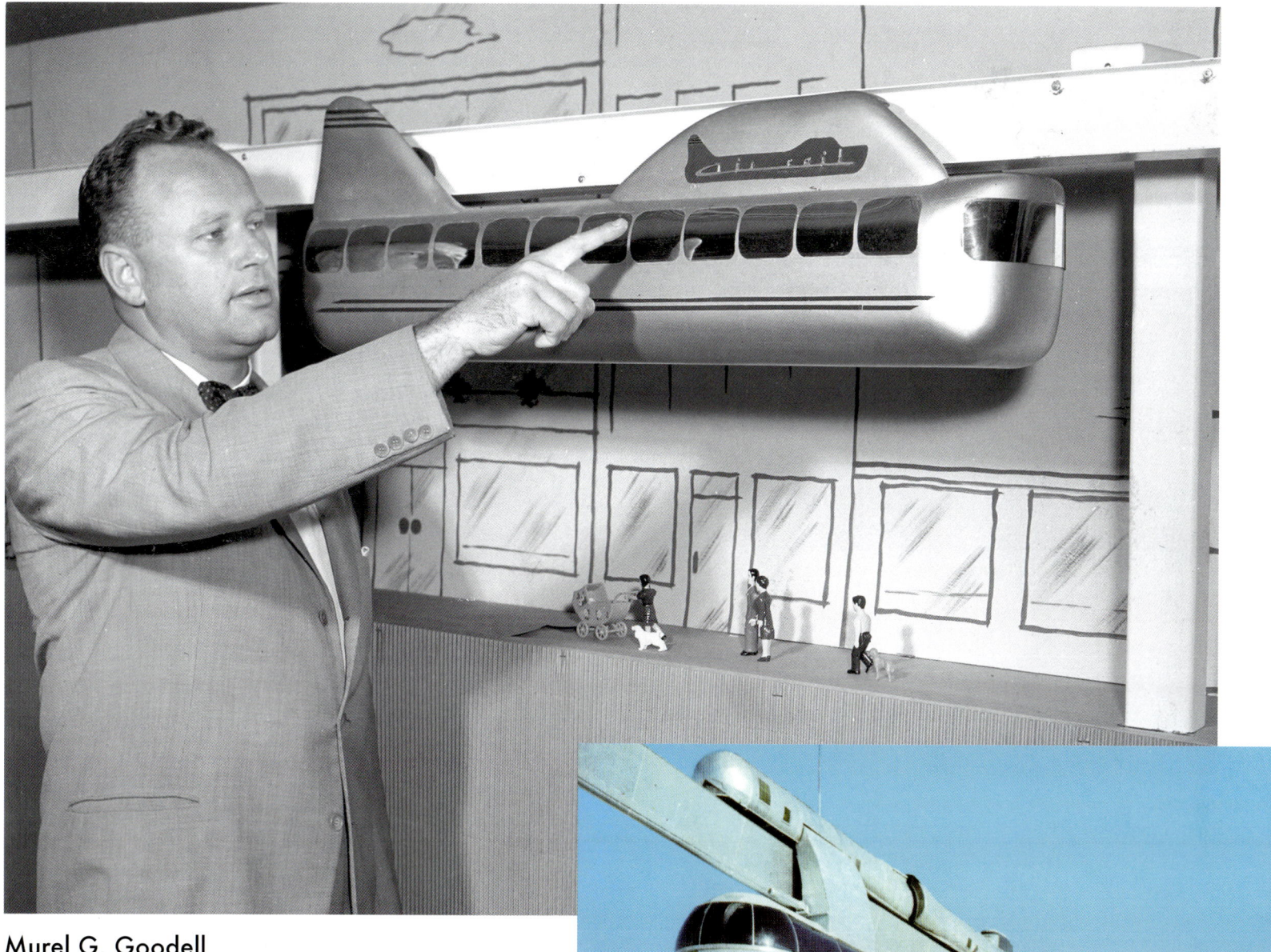

Murel G. Goodell

Texas businessman Murel G. Goodell was another prominent monorail promoter in the 1950s and 1960s. Goodell's Monorail Incorporated demonstrated their technology in Houston and Dallas. Goodell told a Chicago newspaper, "The first city to construct a line will be amazed by the low cost of building, the rapidity of installation and the profit." In 1963 the company received a letter of intent from Los Angeles's MTA to build a city to airport monorail, yet it was never built. Goodell proposed numerous other monorail systems in North America, but only short lines at the Dallas State Fair and Houston's Hobby Field were put into commercial operation.

ABOVE: Goodell's first prototype operated at the Dallas State Fair from 1956 to 1964. Originally a ride was 25 cents, making the Trailblazer the USA's first commercially operated monorail.

MONORAILS

Axel Lennart Wenner-Gren

Swedish philanthropist/tycoon Axel Lennart Wenner-Gren succeeded with his monorail technology beyond all others, yet he didn't live to see it happen. Wenner-Gren had a life-long interest in applied research, and in particular he had an interest in transportation starting in the early 1900s. While involved in many things, the device that helped make him one of the richest men on earth was the vacuum cleaner. He founded Electrolux and through brilliant promotion and sales, vacuum cleaners became an every day reality around the world. His business ties with Germany would lead to a politically motivated wartime blacklisting by the USA government, despite the fact that earlier Wenner-Gren had personally warned President Roosevelt about Hitler. He even served as a self-appointed emissary between Germany and Great Britain in a failed effort for peace. After World War II, he gained much international attention with the invention of his Alweg monorail system. Several different test tracks were built in Germany starting in 1952. Wenner-Gren lived while Alweg monorails were built in Disneyland, California and Torino, Italy. After a two-year battle with cancer, Wenner-Gren died at age 81 in 1961. His business empire crashed soon after his death. His Alweg companies failed as well, but the technology succeeded as Alweg-type monorails continue to be planned and built today by several other companies.

Wenner-Gren at the 1952 premier of his first test track
PHOTO: Ralph Crane

ABOVE: Kuala Lumpur Monorail, a product of reverse-engineering from Seattle Alweg blueprints.
PHOTO: Author

ABOVE: The last Alweg monorail completed during Wenner-Gren's life was for Italia '61 Expo in Torino.

MONORAILISTS

ABOVE: Lucien Félix Chadenson during his retirement

BELOW: Chiba City Townliner

The Safege test track at Châteauneuf sur Loire, France

Lucien Félix Chadenson

Lucien Félix Chadenson was an engineer for his entire career. His specialty was the design of bridges. In the late 1940s his interest in the improvement of transit led him to combine rubber tire and suspended rail technologies. He enclosed the running surface inside the beam, which protected it from weather elements. With the support of the French government and the formation of the Safege consortium of numerous French companies, Chadenson succeeded in getting a test track built and operating by 1960. The prototype was used for extensive testing until it was dismantled in 1970-71. The French never used the technology, but the Japanese did. First they built their own Safege prototype in Nagoya, then went on to build successful Safege lines in Shonan and Chiba City. Siemens of Germany later developed H-Bahn, a small-scale monorail based on the Safege configuration. Chadenson served as the President/Director General of Safege Transport from 1961 to 1977. He made several international trips to promote the technology. He died in 1978.

MONORAILS

Walter Elias Disney

Walt Disney is well-known for his enormous contribution to the world of entertainment, but less known was his avid enthusiasm for futuristic technology. Disney reportedly made an offer to Goodell's Monorail Inc. for their suspended monorail. He asked that they build it at their expense in his new theme park. If it were successful, The Walt Disney Company would purchase it after one year. Goodell felt insulted by whom he referred to as 'the cartoonist' and turned the offer down. Disney received a much better reception from Axel Wenner-Gren. While the starting point technology was from Alweg, Disney's company put their mark on monorail with sleekness as well as impressive turn and climbing capabilities. Imagineer Bob Gurr didn't like the "loaf of bread" look of the German Alweg prototype. He added a

In early 1959, Walt Disney points to Bob Gurr's Disneyland Mark I monorail rendering (later colorized by John Hench)

PHOTO: Bettman/CORBIS

MONORAILISTS

rocket ship nose and tail fins, as was popular with automotive design in the 1950s. As for the track, engineers wanted simple straight beams, yet Disney pushed the envelope with tight turning radii and 7% grades. Today the original 1959 track in Disneyland remains as perhaps the most dramatic demonstration of Alweg technology capabilities in the world. When Walt Disney World Resort opened in 1971, the Disney-modified Alweg trains were increased in size, yet were still scaled-down compared to transit Alweg trains. Disney loved to demonstrate his monorail. Joseph W. Fowler, Disneyland's VP and head of construction, told transit officials during a visit in May of 1959, "We will be happy to show it and explain it to officials from any city interested in studying the monorail as a possible solution to mass transit problems."

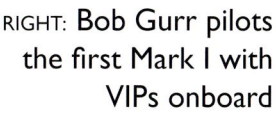

Vice President Richard Nixon's family with Walt and Lillian Disney at the June 14, 1959 opening

PHOTO: Nixon Presidential Library

RIGHT: Bob Gurr pilots the first Mark I with VIPs onboard
PHOTO: Ralph Crane

LEFT: Walt Disney dons a hard hat to take a close look at construction for the 1961 Disneyland Hotel extension.
PHOTO: Author's collection

MONORAILS

Ray Douglas Bradbury

Ray Bradbury inspired generations of readers with his seventy year plus career. As a prolific author he wrote books, stories, poems, essays, operas, plays, teleplays and screenplays. His groundbreaking works include *Fahrenheit 451*, *The Martian Chronicles* and *The Illustrated Man*. He firmly believed in monorail's advantages and argued passionately for them when Alweg extended their 1963 offer to Los Angeles. In an article written for "E" Ticket Magazine in 2001, Bradbury wrote:

In Los Angeles the automobile has taken over and almost destroyed the culture. In my writings and my talks I used the Disneyland Monorail as ammunition. Everywhere I went I said, "Look, the psychology of the monorail is what makes it superior. First of all, it's not an elevated like the old trains in Chicago. It's up in the air, but it doesn't make noise ... you can hardly hear it. The important thing is that it's above the traffic, and would glide past the traffic. We gain about a hundred thousand cars a year on our freeways, and it won't be very many more years until the roads will become unusable. I tried to make that point when I was Mayor Bradley's Advisor on Rapid Transit, and I used the Alweg system as an example, and I said, "For God's sake don't build a subway!"

Bradbury again argued for monorail in a 2006 Los Angeles Times editorial entitled *LA's Future is up in the air*. Bradbury died at age 91 in 2012.

LEFT: Ray Bradbury vehemently protested the Los Angeles County Supervisor's 1963 decision that turned down Alweg's turn-key offer for what would have essentially been a free 70-kilometer monorail system.

PHOTO/Ray Bradbury: Sophie Bassouls/Sygma/Corbis
PHOTO/Seattle Alweg: Author

Dick L. Falkenbury

Having driven on almost every street in the city, Seattle-native Dick Falkenbury had many times witnessed the short-but-effective 1962 Alweg monorail cruising quickly and quietly above the city's streets. He was convinced that politicians were on the wrong track with plans for light rail. Starting out with hand-drawn signs saying 'Extend the Monorail,' signatures for an initiative were gathered. His Initiative 41 for a 87 kilometer, X-shaped monorail system was approved by voters in 1997. Over time, voters said yes to three additional ballot measures for the monorail. Falkenbury had become a popular figure amongst the press and the grassroots monorail backers in the city. He served for six years on the monorail board, never paid for his efforts. Eventually the Seattle Monorail Project succumbed to poor leadership as well as the never-ending efforts of monorail foes. His book *Rise Above It All*, Falkenbury summarized what the Seattle grassroots effort worked for:

The plan was to build a public transportation system like no other. It would be safe. It would be efficient. And it would be economical. It would move people, without accident, quickly. It would make money. It would avoid the taxpayer subsidies, which are the main support of all public transit. It would not interfere with other transportation. It would be non-polluting and clean. The ride would be literally up-lifting.

Dick Falkenbury standing for monorail in Seattle
PHOTO: Rick Dahms, Photographer

Reinhard Krischer

Reinhard Krischer established The Alweg Archives in 2000, an extensive history website (alweg.com). He dedicated the website to his father, Rolf Krischer, one of the original Alweg mechanical engineers. Krischer was a strong believer in Alweg monorail technology and its future. In 2003 he authored a definitive book on the subject, *Alweg-Bahn: Technik, Geschichte und Zukunft der legendären Einschienenbahn*.

LEFT: Reinhard Krischer at the original Alweg test site location. Krischer holds a 1962 Seattle Alweg medallion, fifty years to the day after its opening.

PHOTO: Reinhard Krischer Collection

MONORAILS

The Monorail Society

"Wow, why don't we have these back in our home city?" That's one of the common things said on monorails, yet until the late 1980s there were no all-encompassing information sources on monorail. No advocacy or fan groups existed either. It was common for those pushing other forms of transit to falsely claim, "There are no transportation monorails." That tactic successfully stopped monorails from being developed time and time again.

In 1989, Kim A. Pedersen (this book's author) founded The Monorail Society. It is an all-volunteer organization devoted to foster more awareness and promote monorail technology through education. The Monorail Society (TMS) achieves this with their monorails.org website and through video documentaries. Starting with a modest goal of thirty, membership has reached over 7,000 with members in over 90 countries.

Efforts of The Monorail Society members have helped monorail gain more acceptance as a legitimate transit option. Several monorail projects have directly benefited from the efforts of Monorail Society members. Professionals involved with monorail projects around the world have praised the organization as a valuable source of information on the topic.

Chapter Eight has highlighted the diversity of unique characters that have promoted monorails in history, and the same goes for today's Monorail Society members. The membership includes both fans and professionals. All share the common goal that there should be more monorails carrying people to their destinations.

ABOVE: David M. Ice takes a break from filmmaking at Kuala Lumpur Monorail. Ice has produced several DVDs for The Monorail Society.

PHOTOS: Author

Ken Streit watches Kitakyushu Monorail while on a Japan monorail expedition.

Monorailists gather at the 50th anniversary of a famous monorail.

Transportation engineer Carlos Banchik serves as President of the International Monorail Association

MONORAILISTS

Glenn Barney, onetime General Manager of Seattle Center Monorail, is a longtime admirer of Alweg's ahead-of-its-time technology.

PHOTO: Author

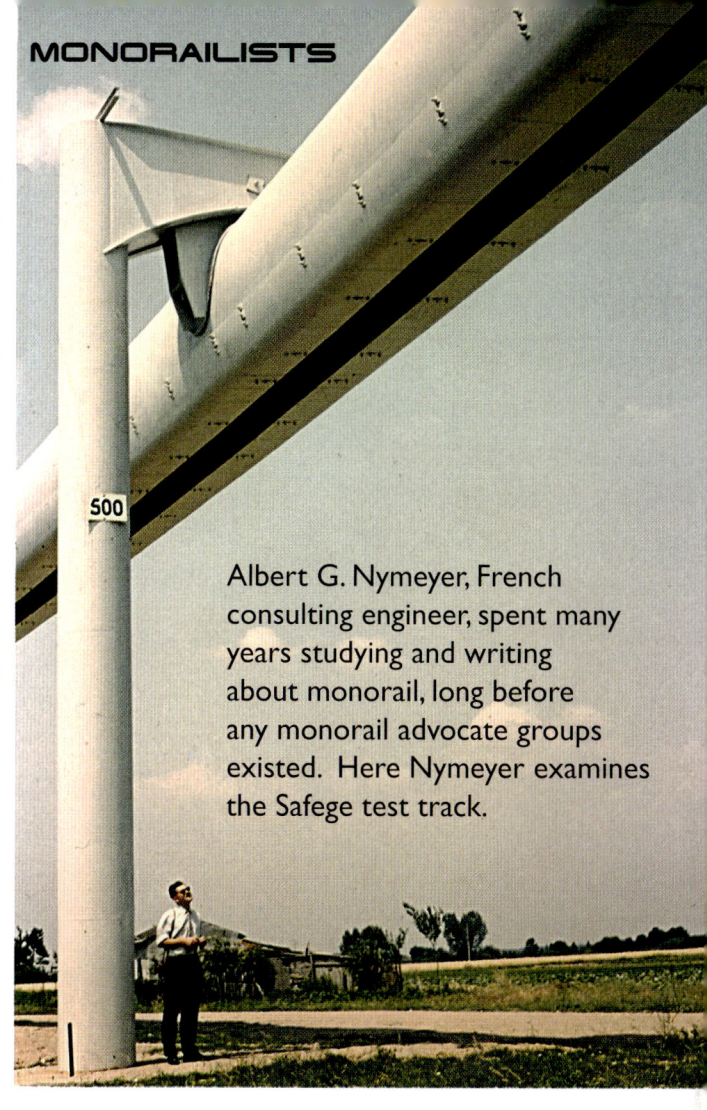

LEFT: Teri-Lynn Wheeler, at the controls of a Mark V, says of monorails, "I love them! I believe in them and their importance as a mode of true transit."

PHOTO: Author

Albert G. Nymeyer, French consulting engineer, spent many years studying and writing about monorail, long before any monorail advocate groups existed. Here Nymeyer examines the Safege test track.

Rob A. Kelly, California filmmaker, spent two years producing *High Tech Monorails* for television and DVDs.

Rail Videographer Luke Starkenburg in Mumbai

PHOTO: RAK Productions

MONORAILS

Marc Horovitz's backyard Lartigue tribute

BELOW: Lutz Hielscher Wuppertal Schwebebahn sets are detailed and functional.

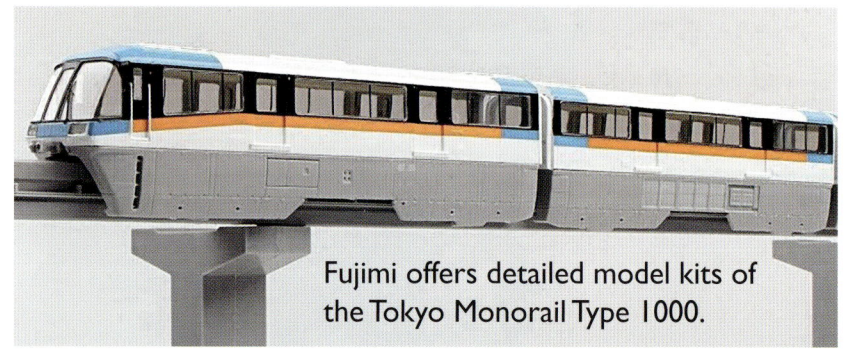

Fujimi offers detailed model kits of the Tokyo Monorail Type 1000.

Monorails for Makers

Scale modeling has been a hobby of railroad fans since the early days of rail. Schuco sold the first operating HO scale monorail sets in the 1960s. Those Disneyland-Alweg Monorail sets have now become high-priced collectibles. The recent increase in monorail development activity has inspired new interest in monorail modeling. Hobbyists are coming up with their own creative designs and some hobby companies are now offering both operating and static monorail models. At the high end of the ready-to-assemble list are the Lutz Hielscher HO and N scale Wuppertal Schwebebahn kits and Fujimi's Tokyo Monorail 1/150 model train and track sets.

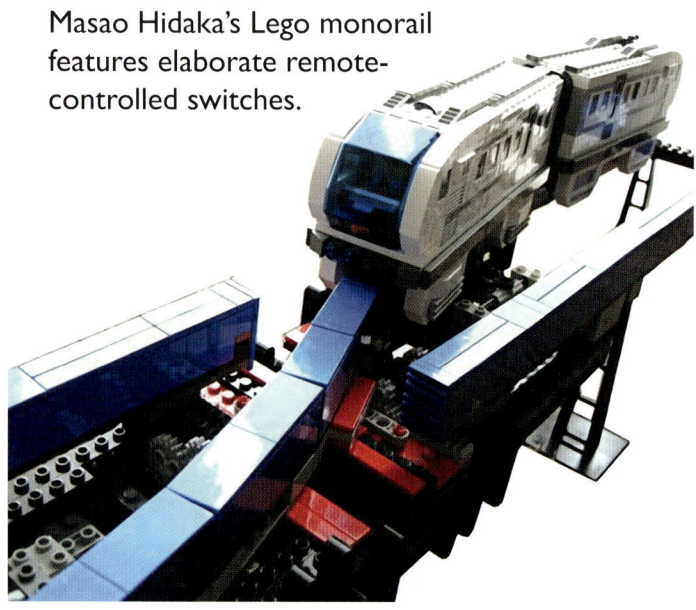

Ryoji Wada's one-of-a-kind tribute to the short-lived Yokohama Dreamland Monorail

Masao Hidaka's Lego monorail features elaborate remote-controlled switches.

222

MONORAILISTS

James Horecka turned a 'weekend joke project' into a fully-functioning Puppy Mover Monorail. With the help of Shirley Allen, Horecka displayed his PMM at Maker Faire.

Extreme Modeling

PHOTOS: Author

The author's Niles Monorail was the first rideable backyard monorail of its kind. Skyler Pedersen drives it along the back side of the house and brother Kory Pedersen departs 'Kitchen View Station.'

Collectibles

Collectibles conclude the Monorailist chapter. Like with many other hobbies and interests, collecting is a favorite pastime for the ultimate fan. Monorails don't disappoint either. There are thousands of items, old and new.

PHOTO: Author

Shanghai Maglev
Transrapid train departs station for Pudong Airport
PHOTO: ThyssenKrupp Transrapid GmbH

Monorail of the future?
FACING PAGE: Futuristic train rendering
ART: Gensler & Associates

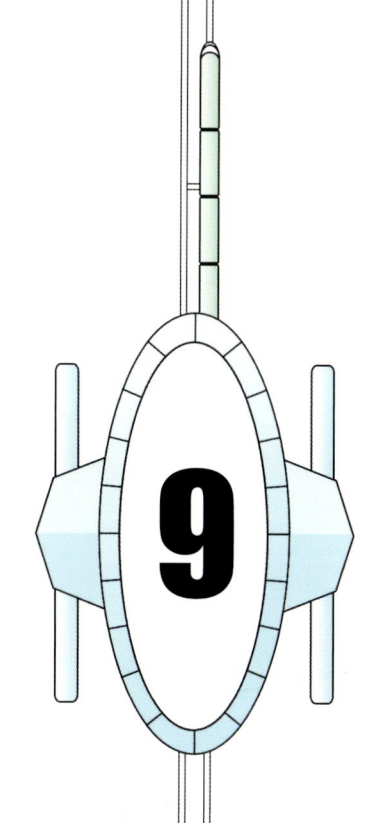

9 Trains of the Future

What can we expect next?

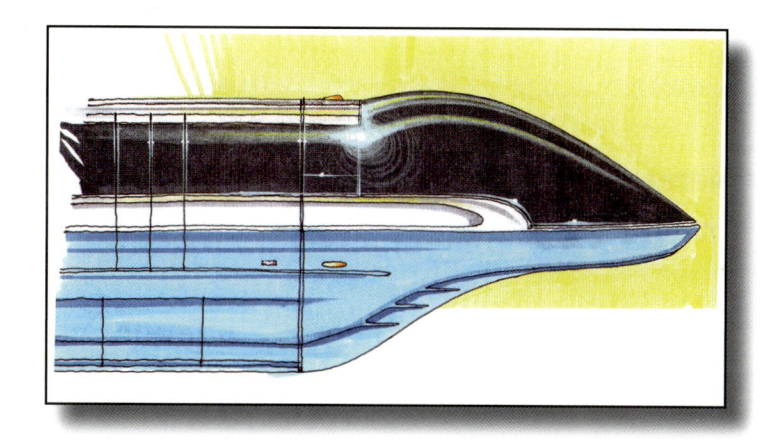

Monorails have been pegged as 'trains of the future' for over 100 years. In many corners of the world, that future has arrived. Systems are currently being built at an increased pace, but what else can we expect in the future?

227

MONORAILS

Futures past vs. the real future

Futuristic art renderings have a way of exciting us about our lives ahead. As shown on these pages, the skills of an artist don't always mesh with the knowledge of engineers.

After Wuppertal's Schwebebahn opened in 1901, the groundbreaking technology captured the imagination of artists worldwide. An *In the Future* postcard series was made for many notable cities, and they included superimposed images of the Schwebebahn over well-known local landmarks. Then-futuristic transportation modes of the era were also superimposed, such as Zeppelins and hot-air balloons.

Visions of the future sometimes do become reality, but one shouldn't believe every prediction. The practice of imagining a future beyond common sense continues today. So what can we really expect for monorail in the future? Where will they be built?

While preparing this chapter, I asked professionals involved directly with monorail to speculate on the industry's future. Their responses are reflected in these pages, along with some of my own observations and thoughts. Many predictions that may seem fanciful today are indeed possible, yet time will tell as to the real future. The acceptance and application of monorails worldwide is still an evolving story.

BOTH PAGES: Monorail renderings from the 1930s through the 1960s reflect an aviation theme.

TRAINS OF THE FUTURE

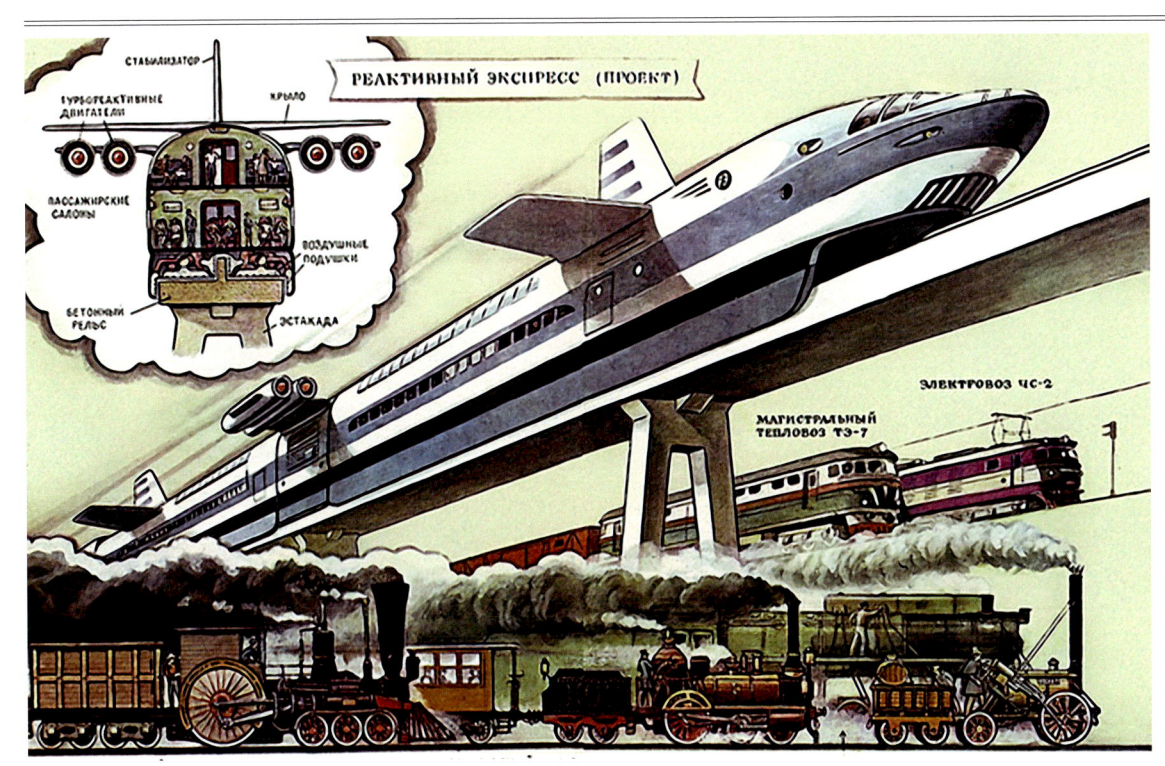

LEFT: A mid-20th Century Russian illustration celebrates rail history and forecasts massive jet-powered monorails.

RIGHT: USA magazine ad art from the 1960s also suggests jet propulsion for monorails. Evidently the impact of noise was not a serious consideration for some artists.

MONORAILS

Disney's pioneering arched spans
PHOTO: Author

Track

In fifty years of both Safege and Alweg-based modern monorail technology, improvements in ride quality have been strived for. Fabrication accuracy of track is an important factor in those improvements. Impact on environment aesthetics will continue to be worked on as well. In 1971, Walt Disney World Resort introduced gracefully-arched beams, which resulted in longer spans between pylons. Laboratories are working on new materials that could ultimately result in even longer stretches of track between supports.

PHOTO: Bombardier Transportation

ABOVE RIGHT: Bombardier's Kingston, Canada 1.8-kilometer test track for their new Innovia Monorail 300 train. The beams had extremely tight tolerances, pushing efforts toward track perfection.

RIGHT: Artist's view of Intamin's contracted Marconi Express monorail for Bologna, Italy. It is designed to include solar panels along the sunny side of the guideway, as well as on roofs of stations. Is this the future or will the added costs prohibit wide use of solar?

ART: Intamin Transportation

TRAINS OF THE FUTURE

Stations

Architecture is an important element of any public transport system. Monorail stations are highly-visible, and architects have found a variety of ways to improve their looks while maintaining their functionality. When stations are in street medians, it's even more important to make them appealing to the eye of the public. Stations will continue to evolve, with unlimited possibilities for clever designs being built to blend into their local surroundings.

RIGHT: Dramatic arched station design for never-built Portsmouth Monorail in England

BELOW RIGHT: Iran's Qom Monorail station design

BELOW: Modern station for proposed Barra da Tijuca system near Rio de Janeiro, Brazil

ART: Intamin Transportation

ART: Bombardier Transportation

ART: Kayson Company

Canvas-roofed station of Kuala Lumpur Monorail
PHOTO: David M. Ice

MONORAILS

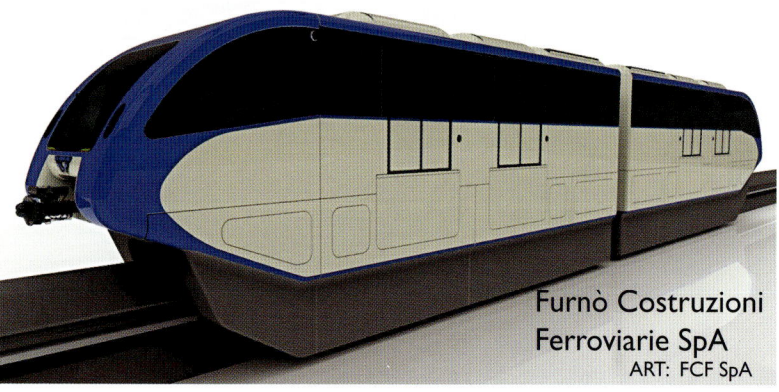

Trains

Monorail manufacturers have made many advances in train technology. All major monorail manufacturers have introduced new trains within the past few years, and each one is better than its predecessor. Every rendering on this page resulted in real trains. New products are focused on mass transit system performance capability and are designed to international mass transit standards. New materials are being used in vehicle fabrication for strength and light weight. As more efficiency is sought after, energy consumption and life cycle costs will get better with the development of even lighter trains. Better software and hardware is being incorporated into their design. The future could bring self-propelled trains, brake regeneration using capacitors, better tires and more comfortable rides with bogies able to 'read' guideways with larger tolerances.

Mitsubishi Urban Flyer
ART: Mitsubishi Heavy Industries, Ltd.

Bombardier Innovia Monorail 300
ART: Bombardier Transportation

Hitachi Large
ART: Hitachi Transportation Systems

Furnò Costruzioni Ferroviarie SpA
ART: FCF SpA

Scomi Sutra
ART: Jack Waller

TRAINS OF THE FUTURE

RIGHT: Metrail's pioneer hybrid train being run through its paces at their Nilai, Malaysia test track. More hybrids can be expected as monorails are brought to smaller cities seeking more economic and sustainable rail.

BELOW RIGHT: High-speed monorails have been talked about for a long time, such as the proposed Colorado Monorail. Will faster monorails be built and tested?

BELOW: Advanced box-beam suspended monorails continue to be touted, including high-speed, steel wheel versions. This rendering is of UbiCiT, a proposal for Montreal, Canada.

PHOTO: Author

ART: Frédéric Laurin-Lalonde

233

MONORAILS

Maglev Monorails

Trains that don't touch their track and operate at aircraft speeds? It's a seemingly impossible futuristic concept, yet maglevs are a reality today. Now that the technology is here, maglev is suffering some of the same stereotype problems that monorail promoters have fought against. Advantages include no contact with the guideway and they are quiet, environment-friendly, smooth-riding, fast and safe transportation. Maglevs have now been proven with extensive testing and in revenue service in Germany, Japan, China and Korea, but numerous high-speed proposals have also been cancelled late in their planning stages. Guideways vary in design, but several are monorail-like with trains straddling their track. Inevitably, the marketplace will decide their success.

ABOVE: Transrapid test track in near Emsland, Germany
PHOTO: ThyssenKrupp Transrapid GmbH

PHOTO: ThyssenKrupp Transrapid GmbH

ABOVE: Shanghai Maglev opened in 2004, the first commercial high-speed maglev in the world.

ABOVE: Besides purchasing a Transrapid system, China has also developed its own urban maglev.

TRAINS OF THE FUTURE

PHOTOS: Korea Institute of Machinery and Materials (KIMM)- Center for Urban Maglev Program.

ABOVE: Korea's Incheon International Airport Maglev serves the airport, a business park and the Yongyoo-Mui leisure complex. The system is 6.1 kilometers long and has six stations. Plans for the future include circling the island the airport sits upon.

RIGHT: Japan has been developing high-speed and urban maglevs since the 1960s. Pictured here is a prototype urban maglev train. After extensive testing, the Linimo urban maglev system opened in 2005 near Nagoya. Linimo operates at speeds up to 100 km/h.

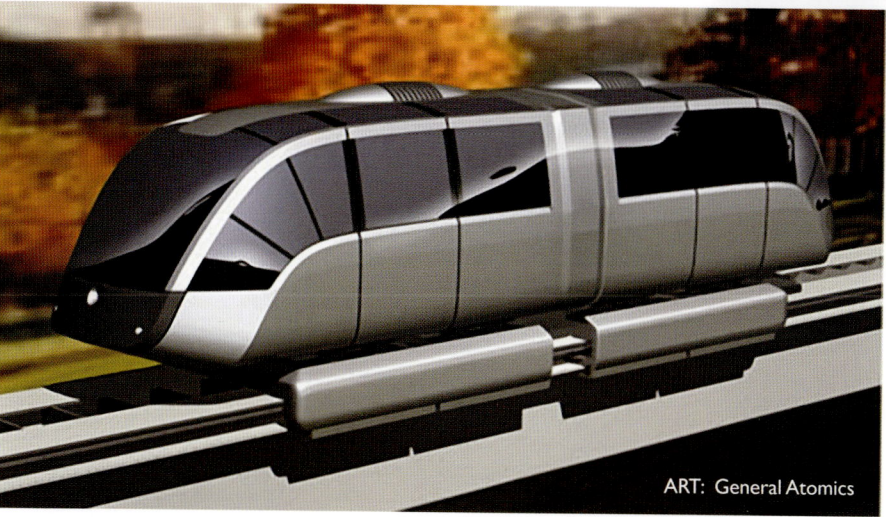

PHOTO: HSST Development Corp.

LEFT: General Atomics built the first full-scale working maglev in the USA on a 122-meter test track in San Diego. The line was established to permit dynamic testing of the company's levitation, propulsion and guidance systems. The lifting NdFeB magnets are passive (no electromagnets) and are mounted in a Halbach Array on the vehicle, and the propulsion is provided by a linear synchronous motor on the guideway. There is no active power system on the vehicle, allowing for a lighter, cheaper, vehicle design.

ART: General Atomics

235

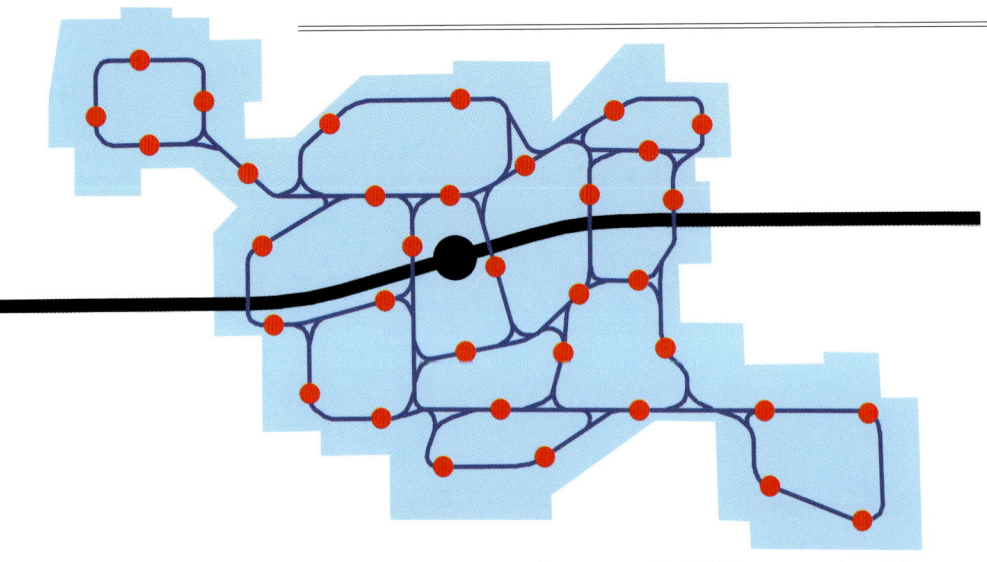

MONORAILS

Personal Rapid Transit

Personal Rapid Transit (PRT) is a transportation system featuring small vehicles operating automatically on a network of guideways. The unique aspect of PRT is the ability for passengers to board a grade-separated vehicle and travel to their destination station, bypassing all other stations without stopping. Stations are on sidings, which permits cars to bypass them. Essentially, a PRT system is an automated taxi on tracks above traffic. Some small demonstrator systems have been built, but no monorail-tracked PRTs (as illustrated) have been built to date. PRT vehicles are small and light, allowing the track and supports to be much smaller than most transit systems. Not all PRT systems use narrow monorail track however. PRT promoters site the privacy of using the vehicles, as well as the comparably low cost to install an extensive network of track and stations. A PRT network can serve as a feeder system to larger transit systems, quicker than busses and taxis.

ABOVE: Illustration of a citywide PRT network with connections to a linear mass transit system
ART: Author

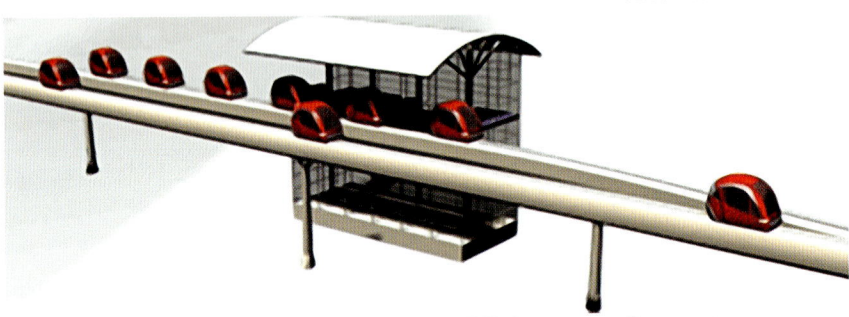

ABOVE: SkyWeb Express PRT station illustration
ART: Taxi 2000 Corporation

BELOW: Intamin's larger PRT monorail proposal for the cancelled demonstrator project for Rosemont, Illinois

PHOTO: Intamin Transportation

SkyWeb Express PRT on a narrow monorail guideway with thin pylons
ART: Taxi 2000 Corporation

TRAINS OF THE FUTURE

PHOTO: SkyTran

ABOVE: A SkyTran full-sized maglev PRT vehicle prototype was developed at NASA Ames Research Center in California. The company has partnered with Israel Aerospace Industries to build a test track near Tel Aviv.

BELOW: Artist representation of a minimalist SkyTran station, siding track and main PRT line

ART: SkyTran

MONORAILS

Pedal power

Scaling down to even smaller than the size of PRT, a new form of monorail has recently been invented. Pedal-powered monorails that leave very small footprints on the environment could find their way into leisure and transit applications. Bicycles are a popular and economic form of transportation, but there are accident dangers and speed hindrances with their use on the surface. Both Shweeb of New Zealand and SkyRide of the USA have demonstrated an alternative with suspended pedal-powered monorails. Backers point out how these small monorails can be built cheaply and provide transit at low cost. Since there is low impact on the track's surroundings, pedal monorails could be located at nature preserves to provide visitors with the unique experience of 'flying' through caves, forests or other scenic routes. Track can be painted to match the surroundings. Both SkyRide and Shweeb are pursuing opportunities to build their pedal monorails around the world.

ABOVE: **Shweeb's first entertainment installation in New Zealand**

LEFT: **Potential applications for pedal monorails can be either scenic excursions or city transport. In 2010 Google awarded Schweeb one-million US dollars for transit research and development.**

RIGHT: **Riders enjoy good exercise while taking in a special aerial view.**

PHOTOS & ART: Shweeb

TRAINS OF THE FUTURE

ABOVE: SkyRide's test track in Waconia, Minnesota

RIGHT: SkyRide's enclosed box beam track allows riding in a variety of weather conditions without affect on the running surfaces.

PHOTOS: SkyRide Technology

MONORAILS

Green trains into greenery

In 1991 Wyoming Senator Malcolm Wallop introduced legislation to study monorail-type transportation as a solution to worsening automobile gridlock at Yellowstone, Yosemite and Denali National Parks. Some environmentalists applauded the idea, others scoffed at it as a "Mickey Mouse idea." Once again Disney's proven monorails were used as an argument against the technology. The cynics won and automobiles still rule the day in those parks. Was the national park idea valid? Could safe, clean, cost-effective monorails serve wilderness areas as well as they do urban areas? Can silent trains on camouflage-painted track with vine-covered pylons mitigate the concerns of nature-lovers? There are already examples of monorail in backcountry. Some exist at theme park venues, but true wilderness monorails also operate in remote areas. China and Korea have several examples of monorails taking people where polluting vehicular traffic is forbidden. Others may follow their lead in the future.

Düsseldorf SkyTrain
PHOTO: Baloncici/Dreamstime

ABOVE: Status quo at USA's Yellowstone National Park includes environment-polluting traffic jams. Monorail was suggested once for national parks, yet the idea was ridiculed.
PHOTO: Guoqiang Xue/Dreamstime

ABOVE: Korea's Daegeumgul Cave is only accessible by this mountain-climbing monorail. 
PHOTO: Daegeumgul Monorail

ABOVE: China's remote Xuedou Monorail takes visitors on a view-filled ride, winding past waterfalls and forest scenery in a spectacular mountain canyon.
PHOTO: Xuedou Mono

240

Florida's Walt Disney World Monorail System has demonstrated green trains in greenery since 1971. Humans and animals safely cross below monorail tracks in any wilderness environment, and the quiet-running electric trains don't disturb the peace.

PHOTO: Author

PHOTO: Author

241

MONORAILS

ABOVE: **An early 1990s concept rendering for Las Vegas Monorail**
ART: Gensler & Associates

LEFT: **1970s concept art for suspended monorail**

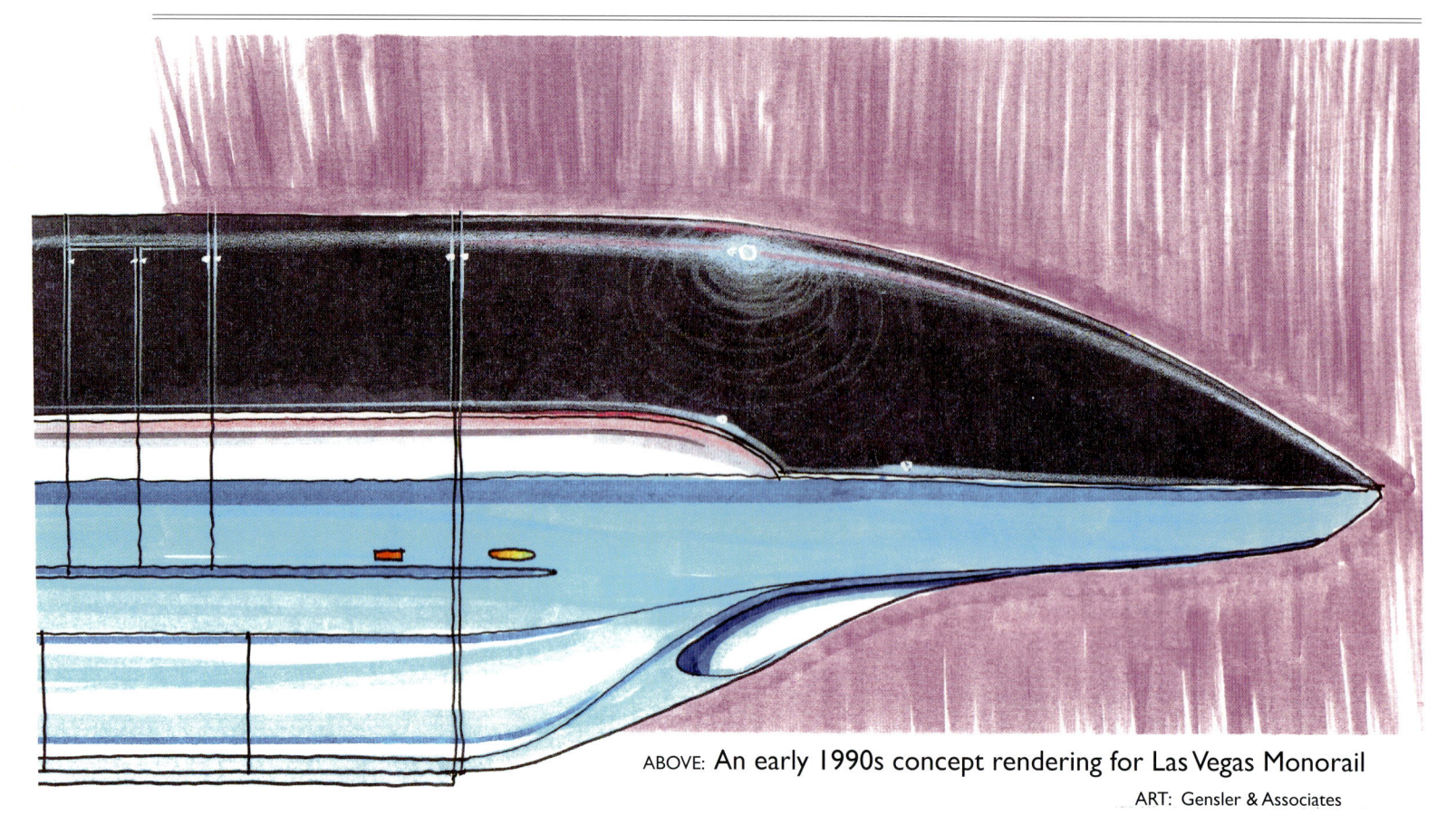

ABOVE: **2000s proposal art for H-Bahn in China**

242

TRAINS OF THE FUTURE

In Summary

Some of the exciting future concepts rendered by artists in the past have come true. When modern monorail technology became available in the 1950s, there was great promise, excitement and hope for the future of transit. With the exception of Japan, that hope for monorail faded for decades. As we have now entered the 21st Century, there is a new awakening amongst transit promoters and transportation planners, in part due to efforts of groups like The Monorail Society. It's been a long time coming, and additional sharing of knowledge will result in the development of monorail transit on a much wider basis.

It is my hope that this book makes more people aware of the potential of monorails in a variety of environments. I've endeavored to give a good overview of monorail's evolution, with a healthy dose of photographs of the many existing systems as undeniable proof of their value. The story continues, and to help illustrate this, an in-the-works Addendum page follows.

Monorails are safe, fast, cost effective, environment friendly, proven and are very popular with the public. Monorails: Trains of the Future, *are* Now Arriving!

ABOVE: Artists continue to render fanciful futures featuring monorails, all while increasing numbers of them become a reality.

Addendum

The story of monorail is constantly changing. As we go to press there are numerous projects being proposed, debated, planned and built. The following list will change quickly, as is the case with all transit history. Still, it's important to include the activity under way to get a sense of the growing value given to monorail transit.

Proposed and Planned Monorails:

Arequipa, Peru
Bali, Indonesia
Bandung, Indonesia
Bangalore, India
Bangkok, Thailand
Beijing, China
Cairo, Egypt
Chennai, India
Columbo, Sri Lanka
Delhi, India
Hambantota, Sri Lanka
Hong Kong, China
Hulhumale, Maldives
Indor, India
Istanbul, Turkey
Jakarta Airport-South Tangerang, Indonesia
Jodhpur, India
Kerbala, Iraq
Kochi, India
Kolkata, India
Lahore, Pakistan
Lusaka, Zambia
Medellín, Columbia
Melbourne, Australia
Nashville, USA
Niteroi, Brazil
Panama City, Panama
Penang, Malaysia
Quebec City, Canada
Republic of Malta
Rio de Janeiro, Brazil
Seattle, USA
Shanghai, China
Tirupati, India
Victoria, Seychelles

Contracted Monorails:

City of Arabia, UAE (awarded to Metrail - on hold)
Manaus, Brazil (awarded to Scomi - on hold)
Sao Paulo Line 18, Brazil (awarded to Scomi)

Under Construction:

Calabar, Nigeria
Port Harcourt, Nigeria
Putrajaya, Malaysia (on hold)
Qom, Iran
Riyadh, Saudi Arabia
Sao Paulo Line 17, Brazil

Existing monorails with expansion plans or construction:

Chiba, Japan
Daegu, South Korea
Dortmund, Germany
Kuala Lumpur, Malaysia
Las Vegas, USA
Naha, Okinawa
Palm Jumeirah, UAE
Osaka, Japan
Tama, Japan
Tokyo, Japan

RIGHT: **Qom Monorail construction**

PHOTO: Qom Monorail

Selected Bibliography

Books
Botzow Jr., Hermann S.D. *Monorails.* New York: Simmons-Boardman Publishing Corporation, 1960
Broggie, Michael. *Walt Disney's Railroad Story.* Pasadena: Pentrex, 1997
Day, John R. *More Unusual Railways.* London: Frederick Muller Ltd, 1960
Eschmann, Jürgen. *Die Wuppertaler Schwebebahn.* Wuppertal: Wuppertaler Stadtwerke AG, 1990
Harvey, Derek G. T. *Monorails.* New York: G.P. Putnam's Sons, 1965
Garner, Adrian S. *Monorails of the 19th Century.* Lydney: Lightmoor Press, 2011
Gurr, Bob. *Design Just For Fun.* Tujunga: APP/GurrDesign, 2012
Krischer, Reinhard. *Alweg-bahn.* Stuttgart: transpress Verlag, 2003
Meigs, Joe V. *The Meigs Railway.* Boston: Meigs Elevated Railway Co., 1887
Sato, Nabuyuki. *Monorail & New Urban Transit Systems.* 2001
Silva, Julio Pinto. *Combate Dialectico de un Innovador-Tren Monoviga.* 1989
Wilson, B.G., Day, J.R. *Unusual Railways.* London: Frederick Muller Ltd, 1958

Documents and Papers
American Society of Mechanical Engineers, 'Disney Monorail System.' 1986
Bombardier Transportation, 'Innovia Monorail 300.' 2011
Bombardier Transportation, 'Innovia Monorail 200.' 2011
Bombardier Transportation, 'Innovia Monorail 100.' 2011
Civil Engineering-ASCE: 'Walt Disney World Monorail designed for smooth riding.' Magazine, March 1972
CTS, 'Community Transportation Services.' 1974
CTS, 'Mark IV Monorail.' 1979
Disneyland Press Release: 'Inspection of the Disneyland-Alweg Monorail System' by the Los Angeles County Board of Supervisors.' May 4, 1959
'E' Ticket: 'Early Days of the Monorail.' Bob Gurr, Fall 2001
'E' Ticket: 'Walt Disney and Other Memories of the Future.' Ray Bradbury, Fall 2001
Polytechnicsches Journal, 'Entwurf einer Schwebebahn fur Berlin.' Professor M. Rudeloff, November 1905
Railway Age, 'Disneyland Extends Monorail.' August 14, 1961
Disneyland Press Release: 'Disneyland-Alweg Monorail System.' 1991
Japan Monorail Association. 'Japan Monorail Association Guide.' Brochure, 2008
Letter: Arianne Gojon (daughter of Lucien Félix Chadenson), April 30, 2001
Mechanical Engineering (USSR). 'Passenger Monorails.' V.V. Chirkin, O.S. Petrenko, A.S. Mikhailov, Y.M. Halonen, 1969
The Transportation Group, Inc. 'M VI Monorail.' Brochure, 1990
Van Nostrand's Engineering Magazine. 'A Single-rail Tramway.' Jan.-June, 1871
WED Transportation Systems, Inc. 'Mark IV Monorail.' 1982

DVDs
The Monorail Society-Kim A. Pedersen/Karl Parker, *'Why Not Monorail?'*
The Monorail Society-David M. Ice, *Monorails of Japan.* 2003
The Monorail Society-David M. Ice, *Monorails of Malaysia.* 2004
The Monorail Society-David M. Ice, *Las Vegas Monorail.* 2006
RAK Productions-Rob A. Kelly, *High Tech Monorails.* 2007

Images
All credited images are copyright protected by the person and/or entity listed and may not duplicated or transmitted in any way without the copyright holder's written permission. Images credited to the 'Author' are copyright protected by Kim A. Pedersen and may not be duplicated or transmitted without written permission by the copyright holder. Uncredited historic images are from the author's personal collection. A sincere effort has been made to determine original copyright holders of every image and to obtain appropriate rights. Any errors or omissions are unintentional and will be corrected in future printings provided the publisher is notified with updated information.

Interviews (with author)
Gurr, Bob; Interview at Disneyland, Anaheim, California, April 10, 1999
Hoopes, Gordon W; Phone interview, February 10, 2010
Laycock, LeRoy; Phone interview, July 29, 2013
Roberts Jr., George D.; Interview at Palo Alto, California, April 14, 2001
Weston, T.W. Tibby; Phone interview, July 30, 2013

Web articles
A Brief History of the Skyway Monorail. T.W. Weston (January 15, 2008)
A Triste História dos Transportes Urbanos-III. Adriano Murgel Branco (December 20, 2009)
Are You Gonna Go WEDway?-Progress City USA. Michael Crawford (Sept. 19, 2008)
The Famous Palmer Railway-An Early Nineteeth Century Wonder The New Zealand Railways Magazine, Volume 3, Issue 7 (Nov. 1, 1928)
The Monorail Myth: The Rest of the Story-Mouseplanet. Wade Sampson (Nov. 5, 2008)
The People Moving People-Progress City USA. Michael Crawford (Aug. 10, 2008)

Websites
ALWEG Archives. alweg.com
American Monorail Project. theamericanmonorailproject.com
Bombardier Transportation. bombardier.com
Hitachi Rail. hitachi-rail.com
International Monorail Association. monorailex.com
Japan Monorail Association. nihon-monorail.or.jp
Metrail. metrail.com
Progress City, U.S.A. progresscityusa.com
Scomi Group. scomigroup.com.my
The Monorail Society. monorails.org
UbiCiT Quebec proposal: design2012.umontreal.ca/din/ub1
United States Library of Congress. loc.gov
Unknown Russian Monorail, izmerov.narod.ru

Other
This book makes reference to various copyrighted works, trademarks and other intellectual property owned by Disney Enterprises, Inc. All images were obtained from credited sources outside of Disney Enterprises, Inc. References to Disney trademarked properties are not meant to imply this book is a Disney product for advertising or other commercial purposes. This book has been produced wholly independent of the Walt Disney Company or any other company.

INDEX

Acknowledgments, 4
Adams, George, 68
Addendum, 244
Advanced Rapid Transit Systems, 61
Advertising, 18, 19
Adtranz, 130
Aerobus, 69
Aerorail, 104
Ahmadinejad, Mahmoud, 109
Aldeia do Papai Noel, 73
Allen, Shirley, 223
Alphen aan de Rign, 104
Alweg, 7, 15, 41, 54, 55, 58-61, 66, 67, 92-97, 106, 110, 112-117, 134, 142, 152, 176-187, 208, 214, 216, 218, 219
AMF, 68, 98
Anaheim, 101
Appelt, Weldon, 60, 61, 78
Arrow Development, 71, 73
Automated Guideway Transit (AGT), 10
Avatar, 17
Baltimore, 99
Banchik, Carlos, 220
Barney, Glenn, 221
Basics, 8-21
Bay Area Rapid Transit, 88
Berlin, 84-85
Bibliography, 245
Bilger, Anson S., 100
Bogalusa, 9
Bologna, 230
Bombardier, 27, 94, 96, 102, 103, 106, 118, 119, 125, 127-130, 133-137, 230-232
Bond, James, 16
Boyes, William H., 53
Bradbury, Ray D., 35, 218
Bradford & Foster Brook, 44
Braniff Jetrail, 68, 70
Brennan, Louis, 52, 210
Burbank, 101
Bus Rapid Transit (BRT), 35
Busch Gardens, 71, 73
Cable car, 11
Cal Expo, 74
Caracas, 212
Chadenson, Lucien F., 62, 215
Châteauneuf-sur-Loire, 62, 215
Chiba, 33, 36, 62, 98, 154, 155, 215
Chicago, 28, 86, 94, 99
Chongqing, 22, 39, 116, 176-179
City of Arabia, 109
Collectibles, 224, 225
Cologne, 48, 94, 95
Colorado, 61, 78, 105, 233
Community Transportation Services (CTS), 96, 97
Contents, 5
Cost Effective, 26, 27
Could Have, Should Have, 80-109
Daegeumgul, 240
Daegu, 190-193
Dallas, 57, 68, 213

Daniel, Mann, Johnson & Mendenhall, 88
Dedication, 4
Definition, 9
Denali, 240
Denver, 105
Detroit, 11, 94, 212
Disney, Walt E., 6, 7, 58, 96, 97, 110, 112-115, 118-125, 216-218
Disneyland, 6, 7, 20, 31, 38, 58, 72, 96, 112-115, 118, 124, 125, 214, 216-218
Dortmund University, 62, 76, 77, 100, 150, 151
Duchamp, Monsieur, 43
Dulles Airport, 99
Düsseldorf Airport, 62, 76, 77, 100, 139, 168, 169, 240
Elmanov, Ivan K., 42
El Paso, 99
Enos, 40, 47, 82
Erlangen, 76, 100
Environment Friendly, 28-31
Eurotren Monoviga, 61, 78
Evacuation, 34
Fahrenheit 451, 17, 218
Falkenbury, Dick, 6, 106, 219
Fast, 25
Feurs-Pannisière, 44, 45
Film & TV, 16, 17
Foreword, 6
Fowler, Joseph W., 216
Frankfurt, 94, 95
Fühlingen, 54, 55, 58, 59, 112, 208
Fujimi, 222
Fun & Popular, 38
Furnò Costruzioni Ferroviarie SpA, 232
General Atomics, 235
General Electric (GE), 98
Genoa, 53
Gensler & Associates, 101, 227, 242
Gibbs & Hill, 87
Gifu, 64
Goodell, Murel, 38, 56, 57, 91, 108, 206, 207, 213, 216
Grassroots, 17
Greenery, 22, 30, 114, 122, 240, 241
Gurr, Bob, 124, 216-217
Haddon, J.L., 44
Hamburg, 15, 83, 94
Harvey, Derek G.T., 7
Hemisfair, 32
Hidaka, Masao, 222
Hielscher, Lutz, 222
Himeji, 64, 65
History Highlights, 40-79
Hitachi, 94, 106, 107, 138, 142-147, 152, 153, 158-163, 166, 167, 170-172, 176-183, 190-193, 232
Hobby Field, 57, 213
Honolulu, 98
Horecka, James, 113, 223
Horovitz, Marc, 222

Houston, 34, 38, 56, 57, 60, 61, 80, 96, 102, 103, 206, 213
How to build monorail, 194-207
HSST, 235
I-beam, 12, 13, 68-73, 98
Ice, David M., 220
Incheon Airport, 235
Industrial, 12, 13
Intamin, 74, 164, 165, 174, 175, 184, 185, 188, 189, 230, 231, 236
International Monorail Association, 220
Introduction, 7
Inuyama, 29
Inverted-t, 10, 60, 78
Irvine, 100
Jacksonville, 133
Jakarta, 109
Jerusalem, 95
Kawasaki Aircraft, 64
Kelly, Rob A., 221
Kitakyushu, 152, 153
Krischer, Reinhard, 219
Krushchev, Nikita, 99
Kuala Lumpur, 1, 2, 20, 25, 36, 172, 173, 214, 231
LA County Fair, 72
Langen, Eugen, 48-51, 83-87, 140, 141, 211
Lartigue, Charles F., 44, 45, 222
Lausanne, 74
Las Vegas, 6, 8, 24, 27, 28, 33, 71, 125, 128, 129, 195, 197-205, 242
Lego, 222
Liège, 99
Light Rail, 6, 7, 11, 27, 34, 35, 90, 102, 196
Listowel & Ballybunion, 45
Lockheed, 64, 65, 91
London, 42, 83, 94, 98
Los Angeles, 6, 7, 35, 38, 90-94, 99-101, 212, 213, 218
Los Angeles MTA, 90-92, 100
Lumber Monorail, 9
Luxor-Excalibur, 71
Lyon Exposition, 43
Maglev, 10, 11, 226, 234-236
Magnesium Monorail, 45
Makers (modeling), 222, 223
Mannheim, 69
Meigs, Joe V., 46, 210
Metrail, 79, 109, 233
Mexico City, 94
Miami Seaquarium, 74
Minirail, 15
Mitsubishi, 98, 148, 154, 155, 232
Monorail Society, The, 6, 7, 116, 220, 221, 243
Monorailists, 208-225
Montreal, 233
Moscow, 99, 174, 175
MTrans, 172
Mueller, Gerhard, 69
Mukogaoka, 64, 65
Mumbai, 20, 184-187, 221

Nagoya, 98, 215, 235
New York World's Fair, 68, 86, 96
Newark International, 75, 130-132
Niagara Falls, 108
Nihon-Lockheed, 64
Nilai, 233
Niles, 223
Nixon, Richard, 124, 217
Northern Kentucky, 104
Northrop, 90
Novelty Monorails, 14, 15, 72-74
Nymeyer, Albert G., 221
Oasis-Broadbeach, 31, 156, 157
Okinawa, 170, 171
Osaka, 158-161
Pacific Ocean Park, 73
Palm Jumeirah, 182, 183
Palmer, Henry R., 42
Paris, 98
Parsons Brinkerhoff, 88, 89
Pearlridge, 10, 126
Pedal Power, 238, 239
Pedersen, Carol, 4, 7
Pedersen, Kim, 6, 7, 220, 223, 247
Pedersen, Kory, 223
Pedersen, Skyler, 223
Personal Rapid Transit (PRT), 236, 237
Philadelphia Centennial, 43
Pinellas County, 105
Pop Culture, 16, 17
Portsmouth, 231
Presley, Elvis, 16, 67
Problem & solution, 24
Puppy Mover, 223
Putrajaya, 108
Qom, 231
Rainbow Springs, 73
Reliable, 26
Rio de Janeiro, 231
Road Machines Ltd., 12, 16
Roberts, George D., 87-90, 212
Rohr, 126
Romanov, Ippolit, 47
Rutherford, Rodney, 209
Safege, 15, 62, 63, 68, 89, 98, 99, 104, 148, 149, 206, 212, 215, 221
Safety, 32-34
Samuelson, Dale O., 6
San Antonio, 32
San Diego, 235
San Francisco, 81, 88, 89, 94, 98, 99, 212
São Paulo, 94, 95, 134-137, 194, 199
Scherl, August, 52
Scomi, 94, 172, 173, 184-187, 232
Seattle, 6, 7, 20, 21, 25-27, 37, 38, 67, 106, 107, 110, 116, 117, 209, 214, 219
Sentosa, 180, 181
Shanghai, 226, 234
Shenzhen, 164, 165

Shonan, 23, 62, 148, 149, 215
Shweeb, 238
Siemens H-Bahn, 62, 76, 77, 100, 104, 139, 150, 151, 168, 169, 206, 215, 240, 242
Signs, 4, 5
Silva, Julio P., 78
Simpsons, 17
SkyRide, 238, 239
SkyTran, 237
SkyWeb Express, 236
St. Paul-Minneapolis, 47, 82
Steel box-beam, 74, 75
Stone, LeRoy, 43
Streit, Ken, 220
Stuttgart, 74
Subway, 25, 35, 196
Sustainable, 26, 27
Sydney, 28, 31, 35, 75
Tama, 162, 163
Tampa, 99, 127
Tehran, 109
Tel Aviv, 94, 95, 237
Thunderbirds, 16
Tibidado, 72
Tijuana, 95
Titan PRT Systems, 70
Tokyo, 6, 26, 27, 30, 64, 138, 142-147
Tokyo Disney, 166, 167
Torino, 41, 66, 94, 214
Trains of the Future, 226-243
Transrapid, 226, 234
Transsystem, 75
Trenary, Bryant, 104
UbiCiT, 233
Ueno, 57
Universal Mobility, 74, 127
Vancouver, 100
Vienna, 94
Von Roll, 74, 75, 130-132, 156, 157
Wada, Ryoji, 222
Wallop, Malcolm, 240
Walls, Keith, 209
Walt Disney World Resort, 26, 29, 96, 103, 111, 118-125, 128, 217, 230, 241
Walt Disney World Resort station architecture, 120, 121
Weather, 36, 37
WED Transportation Systems, 96, 97, 125
Wenner-Gren, Axel L., 54, 55, 58-61, 66, 94, 208, 214
Weston, T.W., 61
Wheeler, Teri-Lynn, 221
Where in the East, 138-193
Where in the West, 110-137
Why not monorail?, 22-39
Why not more?, 39
Wuppertal, 32, 48-51, 86, 87, 90, 100, 140, 141, 211, 212, 222, 228
Xuedou, 240
Xi'an, 188, 189
Yellowstone, 240
Yes it is-No it's not, 10, 11
Yokohama Dreamland, 222
Yosemite, 240

PHOTO: Carol Pedersen

MONORAIL

Exit Only

248